Paul Elliott teaches film, literature and critical theory at the University of Worcester. He has published on Deleuze and Guattari, embodied film theory and the cinema of Shane Meadows and has given papers on the intersections between cinema and neuroscience, psychoanalysis and phenomenology.

HITCHCOCK AND THE CINEMA OF SENSATIONS

Embodied Film Theory and Cinematic Reception

PAUL ELLIOTT

Published in 2011 by I.B. Tauris & Co. Ltd
An imprint of I.B. Tauris & Co Ltd
6 Salem Road, London W2 4BU
175 Fifth Avenue, New York NY 10010
www.ibtauris.com

Distributed in the United States and Canada
Exclusively by Palgrave Macmillan
175 Fifth Avenue, New York NY 10010

Copyright © 2011 Paul Elliott

The right of Paul Elliott to be identified as the author of this work has been asserted by the author in accordance with the Copyright, Designs and Patent Act 1988.

All rights reserved. Except for brief quotations in a review, this book, or any part thereof, may not be reproduced, stored in or introduced into a retrieval system, or transmitted, in any form or by any means, electronic, mechanical, photocopying, recording or otherwise, without the prior written permission of the publisher.

International Library of Visual Culture 2

ISBN 978 1 84885 587 8

A full CIP record for this book is available from the British Library
A full CIP record for this book is available from the Library of Congress

Library of Congress catalog card: available

Printed and bound by CPI Group (UK) Ltd, Croydon, CR0 4YY
Camera-ready copy edited and supplied by Randall Pederson

To Katie, each one of these words is for you

CONTENTS

Acknowledgments   ix

Introduction   1

PART ONE: THE THEORY

1. Film Theory and Embodiment: New Sensations in Spectatorship   23

2. Critical Theory and Embodiment: Refiguring the Corporeal Self   45

3. Neuroscience and Embodiment: Exploring the Thinking Flesh   73

PART TWO: THE FILMS

4. On Hitchcock   93

5. On Taste and Digestion   103

6. On Smell   123

7. On Hearing   143

8. On Touching   163

Conclusion   183

Notes   187
Works Cited   209
Filmography   223
Index   225

ACKNOWLEDGEMENTS

My sincere thanks go to Shohini Chaudhuri, Phil Terry and Liz Bailey for their guidance and support throughout the writing of this, also to the late David Musselwhite, whose dedication to literature and critical theory is a reminder of what can be achieved with thought and courage.

INTRODUCTION

Our own physical body possesses a wisdom which we who inhabit the body lack.[1]

The central hypothesis of this book is simple: that there has been a shift in scopic regimes from the modern to the postmodern, the former being exemplified by a conception of vision as a physiological and subjectivising agent and the latter by the image of sight as a synaesthetic experience that is inextricably linked to other perceptual processes and to the body that they form a part of. As this Introduction shall examine, the simplicity of this idea belies a whole range of different assumptions, methodological acts and theoretical outcomes that not only touch upon a variety of different disciplines (history, metaphysics, economics, optics, and so on) but also seeks to challenge certain foundational discourses upon which these disciplines are based. At its heart, this thesis concerns itself with film theory, but film theory in its wider sense: film theory as philosopher Gilles Deleuze might have considered it – as a direct indicator of ontology and epistemology, a form of concretised thought that can be viewed and examined accordingly. The stakes of film theory as a discipline have been raised ever since thinkers such as Deleuze and Stanley Cavell began to view the process of watching cinema as an inherently philosophical act, one that provides pointers to the very fabric and structure of our thought.[2] Since Deleuze's famous dictum that 'the brain is the screen' there have been a number of books that suggest that cinema gives us a valuable insight, not only into aesthetics but into epistemology and ontology also.[3] Perhaps due to its central place in the cultural mind of many twenty-first century societies, and through its continuing reliance on representational realism, film opens up a window onto the very way we think about and construct our own realities.[4]

Unlike some recent studies, this book does not assume that modernity can be characterised by an all encompassing hegemony of the visual or that postmodernity represents its denigration, although this may well be the case.[5] Rather, I seek to characterise and classify the ways in which vision is thought of and how this changes over time and through different fields of knowledge. I also do not claim that postmodernity is any less visual than modernity; Debord's 'society of the spectacle' after all applies equally to postmodern reality television as it does to the golden age of Hollywood cinema: both are concerned with looking, although perhaps in different ways.[6] What I *am* suggesting is that vision is increasingly being seen as merely one perceptual route amongst many, each of which feeds into our overall experience of ourselves and our surroundings. As we shall see, the observer of the modern has given way to the experiencer of the postmodern.

This book as a whole, then, situates itself initially in the interstice between the two scopic regimes, looking at both with equal consideration, discerning their differences and attempting to understand their tectonic movements.

Part One looks at how these ideas are reflected across a number of different disciplines. The tacit assumption of this work is that the importance of the body and its senses in vision is being recognised across a number of different areas and that it is this recognition that characterises this shift as a *scopic regime* rather than merely a number of unconnected and isolated theories. Each of the three chapters in Part One presents a snapshot of the change between the modern and the postmodern scopic regimes, detailing, firstly, with how sight has been connected to the self and the subject and then how the body and the senses have been used to undercut and complicate this notion.

Chapter 1 looks at some recent works of film theory that deal with multi-modal and synaesthetic reception in cinema. These works reconfigure the cinematic experience to include senses such as touch, smell, taste and sound, and how each of these is intimately connected to sight – traditionally, of course, the main object of film theory. This chapter introduces what will be a major trope in the book: the division of theories into those that deal with the body and its senses as an *index of response* and those that deal with them as a *site*, or a *tool, of reception*. The first area describes theories that posit the bodily senses as being affected by what it sees (for instance the feeling of nausea one feels upon witnessing a distressing scene in a film or the raising of the hairs on the back of one's neck). Such theories tend to take the senses and the body seriously as a means of sensual understanding but still rely, to a lesser or greater extent, on sight as the major process of knowledge formation. The latter group assumes sight to be merely *one* of the ways that we orientate ourselves in the world; that even in the cinema, where we do not directly make use of sensual experiences such as taste or smell, we still draw on synaesthetic memory, on multi-modal understanding and on the lived experience of the sensual richness of life, to flesh out our understanding of the images before us. The body and its senses, then, exist in these theories as a tool that can be used to fill in the gaps that are often left by visual recognition. This chapter looks at how both of these processes have been used by contemporary film theorists to look at cinema and spectatorship. This is, of course, a complicated and subtle distinction but, it is hoped, will become clear throughout the course of this work.

Chapter 2 looks at discourses of the self – psychoanalysis, feminism and phenomenology – and, again, traces how theory in this area has signalled an increasing onus on sensual knowledge in the formation of the self and subjectivity. As I will argue, the image of the self we receive from these areas is less stable than that which arises out of the modern scopic regime; the body and its senses disrupt the fixity of the conscious ego by inserting themselves as a third, indeterminate, term into the equation. The self that emerges from such discourses is more evanescent, more fleeting than the self of modernity. It consists not of fixed points of reference but of sites of intensities and instances of sensual experience that cut across the usual co-ordinates of time and space; the self exists here as a process of becoming rather than an instance of being. Here I make of use of works by Merleau-Ponty, Didier Anzieu and Luce Irigaray to explore how the notion of the self has been complicated and broken open by the body and its corporeal knowledge in order to see, later on, how this impacts on our conceptions of film theory.

Chapter 3 looks at how vision has been conceived by, what is arguably the twentieth-century version of optics, neuroscience. It is important for these ideas that we do not merely consider discourses from the humanities; areas such as film theory and gender studies are important elements of the postmodern scopic regime but they are only part of the wider picture, a picture that includes the sciences and disciplines such as architecture and anthropology. This chapter looks at some of the many theories in recent neuroscience that, again, suggest that synaesthesia is endemic to the human experience and that we must view visual reception as being linked to its wider multi-modal context. The image that arises out of contemporary neuroscience is remarkably similar to the image that arises out of the other two areas I have chosen – the brain is viewed not merely as the grey matter that controls the unintelligent body but as part of a system that is spread throughout the individual and that relies on a wide range of sensual inputs for its lived orientation, as sight is viewed as being inextricably linked to the lived and feeling body. I also look at concepts such as mirror neurons and the gusto-facial reflex that suggest sight is inextricably tied to the experience of our bodies and our other senses; again suggesting that this move constitutes a scopic regime rather than isolated acts of theory. Some recent thinking in neuroscience prompts us to re-figure what we think of as thought, feeling, emotion, the body and the brain. Notions like synaesthesia, that links sight to its other sensual modalities, prompts us to re-map the flesh, seeing in it, not the dull animal-like slave of the thinking brain, but a sentient, shimmering thing that allows us access to the world beyond ourselves.

Part Two deals with film itself and, more specifically, how film theory of the postmodern scopic regime can help us understand the spectatorial experience as it is presented to us in the work of Alfred Hitchcock, a director who has, after all, been linked to both vision and the fixed self through discourses such as psychoanalysis and feminism. It is the implicit assumption of the more practical element of this project that the various cinematic tools I garner from different disciplines can be used to understand visual culture as a whole, and not just cinema and the moving image; however, cinema's specificity, as consisting of movement and time, makes an embodied understanding all the more vital.

This book is not a study of an auteur; the work of Hitchcock is used more as a test case with which to examine how theories of embodiment and multimodal reception can be employed to understand the ways in which audiences react and interact with mainstream Hollywood films; in fact, I could have picked from any number of directors and any number of periods in Hollywood's history. However, Hitchcock's films, as I discuss in Chapter 4, offer us a number of distinct advantages for looking at this area: firstly, due to the longevity of his career and life, any study of Hitchcock is inevitably a study of the changing face of cinema and cinematic technology; secondly, Hitchcock's interest in embodiment and in shocking and titillating his audiences mean that his films have always involved some element of corporeality despite, as many critics point out, also being concerned, to a very great extent, with sight and voyeurism. Lastly, Hitchcock has often been used to justify film theory that deals with issues of the self and subjectivity; whether it is psychoanalysis, feminism or political ideology, Hitchcock's films have time and time again been appropriated for critical mandates over and above that of the director's intentions. It seems fitting then that he should be used to offer a counter discourse to these theories and to their theoretical base.[7]

The choice of Hitchcock as a subject for the second half of this thesis, then, is neither random nor essential. I use his films because they offer a stable and fixed body of work with which to look at the processes of cinema spectatorship rather than because they represent any specific generic or thematic whole. Whereas I do look at the films themselves in some depth, I assume that this same process can be used to look at any film and, perhaps, even any visual medium. What interests me is the way that changing notions of vision can aid us in examining the processes of cinema spectatorship, and the work of Hitchcock is an ideal route into this. Part of the mandate of this thesis is to recognise the importance of corporeality, a level of filmic enjoyment that has, traditionally, been downplayed by many critics (see the discussion of Hitchcock and Auteur theory in Chapter 4). I get the sense that, for theorists such as Chabrol, Rohmer and Jean Douchet, Hitchcock's desire to touch the bodies of his audiences – to make them sweat, jump, blush, feel nauseous and so on – was an embarrassing and rather awkward element to a filmmaker they would have rather considered a philosopher or an artist in the Kantian mode. As I discuss later, this was not a mandate that Hitchcock ever assumed for himself nor did he ever seem particularly comfortable with it. However, like many things, this perhaps represents auteur theory's conception of cinema as a whole rather than merely Hitchcock; in taking Hitchcock seriously (to use Robin Wood's famous phrase), I would assert, we may have missed a great deal of his own artistic intent.

The aim of the readings in Part Two is not to suggest that established methods of looking at film are wrong or that they have no currency in contemporary theory, far from it; it is to attempt an archaeological discovery of the many different layers of the filmic experience, layers that have hitherto remained unexamined. The chapters that form Part Two all centre around a specific bodily sense and will utilise a number of filmic examples in order to highlight the ways that films rely on embodied sensation for their meaning. I will also point out how this sensation relates to the narratalogical, conscious experience of the film and how one can undercut, support or conflict with the other. Each chapter will end with an in-depth examination of a paradigmatic Hitchcock film that encapsulates the use of a specific sense and I will place my embodied reading alongside a more traditional canonical one to, firstly, show how the former differs and, secondly, how the two methods of viewing film can work side by side.

For expositional clarity, I have chosen to look at the different senses in their specificity rather than, as this thesis would suggest, as an interconnected and synaesthetic network of sense-making. The reality is that, in the multi-modal experience of cinema spectatorship, it is impossible to separate the senses in this way – sounds trigger tastes, sights are dependant on touch, smells rely on taste, and so on. However, adopting this stance here would complicate the discussion beyond measure, so a compromise has to be reached. Ultimately, this thesis is an interrogation of a scopic regime, an examination of how our changing notions of what it means to see has affected our ideas of what an audience member is and how they make sense of the images in front of them. This book looks at this, traces a line along the shifting plates of vision and attempts to discern what can be said about the body in the cinema seat.

Scopic Regimes

One of the most comprehensive and suggestive works on the history and development of vision is Jonathan Crary's *Techniques of the Observer: On Vision and Modernity in the Nineteenth Century*. Originally published in 1990, it has, since then, been inculcated into many other works in many areas, most notably perhaps in the discipline of film and cultural studies. Ron Burnett calls Crary's archaeology of seventeenth-, eighteenth- and nineteenth-century vision 'exemplary'; Barbara Kennedy states that Crary's theories allow for 'more interesting models of the filmic experience' and claims that 'the whole of the Cartesian duality that binarily opposed mind against body [can] be abandoned', despite descrying Crary's unwillingness to postulate a gendered body, Anne Friedberg seems to accept without question the larger framework of Crary's philosophical mandate and Vivian Sobchack in her essay 'What My Fingers Knew' makes heavy use of Crary's schema for dividing up scopic regimes and paradigms.[8] Crary's book, although problematic in some senses, has become the beginning point for many theories of the changing nature of vision.

Firstly then, let us summarise Crary's thesis: the basic theoretical thread of *Techniques of the Observer* is perhaps its most distinguished feature and is certainly the one that most of the above mentioned writers have adopted. For Crary, vision can be seen as both a social and an historical construct, the very way we see and the ways in which they manifest themselves are open to change, to alteration and, most of all, to rupture. Crary concentrates on two main paradigms of vision: the classical period that reached its height in the seventeenth and eighteenth century and the modern that began in the early to mid-nineteenth century and extends into our present age. Crary does make a passing nod to postmodernity and to the coming of twentieth-century technology but this is not his primary concern; what interests him most of all is the prehistory of contemporary vision.

Crary characterises these two paradigms through two distinctly different and yet very often erroneously connected technologies of vision: the camera obscura and the stereoscope, and he avoids any notion of technological determination by explaining that what these two items represent are cultural assemblages; in other words, they can be seen both as technological devices and as methods of enunciation – a coming together of sense and object, much in the same way as the home computer is both an item of technological hardware and a method of classifying an age. The camera obscura fulfils the same role in the seventeenth century as the Internet does in the twenty-first century: it aids and facilitates perception but also classifies it. In this way it represents a point of rupture rather than a sign of continuity, as he states:

> The camera obscura must be extricated from the evolutionary logic of a technological determinism, central to influential historical surveys, which position it as a precursor or an inaugural event in a genealogy leading to the birth of photography.[9]

It is obvious from this that Crary's method is highly Foucauldian; what interests him is not the 'quasi-continuity on the level of ideas and themes [that is] doubtless only a surface appearance' but the breaks in continuity, the ruptures and the departures.[10] The technological history of vision, thinks Crary, fools us into thinking that the same eye that viewed the camera obscura also peers into the camera viewfinder; in other words, the visual continuity that critics such as Serge Daney point to can be undercut by a series of ruptures and breaks that ensure vision and our understanding of it is being constantly revised and rethought.[11]

Crary finds the image of the camera obscura being used time and time again in seventeenth-century texts dealing, not only with vision, but with understanding. Descartes, in his *Optics,* cites 'a chamber…all shut up apart from a single hole'; Locke mentions 'a closet wholly shut from light' and Isaac Newton makes use of a form of camera obscura in his *Optics* when he describes his method for measuring the relative refraction of the spectrum. Crary suggests also that Berkeley's use of 'a diaphanous plane erected near the eye' is once again a tacit reflection of the same paradigm's use of the camera obscura as both a discursive and an enunciative object.[12]

If the camera obscura provided both a metaphor and an enunciative object for seventeenth- and eighteenth-century formulations of vision, then the stereoscope provided the same for nineteenth. The stereoscope, or stereoviewer, was mass produced in the middle years of the nineteenth century by companies such as Wheatstone and Brewster and consisted of a binocular apparatus upon which sets of two photographs were placed, each consisting of a slightly different view of the same scene.[13] The result was not strictly three-dimensional but one that appeared to be formed on two planes: a foreground and a background. The stereoscope manifests the underlying thought of nineteenth-century thinkers on vision such as Schopenhauer and Goethe who came to view visuality as a physiologically and subjectively constructed sense, one that is reflective, not so much of an objective reality that can be projected into and onto the eye but that posits 'the inseparability of psychology and biology'.[14] The eye can be fooled, as with the stereoscope; it is no longer merely a conduit for the reality of the world but is a shaper of it – we are no longer seen, states Crary, as spectators but as observers, with all the connotations of agency that brings.

For Crary, this shift in visual paradigm allowed the formation of not only the myriad of visual toys and tricks of the nineteenth century but the visual experimentations of the Impressionists and the early Modernists. Crary notes that theories of vision were altered by advances in physiology and how the empirical mapping of the body through science and medicine prompted new ideas about the relationship between what and how we see. Johannes Müller's work *Handbuch des Physiologie des Menschen* represented a kind of apotheosis of this nineteenth-century position as he 'reduce(d) the phenomenon of life to a set of physiochemical processes that were observable and manipulatable in the laboratory'.[15] For Müller, vision could be prompted by any number of non-objective, non veridical stimuli including 'By mechanical influences such as concussion or a blow/By electricity (and) By chemical agents such as narcotics (and) digitalis…'[16] The stereoscope's view – the view we receive, that is passed to our brain from our eyes (note: *eyes*, in the plural for the nineteenth century also stressed the importance of binocularity over the largely monocular eighteenth century) – does not exist as an objective truth; it deceives us; it is not *of* the empirical world. For Crary, the emergence of the stereoscope would be unthinkable a hundred years before when, as the camera obscura model suggests, vision was thought of as largely an introjection of what is outside, in. What concerns Crary in *Techniques of the Observer* is not some close reading of Descartes or Berkeley or Goethe but organisations and patterns of thoughts on vision and, most importantly, how these are disseminated throughout the rest of the cultural episteme; in art, architecture, manufacturing and so on. Crary's book, however, is notoriously homogenising, his brush strokes are large and his focus is on clear boundaries between time frames and epistemes – what he loses in historic specificity, he gains in heuristic figuration.

Subjectivity and the Modern Scopic Regime

As Crary implicitly states, during the period of modernity, the self was increasingly linked to what it sees, whether this was through the opening up of the arcades that allowed the consumer to realise their own self image, the commodification of vision in terms of optical toys and tricks that relied on individuated perspective for their effect, the valorisation of vision in terms of technology, or its use as a tool of a subjectivising and controlling gaze. The paintings of Turner, for instance, or Monet are indicative of the paradigmatic assertion of the importance of subjectivity in the field of vision. Crary suggests that advancements in our understanding of visual maladies centred the notion of what and how we see firmly in the physiological experience of the individual:

> The 'real world' that the camera obscura had stabilized for two centuries was no longer, to paraphrase Nietzsche, the most useful or valuable world. The modernity enveloping Turner, Fechner, and their heirs had no need of its kind of truth and immutable identities. A more adaptable, autonomous and productive observer was needed in both discourse and practice – to conform to new functions of the body and to a vast proliferation of indifferent and convertible signs and images.[17]

For Crary, the work of Turner represented a turning point, not only in the aesthetic and the representational but in the visual itself. The 1843 work *The Morning After the Deluge*, for example, depicts not only the evanescence and luminosity of the sun (as opposed to a representation of the sun as object) but presents this through a circular iris that both frames and contextualizes the central images, images that are themselves barely recognizable. This painting offers not so much a point of view (in terms of a specific viewer-picture relationship) but an assertion of Turner's own subjective field of vision in the warm afterglow of the amber sun as it gently filters through the damp air. The implicit aesthetic and ontological position behind such an image (as Crary points out) is one that asserts the primacy of the subjective visual experience and *ipso facto* the subject that provides its ground. In other words: Turner's vision is particular to Turner and knowing this can offer us insights into who or what he was. Unlike the representational work of a seventeenth-century artist like Simon de Vlieger, whose seascapes reflect a clearly definable external reality, Turner's vision is shaped and characterized by the emotions and the physiological specificity of the artist himself. The field of vision has become subjectivised.

The connection between the notions of vision and the subject can be seen not only in how science and culture formulated ideas of how we see but also how we are seen. Of course, we need look no further than the work of Michel Foucault to discern the links between the developing discourses of social control and classification and the burgeoning technologies of vision in the nineteenth century. In his monograph on Foucault for example, Deleuze outlines the importance of the gaze in his friend's work:

> A way of saying and a way of seeing, discursive practices and forms of self-evidence: each stratum is a combination of the two, and in the move from one stratum to the next they vary in terms of composition and combination. What Foucault takes from history is that determination of visible and articulable features unique to each age.[18]

Deleuze here makes the prescient point that, in Foucault, that which is articulated is irretrievably linked to that which is seen: the body is observed through the clinician's gaze, morality through the judicial gaze, psychology through the psychiatric gaze, and so on. The institutions of these gazes – the hospital, the prison and the asylum, for instance, simultaneously create their respective subjects – the ill, the criminal, the insane and their normative binaries – the well, the law abiding and the sane. The technologies of vision become not only the tools of those who gaze (the microscope, the telescope) but the architecture the subjects are housed in – the Panoptical prison, the observation clinic and the asylum. Again we see this coinciding with the historical time frame we are examining in this Introduction: Millbank prison in Pimlico, for instance, was built between 1812 and 1821 on plans taken directly from Jeremy Bentham; as Foucault details, 'doctors in the nineteenth century described what for many centuries had been below the threshold of the visible'[19] and Jean Martin Charcot, Freud's teacher and the father of modern neurology, was in residence at the Hopital de la Salpetriere, that has, since Foucault's work *Madness and Civilization,* been seen as a kind of objective correlative for the topographical changes in medicine, vision and society.[20]

For Marx also, the self was inherently linked to the rise of commodity culture in this period; what elevated the object of use value to the commodity of surplus value was not some intrinsic material property belonging to the thing itself but the extent that it 'satisfies human wants'.[21] Notice here of course that Marx does not use the term 'human needs' – wants, unlike needs, are based in the sense of self and the subject. As Baudrillard suggests in *The System of Objects*, the modern object can be characterized by what he terms its 'secondary function'; that is to say, the sense that an object is simultaneously grounded in individual desires and the circulation of a system of commodities.[22] The modern object grounds the subject within a society of subjects and assures us that we are individual whilst at the same time reassuring us we are not alone. Advertising constantly plays upon the connection between vision and the self, appealing to our visual sense by imbuing images with mirrored reflections of who we think we are or who we might like to be. During this period, vision itself was increasing commodified, encouraging consumers to not only see themselves as individuals with purchasing power and economic choice (choice also, of course linked to subjectivisation) but as single perspective beings who could experience the thrill of visuality from a privileged optical position. Such a view manifested itself in the host of visual ticks and toys that were produced in the nineteenth century. In 1816, Sir David Brewster developed the kaleidoscope that created virtual patterns and shapes out of coloured glass and mirrors; in 1824, John Aryton first documented the thaumatrope, a piece of card with a picture on either side that, when spun by the string attached to it with the fingers, would produce a hybrid image formed by the persistence of vision; in 1832, Joseph Plateau developed the Phenakistoscope, a visual illusion of movement involving a spinning disc with slits cut out for viewing; this was itself a variant of Simon von Stampfer's stroboscope. In 1834, George Horner invented the zoetrope; in 1838, Charles Wheatstone demonstrated the first stereoscope to the Royal Society; 1839 saw the perfection of early photography in Louis Daguerre's Daguerrotype. In 1859, A. W. Volkman developed the Tachitoscope, an early psychological device that displayed visual information for a brief period; in 1862, Carlo Ponti invented the Megalethoscope, a large cinematic form of the stereoscope; in 1891, Edison invented the kinetoscope and in 1895 the Lumiere Brothers unveiled the first of their cinematographs.

Of course, the emerging discourse of Freudian psychoanalysis can be seen to embody both the importance of seeing and the importance of the being seen in this period; on the one hand it asserted the value of the primal scene in the creation of the ego and, on the other, it represented an opening up – a making visual – of that which had remained hidden: the unconscious. The psychoanalytic subject could be viewed as the modern subject *par excellence*; not only is it founded upon social and historical discourses such as gender and the family but it also assures us of our subjectivity, our uniqueness and our individuality. The importance of vision on the process of individuation as envisaged by Freud is clearly outlined by Jacqueline Rose in her essay 'Sexuality in the Field of Vision':

> Freud often related the question of sexuality to that of visual representation. Describing the child's difficult journey into adult sexual life, he would take as his model little scenarios, or the staging of events, which demonstrated the complexity of an essentially visual space...

sexuality lies less in the content of what is seen then in the subjectivity of the viewer.[23]

As we have seen, this situation was not only limited to Freudian psychoanalysis but instead traversed a whole paradigm of vision. No longer was sight seen as something that the human eye was a mere tool of, but it was seen as being shaped by and simultaneously shaping the viewer themselves. Vision, it was thought, contributed, in fact was a major constituent of, the shaping of the ego and the personality – whether that be in terms of how we see (Freud, subjectivity of visual experience and so on) or how we are seen.

As I stated earlier, unlike some studies (most notably Martin Jay's monumental *Downcast Eyes: The Denigration of Vision in Twentieth Century French Thought* and David Levin's collection of essays *Modernity and the Hegemony of Vision*), I am *not* positing here the thesis that modernity represented a simple privileging of vision above the other senses. As Viet Erlmann (2004) states:

> To assert that modernity is essentially a visual age…is no longer of much heuristic value.[24]

What interests me is how the character of vision changes over time and how this feeds into discourses such as cinema and visual culture. The twinning of vision with a fixed and stable ontological subject is a major trope of modernity and one that I will revisit time and time again throughout this book. It is little wonder then that cinema studies, especially those formulated in the 1960s and 70s, relied so much on the notion of subjectivised vision and that the idea of watching a film was inextricably linked to the notion of the fixed subject and the self.[25]

However, the equating of the visual with the subject in film theory should not be seen as merely an outcome of a faith in psychoanalysis or semiotics during the 1960s and 70s, but is, instead, ingrained into the very history of cinema itself and not only this but is part of the wider paradigm of vision that saw the latter part of the nineteenth century and most of the twentieth placing ever greater onus on the individuating power of the eye. The image of the cinema viewer, as a passive observer of the images that flicker before them on the screen and of a cognitive mind that translates these into formations and reflections of their own self was constituted, I would assert, by the very scopic regime that allowed cinema to come into being.

The Postmodern Scopic Regime

The notion that many concepts of spectatorship are linked to the modern paradigm of vision prompts us to ask: how do changes in the scopic regime effect what we think of as cinema and film theory? As postmodern theorists have attempted to deconstruct the self, replacing notions such as the fixed subject with anything from performativity to the existential fold, we need to ask ourselves: what exactly is the impact of this on film theory and, more importantly, its basic theoretical assumptions?[26] In a paradigm where the ego is in constant negotiation and where the importance of subconscious, non-visual perception is asserted, we need to re-examine constructs such as the cinema viewer and the spectator and how we frame these in our theories, not so much challenging the importance of vision but gaining a better understanding of how modern science and ontology views it. I am suggesting here a consideration of what we could call, following on from Crary, a 'postmodern scopic regime'.

As I shall attempt to determine in the next three chapters, the postmodern scopic regime can be characterized by an opening up of the perceptual faculties of vision to include the other senses and the lived experience of the body. If the modern scopic regime presented vision as being linked to the individuated physiological and psychological self, then the postmodern scopic regime can be characterized by a faith and an interest in embodied perception and most importantly, the notion of synaesthesia.

The term 'postmodern', however, is notoriously problematic and should always be used lightly; postmodernity here does not refer to notions of intertextuality or to the proliferation of popular culture but, in the spirit of Lyotard, a disillusion with grand narratives – of vision, of the self, of the body, of knowledge, of reason and so on. The postmodern scopic regime is characterised by a gradual erosion of an autonomous visual sense and its links to the fixed ontological subject. By exposing the extent that vision is inherently linked *to* and founded *upon* the other senses, the workings of the body and the sensorium, recent studies in neuroscience, Deleuzian philosophy, second-wave feminism and psychoanalytic studies have all contributed to pushing touch, smell, taste and other sensual experiences into the foreground of the academic arena and, in this way, forms the basis of many re-presentations and revisions of what it means to see and to perceive.[27] The term 'postmodern scopic regime' also is specifically chosen to provide a continuation of Crary's ideas and assumes the same basic heuristic devices.

Now, before we are in danger of conflating several irreconcilable philosophical systems, let it be stressed that what is being proposed here is a way of characterising an epistemic shift, not a unified theory of vision, but many different and, to an extent, otherwise unconnected or conflicting ways of approaching the same thing. Despite there being fundamental differences and conflicts between thinkers such as Didier Anzieu and Gilles Deleuze for instance – in the area of vision, I think, they are united in their efforts – they present merely different ways of answering the same question. The polyvocity of the many often-conflicting theoretical positions is another reason why the term *postmodern* scopic regime seems so apt. It must also be stated that the term 'postmodern' does not refer to the thinkers themselves – it is difficult to declare Merleau-Ponty a postmodern thinker, for example, but I shall assert, he does fit into a general move in the area of vision.

In order to exemplify where theories of the postmodern scopic regime take us let us take one example, Juhani Pallasmaa's architectural textbook *The Eyes of the Skin: Architecture and the Senses*.[28] For Pallasmaa, architecture's obsession with sight, with how our environment looks, has alienated the human being within it and robbed them of their sensual core. He cites, for instance, the ocular reliance of Le Corbusier as an exemplar of modernity's fascination with vision and seeing. At various times Le Corbusier claimed that, 'I exist in life only if I can see', 'I am and I remain an impenitent vision' and 'Man looks at architecture with his eyes, which are 5 feet 6 inches from the ground'.[29]

We are used to looking at buildings from a distance, so much so that if we get too close (much like an impressionist painting) somehow the overall effect is lost. For Pallasmaa, this misses the point of buildings altogether that are, he asserts, to house the body and not the mind: a doorway under the auspices of vision is one thing, it needs to be in proportion to the rest of the façade, it needs to present a pleasing symmetrical outline, its size should be in relation to the windows or other external features; but for the body, the doorway is something to be walked through, to be brushed up against, to be experienced. Architecture, asserts Pallasmaa, should be smelt, touched and felt as well as seen. He also makes the point that the eye somehow ensures a metaphysical distance that has become a major preoccupation of Western thought; he says,

> The gradually growing hegemony of the eye seems to parallel with the development of Western ego consciousness and the gradually increasing separation of the self from the world.[30]

Architecture of the senses uses smells, textures, and temperatures to create different sensual experiences, experiences that the clean lines of Le Corbusier, Gropius and Lloyd Wright forget. It relishes the coming together of self and world and celebrates the fact that we can never divorce the one from the other. Pallasmaa's work represents more than the desire to assert the importance of the body in architecture, as his article 'Six Themes for the Next Millennium' details, his interest was shaped by the cultural shifts of postmodernity and, as such, in turn provide a pointer to how such discourses manifest themselves in practical disciplines such as building design.[31] It is this same shift in thinking that we can recognise in the various areas I look at in this book.

Technological Assemblages of the Postmodern Scopic Regime
Like the classical and the modern, the postmodern scopic regime has produced various technologies that could be thought of as visual assemblages, objects that fulfil both a practical and an enunciative role within the episteme. One of the problems in isolating these objects however is that such technologies are still in development and evolution; in fact, it is likely that the true material manifestation of postmodern vision has yet to be developed at all, caught as we are between the two regimes of understanding, still dependant to a very large extent on the science and epistemology of modernity. So young are the technologies of the postmodern scopic regime that there has been very little academic work dedicated to them at all. Here, however, I would like to present a brief discussion of what could be viewed as first steps towards understanding how recent changes in thinking about vision have manifested themselves in the production of objects like the camera obscura and the stereoscope.

'Virtual reality' (VR) has been lauded as the next generation of sensual technology since the term was first coined in the early 1980s.[32] The image of a reality that is both present and absent, that can be perceived and yet is intangible, and that can be endlessly manipulated by the user or programmer, has been attractive to both scientists and artists alike for decades. VR is total environment; it is the concretisation of McLuhan's 'the medium is message' because it transcends the usual technological binary of software and hardware and offers instead a form of pure medium, a total environment that immerses the user in real time.[33] Reading the scientific literature surrounding virtual reality you could be forgiven for thinking that you were reading works of existential and phenomenological philosophy, as phrases such as 'being there' and 'telepresence' attempt to centre the user within a world that, like Heidegger's, is shifting and ontologically unstable.[34]

'Virtual reality' is a broad term that is used to describe a number of different technologies, some of which offer complete immersion some of which don't. *Desktop VR* or *Window on the World* (WoW) systems offer a purely visual experience for the operative, one that relies on a coming together of user and on screen avatar. The worlds here may look authentic, but the experience is very definitely centred in the real, the user understanding the physical distance that exists between them and their virtual self. WoW systems have grown in popularity since the proliferation of Internet technologies and the development of greater bandwidth and faster downloads, with whole virtual environments being created and populated by thousands of individuals around the world, each of whom can engage with each other on a variety of different levels from the economic to the sexual.

What classifies VR systems as being inherently linked to the postmodern scopic regime however is the development of immersive systems where peripheral devices are used to combine the user's body movements with system input. As a report by the *National Research Council of America* outlines, VR development inherently involves an understanding of both human psychology and physiology, using knowledge gained from the humanities as a basis for technological innovation.[35] Thus the terms used to describe the various input devices in VR systems will become familiar to us over the course of this thesis: 'haptic interfaces', for instance, 'enable the manual interaction with virtual environments (VEs) or teleoperated remote systems';[36] 'whole body motion' sensors combine the visual with the proprioceptive areas of the amygdale, and motion sickness, nausea and dizziness are often taken as effects of a virtual experience on the lived human body.

What characterises these systems is the nature of the I/O devices and their acceptance of the physicality of vision – somehow a moving arm is more 'real' to a user than a command typed upon a keyboard. However, VR systems have never lived up to the promise of science fiction and this may have more to do with the changing sense of the real than the developing nature of the virtual. Baudrillard's fear of deserts of the real and 'the vertigo of a world without flaws'[37] seems only to have currency if one has a faith in an original real in the first place; the bewilderment and confusion of the hyperreal is often, we could assert, palliated by the development of consciousness. Technology does leave its trace on the human psyche but no matter how fast the former develops the latter is often well prepared for it.

This is at the heart of Akira Mizuta Lippit's article 'Virtual Annihilation: Optics, VR and the Discourse of Subjectivity' published in *Criticism*. Lippit sees in the relationship of cinema and VR, exactly the same kind of discourses we have been covering here: the reliance on vision and the subject in modernity and the loss of faith in such notions with the coming of embodied postmodernity, He says for instance that:

> It is important to note that cinema marks a break from the vision of the world as given – the world of the camera obscura – and co-

incides with the advent of the subject...Constituted by others – by the other – both VR and the unconscious share the supplementary logic of psychoanalysis: however the drive toward a screenless reality, a pure community, separates VR from the topology of the subject. In this sense, VR's desire to create a screenless, that is, virtual world, can be seen as the desire to create a world without subjectivity, a world without alterity.[38]

VR could be considered an assemblage of the postmodern scopic regime because it attempts an effacement of the subject so necessary to modernity and does this through an insertion of the body within the binary of software/hardware. However, it is also limited as the technology stands: VR environments are currently not stable enough nor the hardware cheap enough to allow the kinds of mass involvement that characterised the camera obscura or the stereoscope, so rather than being a reflector of optical thinking it is, to an extent, a driver of it, offering a sense of what could be possible rather than a manifestation of what is.

Perhaps the best candidate for an assemblage of the postmodern scopic regime is the Nintendo Wii, a games console that relies on physical as well as visual interaction with a console and screen. Released in 2006, the Nintendo Wii not only represented a coming together of body and eye but also sold over 600,000 units in the first eight days of its release making it, like the stereoscope and the camera obscura, a technological object that was available to everyone.[39] The Nintendo Wii uses a series of accelerometers and gyrometers in the controller to translate the user's physical movement into a visual experience, creating not so much a virtual world as an embodied sense of vision.

Eugenie Shinkle highlights the extent that technologies such as the Nintendo Wii represent a definite shift in scopic thinking:

> Though cultural criticism has tended to privilege the role of vision in perceptual experience, the other sensual modalities, such as touch and movement, have an important part to play in such experience.[40]

Yet again we see here an example of how postmodern scopic thinking asserts the value of the lived body in the field of vision and how this differs from the subjectivised notions of the previous regime.[41] A paper presented by Stephen Griffin at the 2005 DiGRA conference, for example, outlined the issues concerning traditional gameplay's reliance on the button controller:

While the button successfully affords the video game 'play', its lack of support for embodied interaction possibly impedes the development of the medium. Current buttons are not suitable for intimate, performance-based play. They are incapable of creating the nuance of corporeal expression.[42]

The traditional game button is a semiotic; it reduces the complexity of embodiment to a sign. Griffin makes the point that, to the outsider, the player of the video game is merely staring at the screen pushing buttons, but to the gamer themselves they are caught within a web of signification and meaning, each press of a button denoting a move, an action or an intention. Such meaning, of course, like the interpretation of cinema, depends upon a fixed and stable cognitive subject who is able to understand and relate to meaning over time. Notice how Griffin here also uses terms that we have seen become more and more important in scopic thinking during the latter half of the twentieth century: embodiment, intimate, interaction and corporeal expression.

The introduction of motion sensitive controllers like the Nintendo Wii's (or the recently released Sony Eye Toy that uses a webcam based I/O system) shatters the simple arithmetic of the game button, inserting fluid bodily movement into the binary structure of signification. As Griffin's paper makes it clear, embodied controllers should not be seen in terms of technological determination (this is where Shinkle's article and its reliance on Benjamin breaks down), but as manifestations of desires and scopic thinking, thinking that stretches across many different disciplines. Unlike the game button, the movements on the Nintendo Wii controller are not fixed, their variation, theoretically infinite, problematising the usual distinction between hardware/software and user.

The Nintendo Wii, whilst not exactly capturing the relationship between eye and body we will be looking at in this thesis (cinema does not after all encourage you to actually move whilst watching a film) does exemplify the shift in scopic thinking between modernity and postmodernity, in the same way that the camera obscura and the stereoscope did for classical and modern. The introduction of the body in the notion of gameplay freed software designers from a whole tradition of scopic thinking linked to signification and its related subject, as Ernest Adams details:

> The Wii remote gives players new things to do, which means it challenges us designers to come up with those things. Furthermore it takes away the functionality found on other consoles. Instead of eleven but-

tons, two analog joysticks and a D pad of the PS3 controller, it only has six buttons and a D pad. To design for this we have to think differently – we have no choice about it.[43]

This need to think differently arises from the shift in scopic thinking, a shift that has resonance across many different areas.

§

So, theories of the postmodern scopic regime look for ways that we use registers of understanding that are not only based in vision and the self, but suggests that we need to expand phrases such as 'I see' (meaning 'to understand') into 'I feel' , 'I taste' and 'I smell' and to assert their value in the formation of knowledge and perspective. The rest of this book is a first tentative step at defining what has become an increasing interest in the role of the senses and the body in cinema spectatorship; in trying, if you will, to apply theories such as those outlined by Pallasmaa and others to film theory.

We come almost immediately upon a problem here, the age-old one of language. Film is primarily a visual medium; it would be futile to doubt or refute this, and the language of film is based upon the eye and the gaze. 'Spectatorship', 'viewer', 'photography', 'theatre' and so on, all attest to the links between cinema and vision and to invent an entirely new language in order to deal with film theory of the postmodern scopic regime seems to be somewhat pointless. When we talk about a cinema 'viewer', although the word obviously has visual etymological links, its sense surely refers not so much to the eyes as to the body that sits in the cinema. Do I cease being a viewer in a film like Derek Jarman's *Blue* (1993), for instance, merely because I do not actually look at anything other than a blue screen?

Also, it should be stressed that the body that film theory of the postmodern scopic regime is interested in is the body of the spectator and not the body on or of the screen. Work has already been done in various areas concerning 'embodied images', bodies for instance in early documentaries, action or horror films – where the flesh of the actor or actress becomes a text for critical thinking. Whereas studies such as this obviously have relevance to our subject here, they still rely, in the main, on accepted processes of film theory: vision, cognition and the sense of a fixed self.[44] Film theories of the postmodern scopic regime, then, should be viewed as rooted more in the area of spectator studies than film language or aesthetics (and here again obviously the term is used in its wider rather than its purely specular sense), they are concerned not so much with what is happening on screen (in a narratological or semiotic sense) but what is happening in the audience and how its members use their bodies to make sense of and to interpret visual images.

Whereas there has always been some small consideration of the body in film theory it is only over the last fifteen years or so that theories have begun to coalesce into a distinct, though disparate, perspective. I would suggest that this is due to a number of reasons: firstly, the increased general academic interest in the body and its senses that we have already looked at; secondly, the proliferation of certain philosophical discourses into film theory (not least of all Deleuze and notions such as affect and molecularity); thirdly, attempts to view cinema as reflective of a wider ontology and, lastly, an increasing interest in sensual involvement and immersion through developing technologies such as VR, IMAX, and, of course, the Nintendo Wii.

Film theory of the postmodern scopic regime is often allied to other discourses such as post-colonialism, feminism and Deleuzian philosophy and this is because it considers perceptual systems that subtend the usual practices of Western metaphysics and offers alternatives to the processes of cinematic reception. As we shall see, Laura Marks, for instance, has studied the heavy onus placed on the sensuality of touch in films from the African and Asian diaspora, there have been studies on the surprisingly frequent use of taste in films from Latin and central America and feminist filmmakers have often attempted to appeal to registers of understanding that make use of sensual and bodily experiences in their work. Embodied cinema reception, however, as I shall assert, can also be used to help us understand how all films (and perhaps even all visual images) work, even when the filmmakers are not conscious of appealing to the body.

PART ONE: THE THEORY

1

FILM THEORY AND EMBODIMENT: NEW SENSATIONS IN SPECTATORSHIP

Over the past ten years, we have discarded one type of theory, gradually switching to another, as yet to be defined, paradigm. Rather than continue to think about the cinema as an ocular-specular phenomenon, whose indexical realism we either celebrated or whose illusionism we excoriated (which was the case in 'classical film theory', and subsequently, during the decade when psycho-semiotic 'apparatus theory' held sway), scholars now tend to regard the cinema as an immersive perceptual event. Body and sound-space, somatic, kinetic and affective sensations have become its default values, and not the eye, the look and ocular verification.[1]

As Thomas Elsaesser suggests in the quotation that opens this chapter, since the late-1990s a number of different studies and theoretical works have been published that attempt to characterise cinema spectatorship as a process rather than a fixed point of meaning and furthermore one that uses and encompasses a whole range of senses and embodied experiences rather than merely the eye and the sense of self. Like many areas of theory, however, this process is less one of revolution and more one of evolution and the temporal flow of such changes (especially considering we are still within them) is not simple or clear cut. This book attempts the very exercise that Elsaesser suggests in his article – to classify the scopic paradigm that he terms 'yet to be defined' and to attempt to unravel the many threads of embodied film theory that have emerged over the past two decades. This book is a first tentative step at defining the move towards embodiment in film theory, in isolating its central ideas, highlighting its precedents and outlining its many methodological tools. Unfortunately, this exercise is complicated, firstly, by the fact that such theories are still in development and, secondly, because they arise out of widespread epistemic changes rather than present a distinct, shared theoretical position.[2]

With this in mind, this chapter aims to look at some of these emerging film theories in depth and moreover relate them to both each other and the wider cultural episteme. All of these works represent an expansion in thinking regarding vision and a move away from subjectivised optical thought into the area of the lived body, multi-modality, the emotions and sensation. However, in order to give this overview a sense of coherent structure, I have isolated what I see as the two major trends in this area: firstly, theories that deal with the body and its senses as an *index of response* regarding film; that is, theory that concentrates on the importance of the body as a receiver of affects, sensations and corporeal experiences (nausea, dizziness, excitation and so on); and, secondly, theories that view the body as a *site of reception*; that is, works that view the body and its senses as active tools for the *understanding* of moving images when knowledge arising from optical vision is found wanting (synaesthesia, haptic vision, physical sound reception and so on).

The distinction between these two areas is subtle but crucial to an understanding of the theoretical aims of this book and the ways in which film theory has begun to widen its field of reference. As we shall see, this move in film theory broadly reflects the epistemic shift in scopic thinking that was highlighted in the Introduction. Rather than merely representing a series of isolated critical acts, this book makes the claim that embodied film theory is part of some larger scene, one that is still in the process of becoming, one that is in constant evolution. Some of the theories outlined here are related to each other but many have been produced outside of mutual influence, the only thing that connects them is a sense that the field of vision is being expanded and that the body is being re-figured.

Theorists like Karin Littau and Linda Williams take the body of the spectator seriously, they value corporeal experience and what it adds to the process of observation; they examine the ways that films are registered on the bodies of those who are viewing and seek to find more corporeal or visceral levels of enjoyment, engagement and pleasure.[3] However, they do this using what could be thought of as more traditional theoretical tools and with the assumption that sight and sound are the only ways we can interact with filmic images in a primary sense. Their cinematic bodies are feeling things that centre us in a world of sensation: shaking, sweating, beating, quaking, feeling nauseous, horny or scared. Their cinematic bodies are imprints of the film's intentions, passive in some respects, but still vitally important. These are the theories that I see as viewing the body as an *index of response*.

Theories that I have characterised as viewing the body as a *site of reception* are far more akin to the kind of postmodern scopic thinking that was highlighted in the Introduction to this book (Pallesmaa, Nintendo Wii and so on). Their major theoretical tools are noticeably different from both theories of the body as an index of a film and from the vast majority of mainstream work on cinema, asserting as they do, the value of the other senses in spectatorship and the mimetic processes. These cinematic bodies use all their senses to understand the world, sensation becomes knowledge; corporeality becomes sentient. No longer is the flesh a passive receptor of sensation; it is its translator, bypassing the cognitive mind and the eye and reaching more visceral sites of affect. These cinematic bodies think and remember for themselves, they make instinctual choices and sub-cognitive selections; it is a synaesthetic thought, based in sensual memory and the flesh as chiasm, pointing inward and outward, existing in both a present and a past.

Both of these strains of thought serve to redefine what we think of as the cinema goer, redrawing the experience of film and those who view them, making the image of the detached voyeur that sits in the theatre as fragile and as evanescent as the very lights that flicker before them. As much of the film theory that will be examined in this chapter suggests, the embodied spectator constantly negotiates meaning between its many experiential levels and these include the sensual and the corporeal.

The Body as an Index of Response

The body has always figured, to some degree, in film theory; there has always been some consideration of the way in which an audience member's flesh is made to creep, tingle, jump, or otherwise respond to the images that they witness on screen. In his book *The Corporeal Image*, David MacDougall rightly traces embodiment back to the very earliest film critics; Hugo Munsterberg, V.I. Pudovkin and Sergei Eisenstein all flirted with issues of corporeality in the embryonic days of cinema, they were interested in the 'new ways of creating bodily sensations' that cinema offered and sought to understand the underlying 'kinaesthetic potential of [its] images'.[4] However, as many recent critics have asserted, such interest in the body and its senses was soon outweighed by the dominant discourses of the self and its relationship to vision.[5] The three major tropes of post-war film theory – Marxism, Semiotics and Psychoanalysis – all not only rely on the fixed visio-ontological self but elide the importance of corporeality within the processes inherent in spectatorship; all three are based in the removed contemplation of the modern scopic regime, and, as such, make use of its heuristic devices:

identification, empathy, interpellation and on so, that rely on cognition and ontological fixity.[6] As we saw in the Introduction, cinema has been seen as a form of apotheosis of the visual; Bazin's teleological conception of its history in his essay 'The Evolution of the Photographic Image', for example, traces a direct line of ancestry from perspectivalism in painting, through the photograph, to the cinematic film; it is little wonder then that subjectivity and sight in film theory has always been so clearly linked and that the more corporeal, less distinct and more evanescent area of embodied theory has only recently been making itself felt in academic work.[7]

Often, when the body *is* directly seen as being targeted by a film it is considered as a detriment to its artistic worth and negated under the pejorative banners of pornography or cheap sensationalism. This point of view is highlighted in Jon Boorstin's *Making Movies Work*, a book that that has the unintentionally telling subtitle of 'Thinking Like a Filmmaker':

> Visceral thrills are filmmaking's dirty little secrets. Though they can require considerable art to achieve, there's nothing artistic about the results. The passions aroused are not lofty, they're the gut reactions of the lizard brain – thrill of motion, joy of destruction, lust, blood, terror, disgust. Sensations, you might say rather than emotions. More complex feelings require the empathetic process, but these simple powerful urges reach out and grab us by the throat without an intermediary.[8]

Boorstin is not alone in this view, in Linda Williams' study of filmed pornography *Hard Core*, she makes the prescient point that academia has been unusually slow in recognising the merits of 'film genres aimed at moving the body, such as thrillers, weepies and low comedy, [and that they] have [also] been…slow to be recognised as cultural phenomena'.[9] The subtext of this is clear: only low culture affects the body, true art is for the mind only. As we shall see, embodied film theory attempts to overturn this position and, not so much privilege the body, as reassert its value as both an index of a film and a method of knowledge formation; in doing so, such theory also both reflects and taps into the prevailing scopic zeitgeist that was identified by Elsaesser.

It is tempting to view embodied film theory as coming closer to the experience of most cinema goers than more established approaches such as Marxism or Semiotics. The adjectives used to describe the average Hollywood blockbuster or thriller alone asserts the value of the body as both a barometer and a receptor of the intentions of the film: spine chilling, spine tingling, blood boiling, hair raising, heart thumping, skin crawling and others, all attest to the fact that, for the filmmaker, the desire to touch the skin, flesh and bone of the audience is far from the guilty secret outlined by Boorstin, it is an integral aspect of the filmic experience and one that the audience knows instinctively but is perhaps unaware of. The seminal Russian filmmaker, Dziga Vertov, for instance, articulated what, we could assert, is at the heart of many film directors' artistic intents:

> The most careful inspection does not reveal a single picture, a single searching, which tries correctly to unserfage the camera, now in pitiful slavery, under orders of an imperfect shallow eye.
>
> We do not object if cinematography tunnels under literature, under theatre; we fully approve the utilization of cinema for all branches of science, but we recognise these functions as accessory, as off shoots, as branches.
>
> The fundamental and the most important: cinema – the feel of the world.[10]

Of course, it is telling here that Vertov does not speak of the *sight* of the world or even the *sound* of the world but its *feel* – the sensual experience of life that allows, as he says, film to 'tunnel under' the usual practices of aesthetics developed mainly by disciplines such as literary and dramatic criticism. Film here becomes something other than a visual experience, it becomes one that is less easy to classify, difficult to discern and, perhaps, even constantly renegotiated.

The insertion of the body and its feelings into the filmic equation breaks down the barriers between the audience and the screen; the spectator no longer identifies with what is happening but experiences it in a kind of shared space between the body of the film and the body of the audience. In the language of Deleuze and Guattari, the film no longer exists as a representation of an emotion with which the spectator identifies but as a rhizome that connects with the senses of the audience member (or the audience as a whole) and triggers new, unthought of connections based in sensation and sense appreciation.

Ironically, some of the most noticeable redefinitions of modern cinema spectatorship have come from works dealing with its very earliest films. This is both a testament to the continuing relevance of these early examples of cinema and to the sense that embodied theory represents an archaeological rather than a revolutionary process – the critical strategy is one of uncovering hidden tropes and existing ideas rather than inventing new ones. Paul

Stoller, in his text *Sensuous Scholarship* makes the prescient point that for an artist such as Antonin Artaud, the body played a major part in the cinematic experience:

> Although the cinema can seduce us into highly personalized but relatively inactive dreamlike states, its culturally coded images can at the same time trigger anger, shame, sexual excitement, revulsion and horror. Artaud wanted to transform his audiences by tapping their unconscious through the visceral presence of sound and image, flesh and blood.[11]

For Artaud, the cinema was an inherently embodied experience, in his essay 'Cinema and Reality', for example, he makes the surprising claim that 'The human skin of things, the epidermis of reality: this is the primary raw material of cinema',[12] a statement that, as we shall see, mirrors some of the theories emanating from the postmodern scopic regime and the body as an index of the film's intentions. As Lee Jamison asserts however, Artaud's embodied theory was seldom taken up by critics as a realistic method of examining film, only recently have theorists like Paul Stoller and Jennifer Barker begun to take his ideas seriously, an indication perhaps that it is the surrounding episteme, not cinema criticism itself, that is changing.[13]

Tom Gunning's essay 'An Aesthetic of Astonishment: Early Film and the (In)credulous Spectator' is an attempt to understand both the impact and the interest of the very early cinema shorts produced by the Lumière brothers and the Edison company.[14] What, asks Gunning, was the attraction of these films for the early cinema goer, seated in the dim light of the café bar, considering they had no story, no plot and no characters to suture them into the action, and, moreover, what caused the reaction of near hysteria when faced with the oncoming train in the Lumière short *Arrival of a Train at the Station*?[15] For Gunning, far from being the infantile figures of cinema's early childhood that the popular imagination would suggest, these early audiences were well aware that what they were witnessing was a shadow of reality. The appeal of these early shorts was not that they mirrored actuality but that they existed at all, says Gunning, that they turned the stillness of the first frozen image into a series of moving pictures:[16]

> Rather than mistaking the image for reality, the spectator is astonished by its transformation through the new illusion of projected motion. Far from credulity, it is the incredible nature of the illusion itself that

renders the viewer speechless. What is displayed before the audience is less the impending speed of the train than the force of the cinematic apparatus.[17]

The astonishment, the interest, in these early shorts, then according to Gunning, lay not with the images on the screen *per se* as with the apparatus itself: the very fact that they were visually witnessing cinema. Gunning uses the phrase 'the cinema of attractions' to describe this period of growing spectatorship.

Perhaps the real interest for our discussion here concerning the postmodern scopic regime, however, is not so much Gunning's essay as that of Karin Littau's, whose paper 'Eye Hunger: Physical Pleasure and Non-narrative Cinema' can be seen both as a direct response to Gunning's work and as an entry point into embodied interpretations of film theory, especially those that I have suggested view the body as a responsive index.

Littau's essay is published in an anthology of writing concerned with crash culture, and this image, the crash, is an important one when we come to consider how she interprets filmic spectatorship. For Littau, Gunning's argument explains only part of the attraction of early cinema; she agrees with him that modernity was characterised by an increased interest in the use of vision and the development of what she terms *Schaulust* or eye-hunger – part of the attraction of early cinematic performances, she asserts, was the sheer optical pleasure of viewing. However, Littau moves this argument a step further and posits that a more embodied response could also play its part in the cinema of attraction, that there could be a corporeal, physical aspect to cinema viewing that compliments any sense of ego-driven awe or astonishment; there is an animal aspect to vision that provides the viewer with an embodied sensation:

> Whether the crowd gathers at the crash site or gathers for a crash film in the cinema, it is their readiness to be thrilled which has brought them together. Thus, whether the crash film has quickened the audience's heartbeat through kinaesthetic motion (*The Haverstraw Tunnel*) or confused their retinas through the collision of images in montage sequences (*Un Chien Andalou*) or conversely, has commented on spectatorial sensation (*Uncle Josh at the Moving Picture Show*) or on the thematized Schaulust within the fiction of the filmic text (Cronenberg's *Crash*, 1996), with all these diverse films we find, to a greater or lesser extent, instances of physical pleasure in looking.[18]

Straightaway here we can detect a shift in scopic thinking; vision is still assumed to be the functionary sense in the cinematic experience but now it is viewed not as the sole arbiter of meaning but as a conduit for an embodied experience of sensation. Littau suggests that, before conscious meaning is assumed, a physical sensation is felt; our pleasure in viewing, in other words, is inextricably connected to the visceral and the corporeal. Under this notion, the cinema viewer ceases being merely a pair of eyes connected to an autonomous self and becomes instead a seeing, feeling, experiencing body whose kinetic rhythms, neuro-chemical balances and even free flowing digestion can be manipulated by the film maker:

> From the cinema of the Cinematograph to the home VCR: from R. W. Paul's fantasy film *The ? Motorist* (dir. Walter R. Booth, 1906) to the sporting highlights of the 'most breathtaking' and 'the very best and the worst thrills and spills, spins and bashes, smashes and crashes' which announces the 'adrenalin inducing' Crash Impact video tape (Telstar, 1997) the aim has been to satisfy the eye's hunger for sensation and stimulation. And all this is addressed to a flesh and blood audience…the physiological being who sits at the edge of their seat and whose pulse is racing and whose spine is tingling.[19]

Littau here is examining the corporeality of the process inherent in spectatorship but more importantly perhaps she is valuing the experience. The physical sensations felt during a film are, for her, not contingent to the narrative they are inextricably bound up with it; they are not so much cinema's dirty secret, as the mechanisms through which it encourages involvement. In this way, the body becomes an index of the film's effectiveness, connecting with the audience member, inviting them to share in the narrative and mimetically knitting them into the action. In Littau's work we see a shift in thinking – one that, as we will see, is indicative of a more postmodern scopic regime: the characters in her essay (the viewers in the cinema, the viewers of the train crash, etc.) are not only watchers but feelers, experiencers and sensation-seekers; the eye has become inextricably linked to the *lived* body that it forms a part of. Despite taking as a text one of the earliest examples of cinema, Littau's work presents us with a highly contemporary theoretical stance, one that, as we shall see, is in keeping with recent notions arising in neurobiology and corporeal philosophy.

The work of Linda Williams exemplifies the body of work that I have characterised as that which views corporeality as an index of response to moving images. Williams has sought to examine what she calls the area of 'body genre', that is, filmic and photographic work that not only features images of the flesh in terms of representation but, more importantly for our thesis here, that examines the effect of these images on the bodies of those that view them. In centring her work on genres that appeal directly to the desire for cinematic thrills and spills (horror, pornography or tearjerkers for example) and by taking such experiences seriously, Williams attempts to redress some of the imbalances that have arisen in post-war film theory regarding the body and the mind.

In essays such 'Body Genres: Corporealized Observers and the Carnal Density of Vision'[20] and 'Body Genres: Gender, Genre and Excess'[21] Williams stresses the importance of what she calls 'carnal density' in the process of cinema spectatorship, a term she borrows from Crary.[22] The crucial aspect of Williams' work to us here is the fact that this carnal density refers not to represented bodies but to the body of the spectator themselves and as such represents a questioning of the importance of the visual (and the psychoanalytic) gaze in film theory, and, most importantly perhaps, as it relates to gender and sexuality. In a passage concerned with early pornography for instance she goes so far as to anticipate some of the postmodern scopic thinking that will we see is characteristic of more Deleuzian scholars:

> Touch…is activated by but not aimed at, so to speak, the absent referent. Though quite material and palpable, it is not a matter of feeling the absent object represented but of the spectator-observer feeling his or her own body. It is also possible that this arousal and satisfaction may consist of much more than penile erection and ejaculation aimed at intangible, hidden recesses of the imaged female body.[23]

This is a seemingly obvious point but it is one that is very seldom mentioned in studies of pornography (it is even absent in Williams' own study of porn *Hard Core*): that touch (the actual touch of the hand on the genitals) is a crucial aspect of the process of porn viewership and should thus be viewed in terms of spectatorship and spectatorial processes. Williams suggests that the feel of masturbation is more than a contingent by-product of pornography, it is instead a major part of the experience: a kind of physical suturing of the viewer into the action. By shying away from the physical experience of porn in academic studies we miss its very basic, primary function, a function that also occurs, to a greater or lesser extent, in non-pornographic films as well. Through her focus on body genres Williams questions the supremacy of the gaze in the cinematic experience and thus in film theory; as she states, the experience of the body can undercut and even provide a counterpoint to the narratological and cognitive experience of the mind when faced with a film. For Williams, the body becomes an index of certain films' efficacy and a distinct visceral physical encounter, a notion that, as we have already seen, differs from a great deal of film theory that privileges the subject and vision.

Despite focussing on the body, however, Linda Williams' work differs, in several crucial aspects, from theories that I have grouped below as belonging to those that see the body or the sensorium as a 'site of reception'. Firstly, of course, by positing the notion of body genres, Williams ignores the fact that the body is an important tool in all films – not just those that offer vicarious thrills and spills such as gory horror or horny porn. In fact, by suggesting the concept of specific body genres Williams, in some ways, merely falls into the trap of privileging vision and cognitive identification in those films that do not fall under her generic umbrella. Williams also limits her study (and by extension her definition of body genres) to those moments in film that feature images of bodies on screen – the process then is one of mimesis or identification rather then synaesthetic or multisensory exchange and understanding. Most of all, however, the body in Williams' work is pictured as a feeling yet unintelligent mass of nerve endings and corpuscles that serve to bluntly register the effect of what is happening on screen, unmindful, and a slave to cognition. As we shall see, this is somewhat different from suggesting (as theorists such as Barbara Kennedy, Laura Marks and Vivian Sobchack do) that the body can be viewed as a site, a method of *understanding* that serves to address the paucity of vision and that the body can be as much a generator of important information as the brain.

What is crucial about Williams' work, however, is that it values the bodily every bit as much as the cognitive; she makes the prescient point, for example, that visceral and embodied images should not automatically be considered excessive or gratuitous, they may be *the* defining aspect of the film or even the genre to which it belongs. As we shall see throughout this book, this notion can be linked to the change in scopic episteme. The postmodern scopic regime recognises and celebrates the flesh and values its experience in the visual.

The Body as a Site of Reception

The second category of embodied film theory is that which I have termed the body as 'a site of reception', or the body as a corporeal and visceral tool that aids in the understanding of certain images, encounters and meanings that the eye fails to fully comprehend. In this way the body is not only a feeling machine driven by visual images but an understanding and perceiving machine that draws on encysted memory, experience and knowledge, to provide a subcognitive ground for its own responses. This approach not so much challenges the Cartesianism of Western ontology as attempts to re-value its frames of reference, redefining binaries such as thought/feeling and mind/body without necessarily effacing their difference. Thought and feeling, in these theories, like the mind and the body, are seen more as a Moebius continuum rather than a set of distinct and mutually exclusive categories.[24]

One of the first studies to suggest such a notion was Steven Shaviro's *The Cinematic Body* published in 1993.[25] Taking its cue mainly from Deleuze and Guattari's *Anti-Oedipus* and *A Thousand Plateaus*, Shaviro's book not only attempted to assert the importance of the body in film theory but also suggested that this role could be active as well as passive, that is, that it could be used to understand rather than just be affected by cinematic images.[26]

Although never overtly encroaching into areas that, as we shall see, will be covered by later theorists, Shaviro nevertheless suggests the idea that the body is subject to what he calls the 'new automatism of perception';[27] perception that has become unconscious and corporeal. In the first chapter of *The Cinematic Body*, he cites notions such as tactile images and subcognitive processes as being vital areas of cinematic reception and yet he also studies horror and slapstick comedy (most specifically David Cronenberg and Jerry Lewis) in terms of what Linda Williams might call body genres. Shaviro's work then is interesting to the present study in that it provides us with a kind of hinge point between the two areas of the postmodern scopic regime I have been highlighting: presenting body genres *and* corporeal avenues of perception. Because of its relatively early composition (its publication in 1993 coming only one year after the death of Felix Guattari and two before the death of Gilles Deleuze), it also represents something of an embryonic attempt to understand the body as a thinking and understanding tool as well as an effected and responsive one.

The impact of the work of Gilles Deleuze on film theory is neatly summed up by Robert Stam in his *Film Theory: An Introduction*:

> Film theory has…been feeling the positively corroding impact of the writings of Gilles Deleuze, and especially of his two ambitious books from the 1980s: *Cinema I, l'image-mouvement* and *Cinema II: l'image-temps*. Prior to his specially filmic writing Deleuze, together with Felix Guattari, had already been indirectly influential on film theory through his critique of psychoanalysis in *Anti-Oedipus: Capitalism and Schizophrenia*.[28]

What unites much of the recent interest in Deleuze and cinema is the realisation that Deleuze's ideas (along, as we shall see in the later chapters of this section, with similar ideas in other areas such as body politics and neuroscience) can be used to not only counter the kinds of structures and methodological fixity that provide the base for film theory's notions of spectatorship, but can offer reasonable and working alternatives, a point that is highlighted by Gregory Flaxman:

> Sensations burrow through the determinative and dogmatic structures of thought, but in doing so they reveal that structure as such: in terms of Deleuze and Guattari, sensation reveals our 'molar' existence as a dimension, formation or perspective within a 'molecular' universe.[29]

The questions raised by *The Cinematic Body* provided later Deleuzian theorists with the foundation for more specifically geared concepts; the language Shaviro uses for example resounds with the lexis of the postmodern scopic regime as he outlines the changing mandate of film theory and film itself:

> When I am caught up in watching a film I do not really 'identify' in the psychoanalytic sense with the activity of the (male) protagonist, or with that protagonist's gaze, or even with what theorists have called the 'omnivoyeuristic' look of the camera. It is more the case that I am brought into intimate contact with the images on screen by a process of mimesis or contagion.[30]

The Cinematic Body is also interesting in that it acknowledges the need to classify theories of embodied spectatorship and, consequently, to give them a name:

> Much work remains to be done on the psychophysiology of cinematic experience; the ways in which film renders vision tactile, short-circuits reflection and directly stimulates the nervous system.[31]

It is of course precisely this that the present work aims to do.

Ultimately, Shaviro's work can be seen as the first step in the evolution of theories of the body as a site of reception for film, it offers tantalising insights into what might be possible, how film studies could utilise the work of Deleuze and Guattari and what a theory of the cinematic body might consist of.

The Brain is the Screen: Deleuze and Film Theory

Deleuze was constantly aware of making the distinction between psychoanalysis and neuroscience, the workings of the mind and the biology of the brain and how this can bear relation to his theory of cinema; he states in an article on the time-image for instance:[32]

> I think one particular important principle is the biology of the brain, a micro-biology. It's going through a complete transformation, and coming up with extraordinary discoveries. It's not to psycho-analysis or linguistics but to the biology of the brain that we should look for principles, because it doesn't have the drawback, like the other two disciplines, of applying ready-made concepts.[33]

For Deleuze, neuroscience offered a way out of the subjectivised impasse of traditional film theory, and its tropes of neural networks, microbiological interdependency and action potentials fitted neatly in with his own post-structuralist notions of the rhizome and molecularity. The subject, in Deleuze and Guattari, is precisely the same as the cinema viewer of the postmodern scopic regime – fractured, many levelled and constantly in internal negotiation with itself; the traditional fixity of the self has given way to a free flowing system of intensities that coalescence and disperse with equal ease. In many ways, the shift we have been tracing here, between the modern and the postmodern scopic regimes, is precisely the same shift highlighted by Deleuze and Guattari's first book, *Anti-Oedipus,* written in 1972; the conceptual terms and tools that they formulated throughout their career (intensity, sensation, affect, hapticity, haecceity, molecularity and so on) without referring directly to the body or to synaesthesia, do describe the same theoretical arc, neither however lived long enough to see how closely their post-structural thought reflected neuroscientific shifts in the late 1990s and early 2000s – this was left to others to examine.

Deleuze's works on cinema, *Cinema 1: The Movement-image* and *Cinema 2: The Time-image*, do not in themselves utilise a great many aspects of the postmodern scopic regime (although, as we shall see, this *has* subsequently been done by other theorists); however, they do contain several conceptual tools, such as the affection-image, the sonsign and the tactsign (see Chapters Seven and Eight) that do broaden the mandate of cinema studies beyond the purely cognitive and suggest other, more corporeal avenues of spectatorship. However, it is in books such as *A Thousand Plateaus* and *Francis Bacon: The Logic of Sensation* that we see the full importance of his ideas to embodied film theory.[34]

Deleuze's use of neuroscience and the brain was perhaps a reflection of his own faith in materiality. For Deleuze, the spectator was a material object who perceived and felt, a collection of potential intensities, a network of neural pathways, each leading to a specific affect or thought process. As Greg Lambert explains:

> In place of the linguistic model of the unconscious whose origins are found in Levi Strauss…or even the later conception of the unconscious in Lacan, which still operates according to the linguistic principles of metaphor (condensation) and metonymy…Deleuze proposes a new schema that is both non-linguistic…and a-centred: that of the relative distribution of organic internal and external environments on a plane that represents an absolute interiority and exteriority, that is, a topological structure of the brain that cannot be adequately represented in a Euclidean way.[35]

In other words, Deleuze posits a continuum between image and brain, outside and inside, the body of the film and the body of the spectator. We must remember here of course that Deleuze is referring to the materiality of the brain and all of its related areas, areas that include the brain itself, the brain stem, the nervous system, the perceptual systems and so on. In fact, when he talks about the brain he is talking as much about the body that it extends into as the grey matter that resides in the skull. Moreover Deleuze, by asserting the importance of affect and hapticity elsewhere in his work, makes the point that such material systems can only achieve significance through sensation, they are at once its channel and its method of achieving actuality.

Deleuze's cinema books cannot be considered works of embodied film theory, their mandate is too wide, their conceptual base too bound by issues of ontology and philosophical method but, as we shall see below, some of their concepts and others harvested from his books on art and those with Felix Guattari have provided the basis for a great deal of film theory of the postmodern scopic regime. Deleuze's own philosophically materialist background and his use of Spinoza and art critics such as Bernard Berenson and William Worringer have ensured that his work is constantly cited as a base with which to better understand the role of the senses and the body in cinema spectatorship.

Laura Marks – Revisioning the Skin

The work of Laura Marks represents a full flowering of embodied film theory. In her two books *The Skin of the Film* and *Touch: Sensuous Multisensory*

Media she explores the use of a wide range of sensual inputs in the process of spectatorship, examining how touch, taste, smell and hearing all interact with, undercut and enhance the visual.[36] She also utilises Deleuze in a number of interesting ways that enable his work to extend beyond the rather limited cinematic areas that he initially concerned himself with. Her work often explores films from avant-garde or independent directors and her main textual base is one outside of mainstream cinema. Her central texts often aim to directly engage with the area of embodiment and sensuality, exploring their connection to intercultural exchange and the stored memory of diasporic cultures.

In her assertions on the importance of embodiment, both in terms of the characters on screen and in terms of the audience, Marks suggests that the cinema viewer can undergo a series of sometimes conflicting sensual experiences that elide the fixed ontological self usually considered to be film theory's main theoretical object, as she states:

> The ideal relationship between viewer and image in optical visuality tends to be one of mastery, in which the viewer isolates and comprehends the objects of vision. The ideal relationship between viewer and image in haptic visuality is one of mutuality, in which the viewer is more likely to lose herself in the image, to lose her sense of proportion.[37]

We could say that this form of mutual haptic exchange can also result in the loss of 'her self', as the delineation of subject/object and felt/feeler becomes hard to determine. Unlike those film theories where the body is taken as an index of the film, in Marks, the skin and the proximal senses become major receptive sites, lending a thickness that might otherwise be missing in the purely optical experience. The body reacts (or becomes an index) only when this initial or more primary stage has been completed and it is this that makes a receptive site of the body, changing its status from a passive flesh to a corporeal thinking machine.

For Marks, diasporic cultures, especially those heralding from Africa and the Middle East, are more likely to be propagated through embodied experience – touch, taste and smell – than the visually based ocular regimes of Western capitalism. This not only produces a cinema that is more haptical and less optical but it also challenges the dominance of the eye over the skin, flesh and nerves. Resistant to, or even excluded from, the dominant discourse, asserts Marks, minority and intercultural cinema has had to forge new connections, new ways of filming reality and new ways of exploring the relationship between viewer and screen to fully realise its aesthetic aims. As with her use of Deleuze's affection-image, the visual, instead of being translated into thought or action, is made to connect with sensuality, with emotion and with memory (recollection-image) subtending the dominant discourse of ideology and the self. Because diasporic cultures are removed from their own land, she asserts, their cultural artefacts are suffused with images of memory, of longing and of mourning, all processes that are best translated by more proximal senses such as smell and taste than the cognitively based ones of sight and sound.

Such theories however do not suggest that sensuous embodied knowledge is exclusive to those born and raised outside of Western culture, merely that such culture has served to repress the body and the emotions, or at least devalued them. New ways of thinking about vision uncover these hitherto buried strata and encourage Western ontology to broaden its perceptual horizons. Marks' work then is as much about vision as it is about embodiment, as much about all cinema as solely intercultural.

Of course here we come up against a problem: what if the images we experience on screen mean nothing to us, what if we do not have the embodied knowledge that is necessary to make sense of a film, if we do not know what the feel of a sari is like or what the taste of a particular spice is like, does that mean we can never access the images at all? Marks suggests not, for her, this only further enriches the spectatorial process; if this occurs, the viewer then becomes locked not only into a network of sensual knowledge consisting of their own present and past, but into a creative act that exposes the virtuality of both memory and time, encouraging them to expand upon what knowledge they do have:

> What is more disturbing is when the optical image cannot be connected to any living memory. When I find a school yearbook at a flea market, or when I contemplate Christian Boltanski's wartime photographs of anonymous Jewish schoolchildren, I confront a virtual image that does not correspond to my experience, nor perhaps to anybody's memory, yet it cries out to have a memory assigned to it.[38]

The result is the creation of a virtual memory that is based in one's own experience but also exists as a form of generalised past; it is through this process that Western audiences can enjoy world cinema, can be corporeally involved in science fiction, can recoil at images of the holocaust, can guess at what its like to be stabbed to death in the shower in a seemingly ordinary motel in the middle of the night and the many other experiences of film that have no direct correlation to our everyday lives.

As we shall see in the second part of this book, Laura Marks' notions have a lot to tell us, not just about intercultural cinema, but about cinema as a whole. I shall utilise and adapt many of her ideas concerning haptic vision and smell, the time-image and sensual memory to look at mainstream narrative cinema and uncover unexplored areas of cinema spectatorship.

Barbara Kennedy – The Aesthetics of Sensation

Sensation is a major concept in the work of Deleuze and Guattari and forms a fundamental notion in Barbara Kennedy's work, *Deleuze and Cinema*. Sensation in this context, however, describes more than a feeling or an emotion (although these do form a part of it); rather, it serves to stimulate cognition or action and, as such, has a privileged place as that which connects us to the world. Sensation is not contained within us as such but is instead a force, an intensity, that affects us in the same way as, say, the feel of a feather on our skin or the feeling of water, which is to say it does not invade our biological space but does open up its boundaries and borders erasing the difference between internality and externality. Deleuze explored the full range of implications for such a theory in his monograph on Francis Bacon *The Logic of Sensation*:

> The violence of sensation is opposed to the violence of the represented (the sensational, the cliché). The former is inseparable from its direct action on the nervous system, the levels through which it passes, the domains it traverses: being itself a Figure, it must have nothing of the nature of the represented object.[39]

As Kennedy correctly asserts, such a notion has a tremendous impact on ideas of spectatorship because we can, with the Deleuzian concept of sensation, dissolve the dividing line between the spectator and the screen. As in the paintings of Francis Bacon, sensation does not rest in the body of the viewer as such but somewhere in its connectivity with the canvas and paint (or the light, time and movement of the screen). The viewer has become a rhizome with the film. As Kennedy explains eloquently:

> These pre-verbal intensities are called 'pathic events', or prehensive events. Rather than a unity, as in a phenomenological or Cartesian sense, these events operate as a multiplicity. This notion of events oc-

curring on multiple strata explains how experiences can occur through feeling, empathy, affective and pathetic awareness rather than logical thought or a discursive schema such as psychoanalysis.[40]

This proto-subjective layer, what could be called the molecular layer, does not so much exist as an alternative to the more solid molar layer of subjective consciousness but as a virtuality, a non-delineated, non-stratified zone of intensity that may or may not coagulate into sentient and, so, conscious thought. Sensation is the raw material of perception and action.[41]

It is easy to see how such thinking not only challenges the traditional, scopic notions of cinema spectatorship but also offers a viable alternative. In Kennedy's exposition, the film viewer is transformed from the removed, impassive observer of Metz and Baudry into a site of sensation that connects to what is in front of it on, not only a psychical level but, a visceral and corporeal one: feeling the film in a myriad of subcognitive ways, through a multiplicity of sensual channels, forming virtualities only some of which will be realised in actual perception, thought or action.

Sensation, in Deleuzian terms, is much more than the sensation of Williams and Littau, here it is knowledge and thought in its own right, not the product of vision but something that undercuts vision, that exists as a perceptual sense. As Ronald Bogue details with reference to Deleuze's work on painting, colour seen as an intensity, for instance, can evoke a host of other sensations – warmth, coldness, strength, calm and so on:

> Deleuze does recognise that value and tone are not antithetical aspects of colour, and that they are often used in combination with each other…both pertain to the eye and vision, and hence are properly visual, but the opposition of bright and dark, or light and shadow, discloses an optic space, whereas the opposition of warm and cold, of expansion and contraction belongs to a haptic space.[42]

The 'sensation' here refers to the intensity of the colour and how it relates to the synaesthetic body. Rather than being *caused* by visual images (the crash, for example) it forms the basis of knowledge. Imagine for instance the difference between viewing a film such as *March of the Penguins* (2005) and a film like *Lawrence of Arabia* (1962), it would be the sensation of the relative temperatures in these two films that would provide the body's primary knowledge of the terrains, such sensation however is neither visual (in that heat and cold are embodied terms) nor is it an index of the film; it is instead a form of corporal phenomenological knowledge that centres us in a world of sense-making and sense usage.

Kennedy's mandate in *Deleuze and Cinema,* however, is not only to explore the possibilities of embodiment and Deleuzian film theory but to relate them to the rising discourses of Second Wave feminism that I outline in Chapter 2 of this work; such theory asserts the value of the body and sensation in undercutting the phallogocentric discourse of modernity and, *ipso facto*, their manifestation in the field of vision. As Kennedy states:

> A post-structuralist and post-feminist pragmatics seeks an engagement with the filmic experience which moves from debates which theorise 'representation' and the 'image' and their concern with pleasure and desire, to theories of 'material affect' and 'sensation' and 'becoming' and a neo-aesthetics as sexuality. Such post-feminist film theory needs to question the very ontological and teleological foundations of language use and meaning, to provide a fresh approach to what it is to 'think' about ideas and concepts…[43]

As we shall see, this view relates to the overall movement of thinking that we have characterised as the postmodern scopic regime, where feminist thinkers such as Luce Irigaray and Hélène Cixous posit levels of understanding that subtend the usually cognitive processes of vision and the mind. We can also notice how Kennedy asserts the primacy of these sensations and affects; they are not secondary experiences of vision or some other sense but intensities that have meaning in themselves; they create new avenues of interpretation because they elide the rational, cognitive parts of the brain. In films, kinetic movement, colour saturation, intensive sound experiences, visual disorientation and others all attest to the power of the flesh to make sense of that which is put in front of the eyes, something that prompts us to draw up new models of the viewer and spectator.

Vivian Sobchack – Cinesthesia and Phenomenology

The work of Vivian Sobchack represents an opening up of the mandates of film theory and, perhaps more importantly, its relationship to the sensorium and its place within spectatorship. Her full-scale work *The Address of the Eye* attempts to create a phenomenology of film viewing in which the 'lived body' of the spectator is addressed and used as a ground upon which to formulate new theories of meaning and sense experience in cinema. However it is the essay 'What My Fingers Knew' published in the collection *Carnal*

Thoughts: Embodiment and Moving Image Culture that I wish to look at here because it represents not only a simplified view of the many ideas and concepts within *The Address of the Eye* but also, through its use of synaesthesia, provides much of the initial impetus for the present study.

Sobchack's essay begins with a small survey of the uses of the body in film theory. As I have done here, she highlights the paucity of studies that address the corporeal spectator since the instigation of contemporary film theory in the 1960s and 70s. Correctly, Sobchack asserts that this situation is changing and that what I have called the postmodern scopic regime is beginning to bear fruit in terms of theories that attempt to include the body or the sensorium. Sobchack, however, fails to make the distinction that I have made here between those studies that address the body as either representation or as an instinctual (what Sobchack herself calls) 'carnal response'[44] and those works that see the body as a site of sense reception and meaning such as Marks and Kennedy. As we shall see, Sobchack's own work is obviously in the latter of these two groups.

Sobchack bases her essay on her highly visceral experience of watching Jane Campion's *The Piano* (1993):

> Campion's film moved me deeply, stirring my bodily senses and my sense of my body. The film not only 'filled me up' and often 'suffocated me' with feelings that resonated in me and constricted my chest and stomach, but it also 'sensitized' the very surfaces of my skin – as well as its own – to touch.[45]

If Sobchack's analysis were to end there we might conclude that her response to Campion's film represented the kind of theory that I have posited constitutes the use of the body as an index of film's appeal to corporeality: the use of the body as a *responsive* medium mediated by sight. However, in the rest of the essay she goes further than this and offers a framework for viewing the sensorium as a site of *reception* that can provide visual images with a multisensory, synaesthetic thickness. Sobchack also, importantly, in this essay, uses such theory to address mainstream film rather than either the specific 'body genres' of Linda Williams or the exilic, intercultural cinema of Laura Marks.

Sobchack's main thesis in the first three sections of the essay is that optically mediated sensual images have no meaning if they are not related to the whole sensorium of the *lived* body. In order to have a sense of the coldness, the wetness or the saltiness of the sea in *The Piano* we must draw upon our fleshy knowledge, the experience of our skin and nerve endings in similar situations, as she states: 'the film experience is meaningful not *to the side of our bodies but because of our bodies*'.[46] The body has become here not something that is passively affected by the film but something that is actively involved in the creation of meaning; the cross modality of the senses allows sensual images to be (literally and metaphorically) fleshed out, to be grounded in a knowledge that does not reside in the brain but in the body and its connection to the world. Sobchack carries this argument further to suggest that, in the opening scenes of the film, her body has an understanding of the images that her eye/brain dyad misses:

> As I watched *The Piano*'s opening moments – in that first shot, before I even knew there was an Ada and before I saw her from my side of her vision…something seemingly extraordinary happens. Despite my 'almost blindness' the 'unrecognisable blur' and resistance of the image to my eyes, my fingers knew what I was looking at and this before the objective reverse shot.[47]

Sobchack asserts that her fingers haptically anticipated the image that her eyes were not yet ready to see, that her body contained a knowledge and a series of sense-making frameworks that existed apart from her eye and conscious self. We can appreciate how, with contributions from the other theorists we have looked at, we could see this as constituting some form of postmodern scopic thinking.

Sobchack coins the term the 'cinesthetic subject' to describe the embodied site of reception that we can view the spectator as representing. The 'cinesthetic subject', Sobchack is at pains to stress, is not a metaphor, it is a model to understand the full thickness of the cinematic experience in all its molecularity and sense-becoming. Sobchack suggests that the cross modality of the senses (synaesthesia) provides us with a key tool in understanding the cinema experience, one which has been missing in much contemporary film theory.

§

The readings in the latter half of this thesis do not deny, as Steven Shaviro does, the validity of traditional notions of film theory; there is still a place for viewing films as carriers of ideology, of visual images, of points of identification, of subjectivisation and so on. What the readings in Part Two suggest is that this cognitive strata is merely one layer in a whole wealth of experiences that make up the full thickness of the cinematic process and that in order to fully understand it as a medium we must look at how these different layers interact with one another and come together in the fractured subjectivity of the audience member.

Ultimately, what is stake in embodied film theory of the postmodern scopic regime is the creation of a new viewer, not one that is seen as a removed and detached voyeur, passively receiving images which are then filtered through ideology or subjectivity but one that subtends this layer of understanding with an corporeal experience that extends into their own personal and cultural memory; if such memory is lacking, the process becomes a creative one whereby approximations are made and embodied information is re-negotiated and re-visited. As we have seen, the process of discovering this new cinema-goer is not one of genesis but of archaeology, excavating layers of assumption and traditional methodology to find different strata of understanding. This process is an exciting one, one that encompasses many theories and many academic disciplines, it is also one that breaches many foundational discourses but ultimately it is one that is necessary if the full rounded thickness of the postmodern spectator is to be understood.[48]

2

CRITICAL THEORY AND EMBODIMENT: REFIGURING THE CORPOREAL SELF

> I do not see anger or a threatening attitude as a psychic fact hidden behind the gesture or read anger in it. The gesture does not make me think of anger, it is anger itself.[1]

In the last chapter we looked at how some recent film theorists have attempted to broaden the horizons of what we think of as cinema spectatorship. We looked at how such theorists are attempting to assert the value of sensory experience in cinema and how this brings into question the notion of the fixed, stable viewer as well as the consciousness that can empathise, sympathise and hypothesise about what they are watching on screen. Implicit in the studies cited in the latter part of the last chapter is the desire to re-evaluate what exactly constitutes the cinematic subject: the expositionary tools offered by late phenomenological inquiry and post-structuralism (among others) allow us to re-present the cinematic subject and his/her experience as a process of involvement rather than detached spectatorship. Whilst not negating the presence of a removed and contemplative observer, theories of the postmodern scopic regime attempt a reappraisal of embodied knowledge, allowing the full thickness of the experience to be examined. Under these auspices, the spectator exists not only as a conscious self mediated by what it sees but as a site of affect, an archive of bodily experience (present and past), a corporeal sense-making machine and a surface of intensities that sometimes upholds, sometimes undercuts, the traditional mechanisms of filmic enjoyment.

As I have already stated, the situation that I have called the postmodern scopic regime is not limited to film theory; in fact, as I shall attempt to outline, many of the foundational tropes and strategies of theorists such as Vivian Sobchack and Barbara Kennedy herald from outside film as a discipline. In this chapter, I aim to look at how numerous theorists have sought to re-evaluate the importance of corporeality and embodied experience in the wider fields of philosophy, psychoanalysis and gender politics, areas I have broadly grouped under the title 'critical theory'. In each of these disciplines we can once again note a shift from a concept of vision that is linked to a fixed ontological subject to a vision that is underlined by embodiment and synaesthetic multi-modality. Again, inserting the body as some kind of third term between accepted binaries complicates the fixity of the self and heralds from changes in visual paradigms.

The temporal arrangement of theories within this section is not clear cut. Despite positing the term 'postmodern scopic regime' (in the sense that it is used to describe a move away from more modernist notions of the 'grand narrative' of vision and the autonomy of the senses), it is difficult to group thinkers like Merleau-Ponty, Luce Irigaray, Didier Anzieu or Elizabeth Grosz under the same heading. It is, perhaps, even difficult to make definitive statements on the seismic shifts of individual philosopher's careers, or even works, within terms as fragile and as porous as modernism and postmodernism. Merleau-Ponty's *Phenomenology of Perception*, for instance, appears at once to feed into postmodern scopic notions *and* to reinforce those modernist tropes outlined by Crary. His later work *The Visible and the Invisible*, as Luce Irigary states, merely confuses the issue all the more by seemingly reinstating the primacy of 'the look' that is so strikingly challenged in Chapter 1, Part 2, of *Phenomenology of Perception*.[2] With the exception of Merleau-Ponty's early work, the theories that I shall look at here all emanate from the second half of the twentieth century, from the 1960s onwards; however, not all herald from a distinctly postmodern perspective (see *The Visible and the Invisible* or Didier Anzieu's work on corporeal psychoanalysis). I would assert, however, that all display a willingness to challenge the primacy of optical perception and, *ipso facto*, its epistemological paradigm.[3] Again, let it be reiterated, that the term 'postmodern' in 'postmodern scopic regime' refers not to any foundational assumption on the part of the individual thinker or even their work but to the larger seismic shifts in vision and visual thinking. A modernist theorist, in other words, may contribute (wittingly or unwittingly) to the postmodern scopic regime and embodied theory.

As we shall see, certain feminist theory offers us key tools in challenging the primacy of optical vision, a vision that has been seen as not only twinned with notions of the masculine interrogatory gaze but with the phallocratic construction of reason itself.[4] These tools reassert and reassess the senses and sensual experiences that have traditionally been seen as feminine and have thus been excluded from mainstream phallocratic ontology. As in the film theory we have already looked at, ideas of what makes a subject, a person, a living thing, in areas such as body politics and critical theory is changing;

however, rather than providing a clear point of rupture, we can detect a certain sliding between the plateaus of the modern and the postmodern scopic regimes and this is, perhaps, how it should be. There is no distinct line to be drawn, no definitive foundational date to be set. Certain discourses, figures and strategies can be detected, especially since the 1960s, that undermine the prevailing discourses reliant on the optical-visual paradigm; certain discourses that stress the value of the closeness of touch instead of the distance of vision (Anzieu), the bodily experience of colour (Merleau-Ponty), the enveloping quality of sound (Anzieu) and the psycho-sociological importance of bodily sensation when it comes to such areas as disgust offer us yet more in-roads into embodied theory and more critical tools with which to examine cinema.[5]

Aside from the fact that many of the film theories examined in the last chapter are based on a great deal of the philosophical texts that shall be examined in this, what is at stake here, for film theory, is a re-examination and re-assessment of what it means to experience the world and, consequently (because it is part of that world) film. Many of the theories examined here will suggest that merely because a film does not present us with the chemical or environmental stimuli for actual sensory stimulation this does not mean that we use our eyes and ears only in the cinema theatre. Part of the underlying, implicit assumption of many of these theories is that we can never detach our understanding of the world from our lived experience of it. The living body is a process of sense-making, our visual perception is constantly checked, validated, undercut and supported by our other interfaces on the world and these other interfaces are constantly interacting with each other, exchanging information, cross-checking and creating virtualities that allow us to understand images – not semiotically through a distanced contemplation – but instantly through a bodily transitivism.

The Shell and the Kernel

There is a small but important section of Freud's *Beyond the Pleasure Principle* that is dedicated to a description of what we could think of as neuropsychological development, both in terms of phylo- and ontogenesis.[6] As Elizabeth Grosz states in *Volatile Bodies*, for Freud, the biological and the psychological were always inextricably linked, despite psychoanalysis and its founding father being portrayed, in the popular imagination at least, as being concerned only with the mind and its functioning. Chapter 4 of *Beyond the Pleasure Principle* is interesting because it details the tacit biological assumptions and foundational tropes that underpin the rest of Freud's project and, as we shall see, it is possible to trace many of his psychoanalytic strategies and mechanisms back to this original picture. The images Freud paints in this dense passage maybe 'speculation, often far-fetched'[7] but they do provide the basis for not only his but many others' notions of what exactly constituted psychoanalysis:

> Let us picture a living organism in its most simplified possible form as an undifferentiated vesicle of a substance that is susceptible to stimulation. Then the surface turned towards the external world will from its very situation be differentiated and will serve as an organ for receiving stimuli. Indeed embryology, in its capacity as a recapitulation of developmental history, actually shows us that the central nervous system originates from the ectoderm; the grey matter of the cortex remains a derivative of the primitive superficial layer of the organism and may have inherited some of its properties.[8]

Here we see Freud introducing a number of concepts that will form the basis of what constitutes the basic object of psychoanalysis – the human being: its mind, its body and its nervous system. We see, for instance, the twinning of phylo- and ontogenesis, the notion that the developing embryo represents a snapshot of developmental history that, as individuals, we consist of not only of our own biological development but that of our species as well. We see also the beginnings of what will become an important thread of this chapter: the development of what Nicolas Abraham and Maria Torok were to call 'the shell and the kernel', the retreat of the sensitive ectodermic layers inward forming an inner core or kernel and the hardening of the outer layer (with a few exceptions) forming the shell or envelope. Freud continues:

> The little fragment of living substance is suspended in the middle of an external world charged with the most powerful energies; and it would be killed by the stimulation emanating from these if it were not provided with a protective shield against stimuli. It acquires the shield in this way: its outermost surface ceases to have the structure proper to living matter, becomes to some degree inorganic and thenceforward functions as a special envelope or membrane resistant to stimuli. In consequence the energies of the external world are able to pass into the next underlying layers…[9]

It becomes clear here that what Freud is referring to is both the phylogenetic development of the organism qua species and the ontogenetic development of the individual, and that the 'shielding' referred to could just as easily apply to the maturing psyche as to the evolving organic body, both in terms of the individual *and* the species. This mirroring of biological and psychic development is in complete sympathy with Freudian methodology, as Didier Anzieu asserts:

> I base my thinking upon two general principles. One is specially Freudian: every psychical function develops by supporting itself upon a bodily function whose workings its transposes on to a mental plane.[10]

Freud's thinking here is commensurate with the surrounding milieu of nineteenth-century German embryology that was, at the time, experiencing a resurgence of interest in the links between phylogeny and ontogeny through the work of the Darwin-informed embryologist Ernst Haeckel.[11]

In order to protect itself from the intensity of exogenous stimulation, the 'little fragment of living substance' not only develops a kind of dead layer on its outer surface but also withdraws its living, sensitive surface inward:

> In highly developed organisms the receptive cortical layer of the former vesicle has long been withdrawn into the depths of the interior of the body, though portions of it have been left behind on the surface immediately beneath the general shield against stimuli. These are the sense organs, which consist essentially of apparatus for the reception of certain effects of stimulation.[12]

We have here a recognisably complete picture of the neuro-biological development of a 'healthy' human being: through organic maturation (both phylo- and ontogenetically) the outer facing layer becomes hardened and that which was once on the outside – the still living, sensitive surface – withdraws inward to form a kernel that must be protected and shielded. Freud goes on to suggest ways in which this schema can manifest itself in maturity:

> The specific unpleasure of physical pain is probably the result of this protective shield having been broken through in a limited area. There is then a continuous stream of excitations from the part of the periphery concerned with the central apparatus of the mind, such as could normally arise only from *within* the apparatus.[13]

The image of the shell and the kernel was not new in the field of Western epistemology, where knowledge and the self were thought to reside in an inner core that needed to be protected by a shield; Kant, for instance, in 'What is Enlightenment' uses a similar image to describe the search for knowledge and freedom.[14] However, it would be misleading to view Freud's notions as simply based on this image alone; Freud's neurological and thus psychic topology is a great deal more complex than the image of a simple shell and kernel would suggest, as Didier Anzieu states:

> Since the Renaissance, Western thought has been obsessed with a particular epistemological conception, whereby the acquisition of knowledge is seen as a process of breaking through an outer shell to reach an inner core or nucleus…Since the nineteenth century, neurophysiology has turned its back on this conception, *though the fact was not recognised at the time.*[15]

The last sentence here is interesting because it highlights the fact that, during this time neurologists such as Freud (because, as Ernest Jones details, Freud was constantly torn in early part of his career, the late nineteenth century, between obligations to his family and his longed for career in neurobiology) and Ernst Haeckel were developing new ways of thinking about how our brains and our bodies are formed, thinking that would be based on concepts and images of invagination, of enfolding and of double articulation.[16] As Anzieu correctly states, however, and as we can see with Freud in *Beyond the Pleasure Principle*, these early neuroembryologists failed to fully realise the potential of their ideas. Unlike later post-structuralist and feminist thinkers, for Freud, and Haeckel, the process of invagination produces a series of intercommunicative strata rather than an organic non-hierarchical enfolding – what could be thought of as a modernist atom rather than the more postmodern image of the Moebius strip or the double helix. Abraham neatly sums up this image:

> …in Freud's intuition, the Periphery itself includes a Kernel with its own Periphery, which in turn includes a kernel and so forth. The secondary and tertiary, etc. kernels, along with those that precede them in rank are related by analogy. Thus the primary kernel, termed organic, has on its periphery a so-called psychic counterpart of secondary kernel…[17]

The overriding image here is one of stratification; although complicating the picture somewhat, with its mise-en-abyme of differing layers, what we have is essentially the shell and kernel schema, whereby a hardened outer layer protects a more organic inner core. Invagination has not resulted in a

Moebius strip but in a stratified organism whose hardened outer layer serves only to protect and shield a more sensitive inner kernel.

It is not difficult to see how such thinking translated into the discipline of psychoanalysis and how it shaped both its objects and its aims. The image of the shell and the kernel (however complicated and stratified) can be seen not only in Freudian metapsychology but also in its notions of what constituted a healthy organism: autonomous, individuated and centripetally balanced. Through such mechanisms as the Oedipus complex, the individual continues its ontogenetic maturation becoming more and more separated from exogenous influences and more and more autonomous from the world around it. The aim of psychoanalysis arguably is to break through the shell of ego-repression and to restore the balance of the kernel within. Although altered somewhat, we see this same process at work in Lacan's faith in the unsymbolised kernel of the Real, the agalma and the *objet petit a*.

This situation has resulted in psychoanalysis privileging a number of traits that it sees as being present in a healthy individual and consequently missing or damaged in the sick: that of autonomy (from the biology of the mother and, ultimately from the social body of the family), that of depth over surface, and that of centripetal balance over rupture and centrifugal imbalance. Ideally, the healthy adult grows apart from the maternal body and then the family, gains autonomous depth of emotion and intelligence and then becomes fixed in a stable and predictable selfhood. Where this does not happen, psychoanalysis steps in.

It is easy to see from this description why sight and the visual are seen as being so important to the maturing consciousness. Despite Freud briefly touching upon bodily contact and perception in such essays as 'Instincts and their Vicissitudes' and in certain parts of the 'Three Essays on Sexuality' we can see that because it stresses the importance of distance and autonomy sight becomes a major factor in psychological maturation: the young child *sees* the lack of a penis in the female sex, the young child *sees* the primal scene, the young child *sees* their specular image in the mirror and through a complex process of prohibition and invitation, the young child learns to develop its scopic drive and eventually to incorporate it into its sexuality.[18] Little wonder then that classical psychoanalysis has lent itself so well to film and art theory. The scopic drive is the ideal vehicle for the maintenance of the psychoanalytic self; it allows involvement without engulfment, it seeks to penetrate into the depths rather than relying on the 'deadened' outer layer of the skin and, more than anything, it creates a fixity – a perspectivalist point of view that has become synonymous with subjectivity. Since the 1960s, however, a number of theories have attempted to broaden the notions of how we mature psychologically; these theories have asserted the value of closeness, of attachment and the sensations of the skin rather than merely the eyes.

The Skin Ego

Didier Anzieu's book *The Skin Ego* is within a tradition of Freudian thought: it assumes its lexicon, it retains many of its salient features and it attempts at various stages to legitimate many of its theories through recourse to Freud's own writing. Elizabeth Grosz discusses *The Skin Ego* along with Freud's text *The Ego and the Id* and draws comparisons between Freud's brush with corporeality and Anzieu's contribution to understanding how the skin centres the ego within a world of anaclisis and anaclitic attachment. When reading Anzieu's text, however, we become gradually aware that what may have begun as an attempt at extending Freudian thought ends up as something completely, although subtly, different. Anzieu retains the basic tenets of the psyche mirroring biology but the picture we receive of the skin is not the deadened protective layer broken only by a number of perceptual openings but a surface of affect or a film of feeling that stretches over the entire body, sending a myriad of sensations to and from the inner core. For Anzieu, the skin is as much a former of the self as the mouth, anus, genitals and inner core; this is also the case, and here is where Anzieu departs most radically from Freud's view of the body, throughout the entire organism's life.

> The skin is both permeable and impermeable, superficial and profound, truthful and misleading. It is regenerative but caught up in a continual process of desiccation. It is elastic, but a piece of skin detached from the body shrinks greatly…It transmits to the brain information from the outside world, including impalpable messages…the skin is both solid and fragile…Its flimsiness and vulnerability reflect our primitive helplessness, greater than that of any other species, but at the same time our adaptive and evolutionary flexibility.[19]

Here we see some of the extent that Anzieu differs from Freud. Although it is not the case that Freud ignores the role of the skin completely, at no point does he imbue it with as much psycho-emotional importance as Anzieu and at no point is touch and corporeal sensation placed, as it is here, alongside vision in creating the self; a point that Anzieu makes specifically in relation to the blind:

> …you find human beings who suffer from blindness or deafness, or

no sense of smell, and this does not prevent them from living, nor from succeeding in communicating, perhaps in a somewhat more complicated way, but they do communicate. By contrast, there is no human being without a virtually complete envelope of skin.[20]

Instead of the stratification of the modern, Anzieu's study could be seen to represent the Moebius strip of the postmodern whereby externality and internality become not only confused but concomitant: the inside constantly becoming the outside and vice versa. An appreciation of the skin's role in the formation of the self brings into question the values of autonomy, distance and depth as we become literally sewn into our environment; that which we are is no longer contained within some hidden inner kernel but is written onto our skin and bodies.

Robert Brain in *The Decorated Body* is quick to assert the value of this in primitive cultures.[21] The scarification, tattooing and body modifications of such peoples as the Shilluk or Dinka of the Sudan attempt not only to bind the individual to the body of the social but to 'indicate the precise status and identity of the person'.[22] The same process can be seen in certain feminist revisions of the body, where closeness and proximity (traditionally linked with motherhood) are transvalued in the formation of the social, sexual and psychological organism.

Towards the end of *The Skin Ego* Anzieu suggests further ways that the psychical-corporeal binary can be questioned through consideration of the combined envelope of sensuality; here Anzieu's mode of thought seems nearer to the kind of thinking we witnessed in the latter part of the last chapter than the Freudian model of the early twentieth century:

> Parallel with the establishment of the boundaries and limits of the self as a two-dimensional interface anaclitically dependant upon tactile sensations, there forms, through the introjection of the universe of sound (and also of taste and smell), a self as a pre-individual psychical cavity possessing a rudimentary unity and identity.[23]

This stage of Anzieu's thinking is especially interesting to film theory because, among other things, he posits the idea of the sound envelope – a sonic bath that can be used as a means of rehabilitation for 'children suffering from language disturbances'. Developed in France towards the middle of the 1970s, 'semiophony' entails immersing the child in a bath of synthesised sound; ensconced in a soundproof booth, the child would frequently respond not to the meaning of the noises (they were often distorted human voices) but to their mere presence. A sound can cocoon us, can envelope us but it can also invade our space and make us uncomfortable; we experience it as a physical sensation first and foremost that relies on more than the ears for reception. Perhaps, even as much as sight, sound is linked to space and our experience of it, as Deleuze and Guattari suggest:

> A child in the dark, gripped with fear, comforts himself by singing under his breath. He walks and halts to his song. Lost, he takes shelter, or orients himself with his little song as best he can. The song is like a rough sketch of a calming and stabilizing, calm and stable, centre in the heart of chaos.[24]

We see the same processes at work here that we saw in the last chapter: a loss of faith in the visual as the primary mode of connection with the world, we see the same re-evaluation of touch and sensation in allowing us to understand the world and ourselves within it and we also see the same questioning of the primacy of distance and depth that allows us to characterise certain strains of early twentieth-century thought as logocentrically masculine or Western.

Phenomenology

Phenomenology, as John Macquarrie states, has a mixed history when it comes to dealing with the body, embodied sensations and corporeal perception.[25] On the one hand, its founding fathers such as Jaspers, Kierkegaard and Heidegger virtually ignore the body in favour of Metaphysics (a situation that mirrors a great deal of Western philosophy) and yet, on the other hand, thinkers such as Sartre, Marcel and, most importantly, Merleau-Ponty assert that 'to be' inherently involves being physical; in other words, that to exist one must exist *in* a body with all its attendant perceptions and sensations. In this section, I shall explore a thread in phenomenological thought that runs through Sartre's *Being and Nothingness* to Merleau-Ponty's *Phenomenology of Perception* and *The Visible and the Invisible,* and that is analogous with the kinds of shifts in thinking that we have seen occurring in Freudian psychoanalysis and in the ontological discourses as a whole. The discussion of Merleau-Ponty's last work *The Visible and the Invisible* will then lead directly to more recent discussions within feminism that, again, reflect this shift in thinking.

It surely is no coincidence that Sartre places his influential chapter on 'The Look' just before his chapter on 'The Body' in *Being and Nothingness*.

Sartre is aware that these two images – Being as looking and Being as feeling – are logocentrically constructed in the vast majority of Western thought, the former being privileged over the latter. Acting as a kind of hinge between these two concepts (metaphorically drawn as two chapters) Sartre attempts to lay the foundation for a phenomenology of individuated embodied experience by challenging the primacy of scientific discourse regarding the body and our experience of it. For Sartre, the experience of our own bodies (and by extension the sensations, perceptions and affects that arise from them) can never be reconciled with our knowledge of them as biological existents. Knowledge gained from biology or medicine can only ever enlighten us as to other people's bodies, we can only ever witness the heart, lungs or brain of other people, never our own.[26] Our own bodies can only be experienced as a collection of feelings, emotions and sensations; we are alienated from their corporeal visibility in the same way that we can never really come under our own gaze. By making this point alone Sartre asserts the value of sensation and perceptions such as touch and smell that have been traditionally dismissed by Western thought and addressed only through biology and physiology.

However, *Being and Nothingness* is nothing if not a work about the value of seeing, of the Look. In his chapter of the same name, Sartre asserts its importance in the formation of the self:

> …if the Other as object is defined in connection with the world as object which sees what I see, then my fundamental connection with the Other as subject must be able to be referred back to my permanent possibility of being seen by the Other. It is in and through the revelation of my being as object for the Other that I must be able to apprehend his being as subject.[27]

The body then becomes here not so much an apparatus of perception but a thing to be seen by an Other; this is so much the case that Sartre even removes the notion of sight itself from the body, positing a kind of imaginary vision unconnected to the 'ocular globes' of biological discourse. In this, Sartre anticipates the Lacanian imaginary gaze, a point that Lacan himself discusses in *The Four Fundamental Concepts of Psychoanalysis*.[28] 'To be', then, for Sartre, is 'to be seen'; the idea that 'to be' could very well also mean 'to be touched', or 'to be smelt' or 'to touch' or 'to smell' does not occur to him. In this, as Elizabeth Grosz asserts, Sartre displays his essential Cartesianism; that is, his unwillingness to address the full thickness of corporeal being despite attempting to re-assert the place of affect and feeling and to challenge the privileging of 'objective' over 'subjective' assertions of the body. Where the body and its feelings do appear in Sartre, it is as a dull, leaden object to transcendence; the nausea of existence is felt in the pit of the stomach, the headache caused by gravity reminds us of the flesh's immanence and like Antoine Roquentin we are made sick by the sheer sensation of living:

> Now I see; now I remember better what I felt the other day on the seashore when I was holding that pebble. It was a sort of sweet disgust. How unpleasant it was! And it came from the pebble, I'm sure of that, it passed from the pebble into the hands. Yes, that's it, exactly it: a sort of nausea in the hands.[29]

In these assertions is not Sartre's view broadly reminiscent of what we have termed in the preceding chapter viewing the body as an index, an index in this case of being?

We should not however fail to recognise the importance of Sartre in the growing interest in embodied perception. Elizabeth Grosz is perhaps overly harsh when she describes Sartre's 'idealism (as granting) primacy to the mind or consciousness'.[30] Whereas this is undoubtedly true to an extent, it fails to grasp the continuum that exists between Sartre's thought and Merleau-Ponty's, despite the latter labelling the former as a 'Good Cartesian'. Monika Langer[31] addresses this point when she states that:

> Admittedly there are passages in *Being and Nothingness* in which Sartre seems to go beyond such a Cartesian dualism to a view of incarnate consciousness more like that which Merleau-Ponty subsequently developed in *Phenomenology of Perception*. In this connection, one might mention Sartre's own criticism of Cartesian dualism…as well as parts of his discussion in The Body.[32]

As we shall see, what changes between these two accounts (*Being and Nothingness* and *Phenomenology of Perception*) is not so much a reconsideration of being but a reconsideration of the body itself and how it functions, especially with regard to perception and sensation and its role as a site of affect. Sartre, like Freud in psychoanalysis, is rooted in the Western ontological traditional that, as we have suggested, promotes autonomy, distance and depth rather than connectivity, closeness and surface; however, also like Freud, we see embryonic attempts at overcoming these traditions, attempts that would only come to fruition in other, later, works.

The image of the body that is presented in Merleau-Ponty's *Phenomenol-*

ogy of Perception and his last work *The Visible and the Invisible* is markedly different to that of Sartre's.[33] Whereas Sartre's body was at best an index of consciousness and, at worst, lifeless flesh to be looked at, in Merleau-Ponty, the body is the stuff of being: sensations, perceptions, and affects constitute the very essence of existence. For Merleau-Ponty, the two main methods of Western epistemology, empiricism and intellectualism, fail to address the extent that our perceptions simultaneously create and allow us access onto the world. As Monika Langer states, empiricism and intellectualism both 'presuppose a ready made world in their analyses; consequently, both are oblivious to the subject of perception'.[34] For the empiricist, perception is merely one aspect, one event, in a world that can be studied, as Merleau-Ponty states, 'as one might describe the fauna of a foreign land'.[35] This view ignores the fact that the philosopher him or herself is subject to perception and its role as both that which understands and that which constitutes. Alternatively, the intellectualist constructs a transcendental ego, replacing being-in-itself for being-for-itself, and therefore attempting to understand perception from a privileged position outside of it. For Merleau-Ponty, neither of these standpoints addresses the central issue that is: firstly, that being is constituted by perception, and, secondly, that that perception is multifaceted, synergistic and all engulfing.

By viewing the body (and by the body here we mean the body as perceiver, as feeler, as sensation) in this way Merleau-Ponty attempts to transcend the Cartesian duality that has dogged Western epistemology and ontology, not through simply adding a 'third term' (as Moniker Langer asserts), but by revising our notions of its role, its intentionality, and, most importantly, its capacity.[36] Merleau-Ponty urges us to rethink what we mean by the terms thought and consciousness and to fully understand the body's role within them. The flesh has become sentient, not merely an index of thoughts emanating in the mind, but a surface of sensation, a mode of being, that enfolds itself out onto the world and back again; a network of feelers that seek out perceptual information in a variety of different ways and that both effects and is effected by its own processes. Unlike Sartre, who saw the body as a barrier to transcendence, for Merleau-Ponty, the body is its own transcendence, created somewhere in the interstices of the perceptual network, in the same way that we sometimes envisaged the Internet as consisting of something other than the myriad of electro-physical bodies that actually make it. For Merleau-Ponty, the body, its perceptions and sensations, are what binds us to the world; it also challenges notions of subject and object (a point that, as we shall see later, has been taken up by feminists such as Luce Irigaray), for touch involves exchange in both perceiver and perceived.

When I feel a stone, for instance, am I perceiving its hardness or is its hardness highlighting the softness of my hand?

However, as Luce Irigaray suggests, despite reconfiguring the body in this way, Merleau-Ponty is still committed to the primacy of vision.[37] In *The Visible and the Invisible*, for instance, he states:

> As there is a reversibility of the seeing and the visible…so there is a reversibility of speech and what it signifies; the signification is what comes to seal, to close, to gather up the multiplicity of the physical, physiological, linguistic means of elocution, to contract them into one sole act, as the vision comes to complete the aesthesiological body.[38]

Here the body's capacity to sense and perceive (the aesthesiological body – see below) can, in some ways, only be bought to cohere by the power of sight; vision, in other words, completes the circle of embodiment left broken by the other senses. Merleau-Ponty then ultimately relies on the centripetal image of vision to complete his picture of what it means to be; he also greatly expands our notions of what flesh is capable of and what its role is in the act of living. The title of the penultimate chapter of *The Visible and the Invisible*, 'The Intertwining – The Chiasm', offers us a further insight into how Merleau-Ponty sought to centre the physical self in its environment. We can clearly see here the sensual interconnectivity (both in terms of synaesthetic reciprocity of the senses and in terms of the self-world rhizome) that characterises the postmodern scopic regime and that, as we have already asserted, is a major facet of recent thinking in both film theory and psychoanalysis. The image of the chiasm derives from anatomy and, more recently, cellular biology and describes the crossing of two chromatids or muscular or optical fibres; this, as we shall see, is useful in allowing us to envision exactly how Merleau-Ponty saw the process of exchange between the senses that, at some points, comes close to recent theories heralding from neuroscience.[39]

Due to the sheer number of concepts that litter *Phenomenology of Perception* and *The Visible and the Invisible* and their concordance to the present book, I have isolated a number of conceptual tools from both works that will not only allow comparisons with the concepts already outlined with reference to film theory but that can be used in the second part of this book to greater understand the experience of spectatorship. I have also confined this act of conceptual harvesting to the two most commensurate chapters: Part 2, Chapter 1, of *Phenomenology of Perception*, 'Sense Experience' and 'The Intertwining – The Chiasm' from *The Visible and the Invisible*.[40] Taken together, the following 'toolbox' attempts to outline the salient points in

Merleau-Ponty's chapters as well as providing the foundation for further exegesis later on in this work.

Colour Corporeality

Merleau-Ponty makes extensive use of the work of a number of pre-war psychologists in his chapter on sensing, not least Heinz Werner's *Untersuchungen uber Empfindung und Empfinden* and Goldstein and Rosenthal's *Zum Problem der Wirkung der Farben auf den Organismus*, both of which deal with the notion of colour and its embodied experience.[41] Using data garnered from patients suffering from disorders of the cerebellum or frontal cortex, Merleau-Ponty posits the idea that our experience of colour does not consist of indescribable quales but 'present themselves with a motor physiognomy, and are enveloped in a living significance'.[42] Goldstein and Rosenthal found, for instance, that a patient's experience of their own body differs when confronted with a visual field of a specific colour; the sweep of the arm takes on a different character when presented with red than when presented with green. Also, the surrounding colour field affected the patient's ability to estimate distance and time, 'with a green visual field the assessment is accurate, with a red one the subject errs on the side of excess. Movements outwards are accelerated by green and slowed down by red'.[43]

Heinz Werner's work suggests that the body adopts a specific physiological stance when confronted with a coloured visual field:

> 'there is in my body a sensation of slipping downwards, so that it cannot be green, and can be only blue but in fact I see no blue', says one subject. Another says: 'I clenched my teeth, and so I know that it is yellow.'[44]

Merleau-Ponty's point here is not that colour presents itself as a signifier (we must be careful not to reduce his idea to simple evolutionary clichés), but that the body adopts a specific stance, a specific physiological readiness for the experience of colour. He likens the experience of colour (and in fact of all the senses) to that of falling asleep; we do not enter sleep so much as adopt the psychological and physiological character of sleep before it becomes us – we are sleep. There is a corporeal aspect to colour that invades our bodies as soon as we are presented with it and Werner's experiments with colour-blind patients have suggested that this process is the same whether or not the colour is visually recognised at all. Sat in a dark cinema theatre, rooted to our seat, unable to move but presented with images usually saturated with bright stark colours, is the body's corporeal response not a major part of how we react to the film? Are our bodies not waiting to be played upon by the spectrum of differing light frequencies that constitutes the modern colour-saturated blockbuster rather than providing semiotic cues for our eyes and our brains only?

The Sensorium Commune

Merleau-Ponty is specific in declaring that, for him, the synergy of the senses is not one carried out by a transcendental ego; for him, the body itself is the synergetic apparatus, providing a method of grounding the self within a world of perception in all its thickness; ironically this is best understood through the use of a metaphor based in vision. Binocular vision, he argues, does not merely consist of the coming together of two unrelated monocular images; it is the three dimensional image here that serves as the psychobiological ground. The splitting of it into two separate images (as in double vision) serves only as an anomaly that highlights the intentionality of the binocular and yet the binocular, paradoxically, also depends upon its monocular constituents:

> The single object is not a certain way of thinking of the two images, since they cease to be the moment it appears. Has the fusion of images been effected, then, by some innate device of the nervous system, and do we mean that finally we have, if not on the periphery, at least at the centre, a single excitation mediated by the two eyes?[45]

In this way, Merleau-Ponty manages to assert the importance of the synergy whilst retaining the identity of the two monocular inputs. In other words, we do not here need to resort to traditional dualities concerning being-in-itself and being-for-itself or the physiological and the phenomenal, for Merleau-Ponty the two can quite happily coexist, if not together in the same body, then in the same body of knowledge.

In *The Visible and the Invisible*, Merleau-Ponty expands this idea to include not only all the senses but intersensual exchange between individuals. What if, he asks, our two hands function in the same way as our two eyes? As if my tactile knowledge of this cup on the desk depended upon my using both hands upon it. The experience would not consist of two separate sensory inputs that were commingled by a transcendental ego but of an appreciation of the cup's physical presence by my body as a sensorium commune, as a sensing thing with all parts working together. For Merleau-Ponty these parts consist just as much of the different senses as they do redoubled body parts:

...while each monocular vision, each touching with one sole hand has its own visible, its tactile, each is bound to every other vision, to every other touch; it is bound in such a way as to make up with them the experience of one sole body before one sole world...[46]

This is the first intertwining that Merleau-Ponty writes of, the intertwining of separate strands of experience to make the one single world. However, within this chapter there is another image of intertwining: the intertwining of individuals who share the same experience:

There is a circle of touched and touching, the touched takes hold of the touching; there is a circle of the visible and the seeing, the seeing is not without visible existence; there is even an inscription of the touching in the visible, of the seeing in the tangible and the converse; there is finally a propagation of these exchanges to all the bodies of the same type and of the same style which I see and touch – and this by virtue of the fundamental fission or segregation of the sentient and the sensible which, laterally, makes the organs of my body communicate and founds transitivity from one body to another.[47]

The sensorium commune then applies not only to the body itself but also to the body in connection with every other body. Questioning the validity of the prevailing mode in Western ontology (and coming surprisingly close to recent notions such as the rhizome) Merleau-Ponty asserts not only the value of closeness but also the inevitability of it.

The Aesthesiological Body

The aesthesiological body appears most obviously in *The Visible and the Invisible* and forms a major part of Luce Irigaray's critique of 'The Intertwining – The Chiasm' in her *An Ethics of Sexual Difference*. It is a concept that stands at the intersection of Merleau-Ponty's notions of the physical and the metaphysical because it describes the body that slips underneath consciousness – it is pre-reflective – it is the body that exists under our egos. In his essay 'Religious Cinematics: The Immediate Body in the Media of Film', S. Brent Plate describes it as 'that which combines both sensing and thinking',[48] for the aesthesiological body can not be described as mere thought nor flesh in the traditional Cartesian sense where the mind thinks whilst the flesh feels, as Plate again asserts:

> The aesthesiological body brings together ideas and the sensible world; knowledge of ideas does not come about through an abstracted, bodiless mind. Rather we finally have to understand it, the pure ideality already streams forth along the articulations of the aesthesiological body. Thoughts and feelings work together in the world-building enterprise.[49]

We could think of this as the flesh of thought, or perhaps even the thoughts of flesh and we have touched upon ideas of a similar vein already with the distinctions between the body as an index of response and as a site of reception. The aesthesiological body undercuts the traditional transcendental ego of much of Western ontology and through this film theory, because it posits a body capable of autonomous sense-making and of sub-conscious, pre-reflective action. This again goes beyond ideas of the simple 'fight or flight' of evolutionism and rests more in the grounding of the body within a world, a world that has to be constantly monitored and adjusted to without making undue demands on the consciousness.

Spatiality

For Merleau-Ponty, the perception and appreciation of space is irrevocably linked to the possession of a body. The classical spatio-visual assertions of philosophers such as Descartes and Berkeley mean very little, asserts Merleau-Ponty, without the experience of touch, and, more still, without the experience of a finite body that can offer us spatial relation. However, *Phenomenology of Perception* posits a notion that undercuts the link between vision and space altogether by describing a space that can be experienced with the eyes closed:

> When, in the concert hall, I open my eyes, visible space seems to me cramped compared to that other space through which, a moment ago, the music was being unfolded, and even if I keep my eyes open while the piece is being played, I have the impression that the music is not really contained within this circumscribed and unimpressive space.[50]

The space here is not simply an imagined space, although it may very well be a remembered one; it is the physical body experiencing the realities of spatiality, a reality that is, very often, undermined by vision. The spatial experience of the listener in the concert hall (or we could even say in the cinema theatre) is being constantly renegotiated, as the sounds they hear or the images they view first contract and then expand their understanding of space. Space, like all other sensations, cannot merely be reduced to that which we see, most of our senses and bodily perceptions offer us some insight into the spatial nature of our surroundings; even smell and taste delineate closeness or distance to some extent. Sound, however, as Merleau-Ponty suggests is very often linked directly to how we perceive space directly, and this is not always based on volume. A film soundtrack offers us a vital window on how we perceive the connections between sound and space: in a whispered close-up, for instance, it is not the volume that allows us to experience the invasion of our personal spatial boundaries, it is the timbre, the breathiness, the nature of the voice that affects us and very often this is linked with other sensual suggestions: sweat on the face, saliva on the lips, the sound of a heartbeat and so on, offering us smell, viscosity and kinetic points of mimesis. If we did not feel as though our personal space where invaded, if for instance the viewing of such a scene was merely an intellectual exercise involving identification and the interpretation of semiotic cues, the scene would have no meaning or power – either for our experience of the film or for us as living human bodies. Filmmakers constantly play on their viewers' understanding of space, an understanding that must, if it is to have emotional currency, be based in a mimetic rather than a semiotic process.

Feminism

In her book *The Man of Reason*, Genevieve Lloyd traces the interconnected, logocentric binaries of reason/nature, male/female and mind/body. There is, she asserts, throughout Western thought, not only a privileging of reason over nature, male over female, and mind over body, but an assertion of their concomitance; the first instances of these binaries (reason, male and mind) forming a locus of stability, knowledge and fixity and the other (nature, female and body) representing points of uncertainty and areas of indetermination. Arising out of biblical exegesis, for example, thinkers such as Philo, Augustine, and Thomas Aquinas, highlight that, in Genesis, it is man that is made in God's image and thus man who can claim the birthright to that which is constant and unchanging. Woman, always a product of biology having been produced from the body of Adam, is associated with the corporeal, the fleshy and *ipso facto* with that which decays, defies reason, and ultimately dies.

During the Enlightenment we see a shift in thinking: whereas pre-Enlightenment thought saw humanity as either being inhabited by both male and female parts or as being the product of some split in an originary soul (as in Aristophanes' famous declaration in Plato's *Symposium*), from the early sixteenth century onwards we see an externalisation of this binary, where science and rationality (strongly associated with maleness) attempts to dominate or overcome the more feminine realm of nature.[51] The image of a male technological science attempting to tame a mysterious and quixotic Mother Nature, creating order out of chaos and understanding through interrogation and dissection, is one that still prevails today.

It becomes clear when assessing Lloyd's notable contribution to understanding ontological patterns in gender politics however that we must be completely sure of our terms. Terms such as 'the body' become problematic, as we have seen, when placed into simplistic binaries, especially ones that attempt to classify whole paradigms of knowledge under specific gender differences. Lloyd does not make the distinction in her work between the body as flesh and the body as feeling and perception, between the body as something to be looked at and the body as a locus, a site, a screen of affects, perceptions and emotions; in short, Lloyd does not make the distinctions we have been looking at in this book. We have seen for instance that, according to Crary, the modern scopic regime was characterised by its use of physiology, there is as much use of the body here as the mind, however the science is noticeably masculine in its overtones, at least according to the rest of Lloyd's thesis. The sixteenth-century physiologist William Harvey is typical of this process when he states in his *An Anatomical Disquisition on the Motion of the Heart and Blood in Animals* that:

> At length, and by using greater and daily diligence, having frequent recourse to vivisections, employing a variety of animals for the purpose, and collating numerous observations, I thought that I had attained the truth, that I should extricate myself and escape from this labyrinth, and that I had discovered what I so much desired, both the motion and use of the heart and arteries.[52]

We can see here that the body is not opposed to reason and, perhaps more importantly, is not subjugated by it, instead the body reflects and exposes reason; it becomes a way that reason manifests itself. Harvey does not see the body as posing an unfathomable barrier to understanding but as offering a way out; the labyrinth he talks of is not that of the complexity of the body itself but his own lack of reason, a lack that is breached through interaction with the body as flesh, as thing. The opposing of reason with the body after the Enlightenment (and by extension the twinning of maleness with mind and femaleness with the body) then only makes sense if we assume the body to be the perceptual body, the body of sensation, the body of emotion and, importantly, this is also the point at which the body is, in Western ontology, considered to be at its most feminine.

This is a complexity that is missing in Lloyd's study but is more obvious in the works of Luce Irigaray, Hélène Cixous, Iris Young, and other feminist writers of the 1970s and onwards, who attempted not only to transvalue this felt body that has been at best ignored, at worst subjugated by Western phallocratic science but to celebrate the multivocity and centrifugality that such a project entails. As we shall see, this again, represents an expansion of what it means to perceive, as theorists such as Irigaray and Young assert the value of touch and taste over sight and how this undercuts what we think of as the fixity of the (in their assertions masculine, phallocentric) self. As with the other chapters of this first section, what follows is a toolbox of concepts drawn from a number of contemporary feminist thinkers that not only reflect the mandates of the current study and can be used in the second section of this book but that are taken as being representative of the larger body of work that they come from.

The use of the perceptual lived body by feminist thinkers also represents a politicisation of the debates that have hitherto been framed only in terms of an ungendered, uncultured body. Whereas many of the ideas contained within this section emanate from feminism, many of the founding concepts can be traced back to notions already covered in this chapter, notions that herald from phenomenology and psychoanalysis. Feminism, like Deleuzianism, is capable of working from the inside of the very discourses that it challenges, adopting and adapting tropes and perceptual personae for its own ends. Also like Deleuzianism (although for different reasons), feminism is an intentionally heterogeneous discourse, offering no teleology, no unified perspective and, ultimately, no definitive statements.

The Gendered Body

As previously stated, up until now we have been looking at theories that, essentially, view the body as ungendered and uncultured. Merleau-Ponty's notions of bodily phenomenology for example make no mention either of the various physical differences that exist between men and women or the many differences that exist through enculturation and sexualisation. In many ways, the question of whether one is born a women or becomes one (a notion of course taken from de Beauvoir) is secondary to the fact that women exist as different from men *per se*; the debate as to how this occurs (through biology or culture) is irrelevant in this case, what is important and what feminism lends to the debate is the fact that, very often, 'the body' in philosophy (and discourses such as film theory) refer to a universalised, generalised body that, more often than not, is male and moreover heterosexual and Caucasian. In *The Second Sex*, de Beauvoir famously lists some of these differences:

> On average she [woman] is shorter than the male and lighter, her skeleton is more delicate, and the pelvis is larger in adaptation to the functions of pregnancy and childbirth; her connective tissues accumulate fat and her contours are thus more rounded than those of the male. Appearance in general – structure, skin, hair – is distinctly different in the two sexes.[53]

Luce Irigaray and Iris Young stress the importance of biological differences in forming the ontology of women; the vagina, the breasts and the multiple erogenous zones all challenge the accepted lore of the phallic economy and add new images and different structures with which to view sexuality and, via this, ontology, as Irigaray states:

> Women's autoeroticism is very different from man's. In order to touch himself, man needs an instrument: his hand, a woman's body, language…and this self caressing requires at least a minimum of activity. As for woman, she touches herself in and of herself without any need for mediation, and before there is any way to distinguish activity from passivity. Woman 'touches herself' all the time, and moreover no one can forbid her to do so, for her genitals are formed of two lips in continuous contact.[54]

The crucial aspect here for any study that relies on touch, on sensation and on perception is not necessarily that one must attempt to encompass all possibilities of experiences and the whole spectrum of gendered-based receptivity (this of course would be impossible, and for a male theorist this is doubly so), instead we must be aware that such complexities exist, that the dialogue arising from such a study or such a debate is likely to be effected by these considerations but that that only enriches the scope of a strategy rather than restricting it. More importantly, by citing feminist theorists' exposition of the underlying, covert masculine body in ontological thought and its satellite discourses, we can begin to question the validity of its orginary assumptions.

Phallocentric Scopophilia

In *Speculum of the Other Woman* Luce Irigaray makes, on a number of occasions, the link between gender and vision:

> [What] leads to envy of the omnipotence of gazing, knowing? About sex/about penis. To envy and jealousy of the eye-penis, of the phallic gaze? He will be able to see that I don't have one. I shall not see if he has one. More than me? But he will inform me of it. Displaced castration? The gaze is at stake from the outset.[55]

The relationship between the eye and the penis is not merely an observation by Irigaray but, as we have seen, arises out of the masculine nature of Freudian theories of sexuality and their concomitant reliance on vision. This notion would be reflected in Laura Mulvey's article 'Visual Pleasure and Narrative Cinema' where it was couched in psychoanalytic terms as 'Woman as Image, Man as Bearer of the Look'. Phallocentric scopophilia not only reduces woman to the status of image but projects a fantasy upon that image, capturing it and keeping it within the gaze.[56] The bearer of the gaze and thus progenitor of the fantasy controls its proliferation and projection; this in turn reinforces several of the ontological archetypes we have already established: distance, autonomy and so on.

Asserting the value of other perceptual inputs such as touch, taste and even smell, feminist thinkers such as Irigaray and Sobchack, as well as film makers such as Shauna Beharry have attempted to challenge the primacy of vision in creating the self by highlighting its essentially masculine nature.[57] The notion that the primacy of vision in Western epistemology may be due, not to some innate originary relationship between what we see and who we are, but to the proliferation of masculine modes of being is vital to a study such as this that is based on the hypothesis that technology such as cinema relies on senses other than optical sight for its impact.

Closeness

One of the most obvious tropes of many feminist revisions of the perceptual body is that of closeness. As we have seen, vision maintains both distance and autonomy, the awkwardness of touch, of proximity, where boundaries and bodily borders are compromised and the self becomes less individuated and more symbiotic, is elided in favour of a safe space of one's own, permeated only by the senses of distance and separation: sight and sound. Feminism has not only transvalued the senses of closeness but the wholly feminine experience of pregnancy and motherhood has, as Julia Kristeva argues, challenged traditional, masculine notions of subjectivised autonomy – the maternal body providing the ultimate site of closeness between mother and child.[58]

Irigaray (for instance in the quotation above) makes use of notions originally conceived of by Merleau-Ponty to challenge the binary of touched and toucher. Touching undercuts not only the distinct bifurcation of mind and body but also of the subject/object binary – who is being touched and who is touching in this mutual exchange of sensual information? The hand that grasps the stone not only receives from it information regarding the coldness and hardness of the inert material but the stone also offers up similar information regarding the warmth, the softness and the sensitivity of the skin and flesh that surrounds it. This is, in a sense, what Laura Marks terms 'thinking with your skin' because it is the skin itself, not the brain that governs this exchange.[59]

Closeness is not directly articulated in many feminist texts, however it does represent a central (if sometimes covert) trope and a major strategy for overcoming some of the logocentricisms that are seen as either products or foundations of phallocentric discourse. In her seminal essay 'The Laugh of the Medusa', Hélène Cixous states the full political and ontological ramifications of asserting the value of touch:

> Everything will be changed once woman gives woman to the other woman. There is hidden and always ready in woman the source: the locus of the other…Touch me, caress me, you the living no-name, give me myself as myself.[60]

Here we see firstly a rejection of the traditional abhorrence of physical engulfment that has, since Freud, been attached to motherhood and via this to femininity and, secondly, the suggestion that the physical body can never be framed without a consideration of that which it touches; that we exist at all times as both a toucher and a touched, in a world that we understand through the evanescence of our skin. Closeness is political as well biological because it challenges the traditional binaries of ontology and suggests that the self maybe contained as much in the things that it touches as in itself.

Viscosity

Allied to touch is the thread of feminist thought that deals with viscosity and its role as a displacer of physical and psycho-physiological boundaries. In her work *Purity and Danger* Mary Douglas quotes Sartre and his assertions on viscosity in *Being and Nothingness* again, not only attributing to Sartre a seminal role on the formation of theories of the physical over the metaphysical, but also highlighting the connections between existential phenomenology and late twentieth-century feminism:

> Viscosity, he says, repels in its own right, as a primary experience. An infant plunging its hand into a jar of honey, is instantly involved in contemplating the formal properties of solids and liquids and the essential relation between the subjective experiencing self and the experienced world. The viscous is a state half way between solid and liquid. It is like a cross section in a process of change. It is unstable, but it does not flow…Its stickiness is a trap, it clings like a leech; it attacks the boundary between myself and it.[61]

In Kristeva's reading of Douglas especially in *Powers of Horror* this horror of the viscous would be transformed into the process of abjection, the expelling of that which does not promote and project the sanctity of the physical and psychological border.[62] The viscous and the fluid will also be twinned with the feminine and the maternal as Irigaray points out.[63] Viscosity and its strange power to repel is also a bodily sensation, we understand the nature of a viscous material through touch alone, we may come to recognise it through sight and to steer away from it if we have to, but this (as Sartre correctly states) is a secondary experience, the primary one is based in touch and in closeness, in the body's experience. Douglas suggests that it is the clinging nature of the viscous, its adherence to the skin and to its hairs, that gives it its power to repel. This is the information that fleshes out the visual experience that not only lends it thickness but imbues it with qualities above and beyond its physical make-up.

For feminists such as Irigaray, Kristeva and Cixous, then, it is not only the female body as flesh but as a site of sensation that undercuts and challenges the primacy of the phallus and, by extension, the patriarchy and its primary sense-perception, vision. We can note that it is not merely the two lips of the vagina that are singled out by Irigaray but their function as producers of sensation, of hinges between touching and touched. The feminine body, in these and other writers, is seen as defying the dictates of reason and the singular autonomy of the self. Irigaray and Young work *within* the dominant discourse, unsettling and destabilising it, using the tools that are handed to them, a strategy that often results in the criticism that they accept masculine binaries instead of attempting to work outside of them. In Cixous we not only see this same faith in the body and its perceptions/sensations but the suggestion that the Cartesian privileging of the mind and the subjection of polyvocal desire to the phallus may well oppress men as well as women:

> By virtue of asserting the primacy of the phallus and of bringing it into play, phallocratic ideology has claimed more than one victim… As a woman I've been clouded over by the great sceptre and been told: idolize it, that which you cannot brandish. But at the same time man has been handed that grotesque and scarcely enviable destiny (just imagine) of being reduced to a single idol with clay balls.[64]

This 'scarcely enviable destiny' is not only the primacy of phallocentric desire it is the denial of the full roundness of sensual experience, experience that as we have seen, is slowly being explored in all manner of differing discourses. Cixous does not explicitly make the connection between vision and the unenviable destiny but the notion of sight as a sense that allows distance, detached contemplation, and perspectivalist subjectivity surely underpins her points. She makes it clear that the binary-producing nature of the phallocentric self and its primary sense-perception, vision, is restrictive and harmful for both men and women.

§

The areas under discussion in this chapter form (along with Marxism perhaps) a major part of twentieth- and twenty-first-century academic debate. They are both interconnected and undeniably different, taking different political and ontological stances, relying on different lexicons, different areas of interest, different intellectual strategies and producing different enunciative statements. However, as we have seen, there are points of convergence and each represents, to a degree, the underlying patterns of thought that characterise the episteme. We have witnessed in this chapter one such point of convergence: the re-evaluation of what it means to perceive, how we understand the very basic building blocks of our experience of the world. The Cartesian split between mind and body not only underpinned binaries such as culture and nature and man and woman but thought and feeling. Thought, a product of the mind, was considered not only abstract and pure but eternal whereas feeling was fleeting and at best amoral, at worst immoral. Overturning this binary, as the preceding chapter has attempted to show, is not so much about merely privileging one of its poles over the other but about showing how such terms are more fluid and protean than might first appear. The concepts of skin ego, of the aesthesiological body, of colour corporeality, of viscosity and the others outlined here are all forms of understanding, of thought, but ones that do not depend on the brain or its closest perceptual ally vision for cognition. Each of these concepts falls between traditional notions of thought and traditional notions of feeling; they are based in the body not only as a lived entity but one that understands and evaluates its world sub-cognitively. The body here exists beneath the self, working to its own criteria, feeding and filtering information; to say that the mind thinks and the body feels is to simplify the processes of sense experience and perceptual engagement.

This is the body that sits in the cinema seat; this is the body that reacts to the images and that understands the pictures. It flinches at scenes of violence because it knows the sting of pain, it knows the feel of viscosity and thus understands when presented with its image, it knows closeness through the hairs that reach out and touch other bodies, it reacts to bright colours and to loud noises, it mimetically creates, out of its own toolbox of sense memory, the environment it is witnessing. As we shall see in the last chapter of this section, recent theories heralding from neuroscience will also attest to this process of sensual expansion, an expansion that is challenging the primacy of vision in yet another discourse.

3

NEUROSCIENCE AND EMBODIMENT: EXPLORING THE THINKING FLESH

There are strong indications that among the loose federation of sciences dealing with knowledge and cognition…there is a slowly growing conviction that…a radical paradigmatic or epistemic shift is rapidly developing. At the very centre of this emerging view is the belief that the proper units of knowledge are primarily concrete, embodied, incorporated, lived.[1]

I don't believe that linguistics and psychoanalysis offer a great deal to the cinema. On the contrary, the biology of the brain – molecular biology – does.[2]

This book has set out to look at the process of vision as it is conceived and constructed by successive paradigms. An underlying notion to this is that vision changes, and the way that we think about sight in the twenty-first century is radically different from the way we thought about it two hundred years ago. In the preceding chapters we have looked at how this has manifested itself in various human sciences and arts such as film theory, psychoanalysis and gender politics. However, as this chapter will attempt to assert, the same changes can be detected in the biological sciences and in optics, both disciplines that would seem to be based on more objective and universal assumptions. It is one of the paradoxical aspects of modern film theory that, even in the early twenty-first century, it bases its theories on an optical science that was developed sometime in the nineteenth century – the assumptions about vision that we can detect in many theories of cinema herald from a time before MRI scanning, before brain surgery, before neuroscience and before the advancements in optics that have, inevitably, altered our view of how we see and how we are seen.

As I shall attempt to determine, even in the biological sciences (that place of seemingly objective scientific reason) we can note a shift in the way we view vision – where once sight was seen as being inextricably linked to the physiological self, it is now caught within a network of ideas about synaesthetic reception, multi-modal sense knowledge and the other tropes of the postmodern scopic regime. This chapter, then, is an attempt to assert how two major sciences, optics and neuroscience, have altered our concept of vision over the past ten or fifteen years and have, themselves, been altered.

In order to fully understand this, it is necessary to look back at how science has traditionally viewed the senses and their interaction. This chapter does not offer a history of the senses but it does attempt to trace the trajectory of change that we have already seen in other, less scientific, disciplines. To this end, the first section of this chapter looks specifically at how science has been affected by outside discourses such as management theory and computer technology and thus has been open to epistemic shifts and paradigmatic flux. This exercise is not to suggest that science is conceived in the same way as the humanities but, just as science can influence the arts, so aesthetic discourses, rhetoric and language can influence science providing the conditions for change and the co-ordinates for epistemic evolution. This chapter then goes on from this to look at how recent theories of neuroscience and optics have shown an increasing tendency towards synaesthesia and multi-modal reception and how this matches similar movements in other disciplines. For me, an examination in this area – of the changing face of optical thinking – is long overdue in film theory of the twenty-first century.

In the interwar period, German biologist Fritz Kahn produced a series of illustrations depicting the functions of the human body. Kahn's visions of the body, the brain and its various systems show distinctly how biological knowledge utilises non-scientific disciplines and images to model and convey its ideas. One of Kahn's most famous pictures depicts the inside of a head, the brain, as a telephone exchange that takes inputs from the eyes (for example) and translates them into actions for the body via the central nervous system. Another views the respiratory system as a mine shaft ferrying oxygen around the body using several small roped buckets and expelling the resulting carbon dioxide out of the mouth; this picture is fittingly called 'The Factory of the Lungs'. One of Kahn's illustrations even depicts the brain as a kind of cinema, with a small projectionist aiming a cinematographic image onto the screen of the brain and an equally small organist on the other side translating this firstly into its signified and then into the spoken word.

Kahn's use of models in formulating and explaining biological processes, like sight, can best be summed up using the title of his 1926 work, *Der*

Mensch als Industriepalast ('Man as an Industrial Palace'), and it is not difficult to see how this title says as much, perhaps even more, about the surrounding socio-economic paradigm as contemporary notions of biology or neuroscience. As Eleanor Turk details, Kahn was writing at a time when Germany's industrial economy was experiencing an economic boom, thanks in the main to American loans paid under the Dawes Plan (American loans of some $200 million were secured in return for the payment of war reparations to Britain and France):

> During the next five years, the German economy showed remarkable improvement due to these American loans. Production in virtually all of the basic industries reached or exceeded the prewar levels, with a similar effect on wages and profits. There was an urban building boom and introduction of new technologies. The great prewar industrial firms prospered, aided by the formation of cartels to control production and prices.[3]

Kahn's illustrations, then, of the body and, by extension, contemporary biology's formulations of it, as well as the brain and the mind, were directly influenced by the surrounding socio-economic milieu. Stephen Rose, in *The Conscious Brain* also makes this point (although related to a different time period, 1930s America) when he describes a picture that modelled the brain through contemporary systems of management and organisational theory: the brain – says a 1930s encyclopaedia entry – is like the manager of a factory and the various bodily systems like a well run industrial concern.[4] According to Rose, this process is not new, the brain and the biological systems are, he asserts, very often described as being analogous with the latest technological or social advancement: Descartes, building on the physiological work of Galen and William Harvey, for instance, asserted that the brain served as a hydraulic pump for the nervous system, eighteenth-century physicians and neuroscientists assumed that the brain worked in a clockwork fashion and more recently the brain has been described as a computer, calculator or even the Internet.

As Thomas Kuhn suggests in *The Structure of Scientific Revolutions*, science frequently exports its theories outside of itself creating, what Kuhn calls, a 'change in world view'.[5] However, as Rose suggests, this process can also occur in the opposite direction: science and scientific method can be influenced by spheres beyond scientific borders through the use of models, analogies and the construction of hermeneutic frames of reference. Scientific disciplines such as neurology and biology *can* be influenced and affected not only by technological advances such as computer and IT systems but by theories of managerial organisation, economics and structural concepts such as social networking or the Internet. The relationship we have to our bodies and minds particularly then are open to influences from non-scientific discourses and nowhere is this more obvious than in embodied theory.

The image we receive in Crary's *Techniques of the Observer*, of the forces that shape the scopic regime, is not one based merely in science, or rather, not one that (as Kuhn might suggest) is set in motion by scientific discovery alone. Instead, what we are presented with is a kind of feedback loop between science, technology and society; whereby the objects of science are shaped and dictated (both financially and in terms of specific focus) by the interests, desires and needs of the wider populace. This in turn, of course, promotes and encourages more scientific work in these areas which completes the loop. All of this means that science is as open to epistemic shifts as any other discipline and this, as we shall see, extends to the postmodern scopic regime and contemporary formulations of biology, neurology and optics.[6] Thinking about scientific disciplines in this way allows us to see beyond the simplistic notion that conceptions of the body, its senses and our biological selves are universal and objective, and, somehow, not affected by the surrounding social milieu. Many of the studies looked at in this chapter offer us yet more insight into current thinking regarding the sensorium and its importance in centring the individual within their world. Looking at science in this way attempts to highlight the extent that disciplines such as film theory need to be aware of the changing nature of scientific discourse and the degree to which their development affects our understanding of the very basic elements of cinema reception. Changing theories of vision necessitate alterations in film theory's fundamental assumptions.

Science and the Senses, Science and Sight

As Crary details, the development of scientific models in the nineteenth century assumed the biological and psychological connection between vision and the self by privileging the individuated physiological aspects of sight. Although nineteenth-century vision was linked to the body, it was linked in a way that denied the inter-relatedness of the senses and elided the extent that the flesh could, itself, be a site of reception; he details for instance that:

> The body that had been a neutral or invisible term in vision was now the thickness from which knowledge of the observer was obtained.

This palpable opacity and carnal density of vision loomed so suddenly into view that its full consequences and effects could not be immediately recognised.[7]

Nineteenth-century science, in other words, did begin to understand the importance of the body in vision but had not fully realised its synaesthetic and multi-modal consequences: this would only happen later under the postmodern scopic regime.

Nicholas J. Wade's book *A Natural History of Vision* charts the development of biological optical science from the early Greek thinkers to the nineteenth-century anatomists. As he tacitly demonstrates, the movement of this development encompasses a range of different paradigmatic periods but, overall, we can detect an ever increasing move from natural philosophy to what we might call biological mechanics – from the discussion of vision as a philosophical idea (for instance in the visual philosophies of Plato, Aristotle and Al Kindi) to the assumption that it could be understood through dissection and surgery (for instance early attempts with Galen and then Descartes, right up until the Brewster and the nineteenth century).

Wade (mirroring Crary) details how this shift was commensurate with the increasing assumption that vision was linked to individuated physiology, that vision was every bit as subjective as thought and that this point could be determined through dissection and interrogation of the individual eye under question. He quotes extensively, for instance, from Jan Evangelista Purkyne, the Czech anatomist who researched heavily into subjective visual experience and its physical base.[8] As can easily be surmised, vision becomes linked in the nineteenth century to the self and to discourse of anatomy and more and more divorced from the universal and the philosophical.

What is also interesting about Wade's book is that he does not discuss theories of vision and sight that appear after the mid-nineteenth century and moreover after the advancements made in anatomical surgery. Now, there may be many reasons for this but one of the most compelling is that, by this time, vision was no longer seen as a problem for science; like many aspects of the human body, by the early twentieth century, vision was seen as a closed book – the 'systematic anatomy'[9] of the early 1900s had said all it could about the mechanical workings of the human eye and its relationship to the optical nerves, muscles and arteries of the surrounding body. It is these same scientific assumptions that we have recognised as forming the basis of much film theory.

Increasingly, as we shall see, the study of vision becomes seen as the domain of neuroscience, with the processes of vision being linked to the whole sensorium, not just the senses *per se* but to the non-optical nerves, the brain and the host of other non-mechanical aspects of physiology and neurobiology (areas such as hormone production for instance). Sight also becomes linked to the wider field of psychology with Gestalt theory and studies of subjective perception.[10]

The relationship between the eye and the brain had been recognised as far back as the Persian scientist Alhazen, who lived around 1000 AD and who was himself influenced heavily by Galen. However, for Alhazen, the process of vision worked in the opposite way to the process we might recognise today:

> And it is said that the visual spirit is emitted from the anterior part of the brain and fills the channels of the two primary nerves connected to the brain and reaches the common nerve and fills its channel and comes to the two secondary optic nerves and fills them, and it extends to the glacial humor and confers the power of vision on it.[11]

Vision here was something that the brain conferred on the eye; the process was one of projection rather than introjection, but nevertheless, the relationship of the eye and brain was set. Once vision is seen, not merely as a mechanical process but one that relies on a holistic consideration of the body and the brain, sight becomes a more complex, more evanescent and, perhaps even, more challenging area, and less reliant on monolithic notions such as the stable self and fixed subjectivity.

Neuroscience

We have seen, then, how throughout its history, science has not only relied on non-scientific disciplines for its models and metaphors but also how it is shaped by the wider structures and mandates of epistemic thought. As I have suggested above, nowhere is this more obvious than in recent developments in neuroscience and, in particular, its re-visioning of the importance of synaesthetic experience, the body and their relation to the brain and thought. It is interesting to note that the dividing line between science and philosophy, between neurobiology and the philosophy of mind is becoming evermore indistinct: Antonio Damasio's *Descartes' Error* is an exemplary case but we also notice this in the work of Richard Cytowic, who cites Aristotle, Blaise Pascal; and the writings of Vasily Kandinsky, Ellis and Young, who cite the theories of Plato and Bergson when discussing the neurological processes of memory; and Stephen Rose, who has used all manner of philosophers, thinkers and cultural theorists to convey his ideas throughout his career. In this area, at least, science and the liberal arts are not exclusive: one informs and underpins the other.[12]

Synaesthesia

Science's relationship to synaesthesia can be broadly grouped into three main chronologically determined areas: nineteenth-century interest, which manifested itself in (amongst other things) theosophy and symbolist aesthetics; the middle years of the twentieth century where Skinner's Behaviourism virtually discounted all areas of psychology that were based in subjective experience and thus all but ruled out cross-modal perception as a field of study; and the more recent resurgence of interest in synaesthetes as examples of 'cognitive fossils'[13] that allow us to shed light on how non-synaesthetic perception and memory works. As we shall see, there was a marked shift in thinking regarding the neurological topology of synaesthesia between the first and last of these timeframes that had a noticeable impact on how it could be used to highlight the processes of ordinary perception. Simply put, synaesthesia changed from being thought of as an evolutionary super-sense (in the nineteenth and early twentieth centuries) and residing in the higher regions of cognition, to being thought of as a fossil-like residue of neonatal and phylogenetic evolutionary perception existing within the much more primitive limbic system – the neurological region that processes information *before* cognition. It is crucial to delineate between nineteenth and twentieth-century conceptions of synaesthesia before discussing how it informs recent theoretical thinking.[14]

In a famous poem written in 1871, Rimbaud speaks of assigning a specific colour to each of the vowels:

> Black, A, white E, red I, green U, blue O – vowels,
>   Some day I will open your silent pregnancies:
> A, black belt, hairy with bursting flies,
>   Bumbling and buzzing over stinking cruelties…[15]

The poem paints a fairly typical picture of nineteenth-century notions of the synaesthetic experience: the heightened awareness of the poet uncovers the normally invisible perceptual links that exist between the different senses, creating a kind of hallucinogenic melange of sensations that uncover hidden correspondences between colours and sounds, letters and images – a word and concept also used, of course, by Baudelaire in his poem of the same name. An essay by Robert Robertson on Sergei Eisenstein's interest in synaesthesia gives us some indication of how the condition was thought of in the nineteenth and early twentieth centuries:

> The evidence of Eisenstein's interest in synaesthesia and the interaction of the senses is present in his library. According to Hakan Lovgren, in the 1930s he began to acquire books by the Russian symbolist poets and writers…A marked interest in alchemy and other occult and hermetic traditions was characteristic of artists in the symbolist movement.[16]

Synaesthesia was seen as commensurate with Blavatskian theosophy, with Giordano Bruno, with symbolist aesthetics and with drug experimentation. It also, as the writing of Eisenstein suggests, was seen to refer to the synchronization of the senses – the twinning of colour, sound and movement for instance through montage. This paints the synaesthetic experience as being somehow beyond the everyday, a kind of sixth sense that could be achieved through meditation or mescaline.

More recently, definitions of synaesthesia have distanced themselves from such gnostically-based experiences. Synaesthesia has been defined by a number of more specific experiential phenomena that aim not only to characterise it but to empirically establish its existence. Noam Sagiv outlines that these include establishing that the cross modal sensual experience is the same over time, that they occur without warning or external stimulation (drugs, injury, etc.), that they must be present from childhood and that they must not be simply metaphorical speech.[17] The neurological condition of synaesthesia, according to Richard Cytowic, should also be projected; that is, symptoms should be experienced within the visual field rather than merely in the imaginations of the subject or occur as vague instincts or feelings.[18] Unlike nineteenth-century notions of synaesthesia, its late twentieth-century neurological counterpart assumes that there will be little or no relationship between the sensual experiences – that the word 'blue', for instance, need not necessarily evoke the colour blue or that the word 'strawberry' need not make the subject taste the fruit.

Paradoxically, then, it is not the condition of synaesthesia *per se* that will inform the present study but what it suggests about ordinary non-synaesthetic perception. As we shall see, some current thinking on the neuropathology of the condition places it much further down in the evolutionary and neurobiological hierarchy, suggesting that we all perceive synaesthetically, but that, later, the cognitive functions filter out much of its affects, cognitive functions that are missing or faulty in the synaesthete. It is this aspect, obviously, and moreover its links to memory that can aid us in understanding the fully embodied nature of cinema spectatorship.

The Limbic System

Cytowic's theory of the limbic system is, as he says himself, a product of changing attitudes towards the whole brain and its functions:

> The old view of brain organizations has collapsed…it could no longer bear the weight of having to explain the avalanche of observations made during the recent past…We now know that as a model its generalities are true, while some of its specific predictions are erroneous.[19]

One such departure from accepted neurobiology is the importance attached to emotion and feeling in the thought processes and, consequently, the relationship between the thinking brain and the feeling body. Again, what we detect here is not so much a revision of Cartesian notions of mind and body (this would, arguably, represent merely an upturning of existing binaries) but a revision of what thought and feeling are and the concept that the dividing line between the two is difficult to discern.

In his book *The Man Who Tasted Shapes*, Cytowic outlines the experimental processes that Michael (Cytowic's subject) undertook:

> 'Are you comfy?' I asked. Michael was strapped down on the couch, his head nestled inside the helmet with its electrical devices protruding two feet in all directions. Tons of nuclear, electronic, and computer equipment hummed around him in the darkened room. He looked like a cyborg. I was adjusting the strap on the black anaesthesia mask that covered his face.
>
> His eyes peered at me from beneath the helmet. 'I'm not sure how I look', Michael mumbled through the mask, 'but you were right. I feel like the Bride of Frankenstein.'[20]

The process that Michael was undertaking here was a CBF or Cerebral Blood Flow scan that, as the name suggests, is designed to show the levels of blood flow *to* and thus activity *of* the various parts of the brain during various actions and thought processes. Michael, as Cytowic details earlier, was a gustatory-tactile synaesthete who literally felt different shapes in his hands depending on what he tasted or smelt. During the hour of the test, Michael was asked to inhale a number of pre-selected smells in order to firstly trigger his synaesthesia and, secondly, to monitor the resulting brain activity, activity that was then placed in comparison to non-synaesthetic brains:

> We chose a set of three sessions in one sitting. The first session would establish a resting baseline, against which we would compare two subsequent activation states. The baseline is measured in what is called the resting state: the patient lies on the couch, eyes closed, hearing only the steady white noise of the surrounding machinery…the normal pattern of resting blood flow should be fairly homogeneous, with no brain region standing out from another.[21]

What was interesting and crucial about Cytowic's study was that Michael's period of synaesthesia did *not* produce an increase in blood flow to any measurable part of the brain; in fact, it showed a decrease; as the subject felt the shape of the smells that were administered to him, his brain showed less activity than when he was resting; sometimes dropping to levels that would normally be considered symptomatic of illness or damage in a normal perceptual subject. Despite this specific CBF process not being able to gain access to the limbic system (it only measures cortical blood flow), Cytowic concludes from this experiment that synaesthesia resides in this often overlooked and primal part of the brain – a conclusion that also suggests that we are all party to this process but that it is normally obscured by the cortical activity that is so obviously missing in Michael.

The limbic system is concerned with memory, with emotion and with spatial awareness. As Susan Greenfield states, it especially governs aggression and sexual behaviour and thus, is often, referred to as the reptile or animal brain.[22] Michael O'Shea details that, in terms of neurobiological evolution at least, the limbic system is also linked to the olfactory processes making smell the most primal of all the senses – although in man the link between smell and reflex (fight or flight) is replaced largely by memory.[23]

This last point is interesting in terms of our understanding of the brain and how it works. One of the most well known studies of memory, A. R. Luria's *The Mind of a Mnemonist*, is also concerned with synaesthesia.[24] Luria's subject 'S' was a young man with a remarkable memory; in fact, so great was his powers of recall that they were thought to be virtually limitless and for many years he earned fame and fortune on the cabaret circuit as a memory man, commanding meetings with artistic and cultural luminaries such as Eisenstein and L. S. Vygotsky. Luria asserted that it was S's synaesthesia that enabled his fantastic recall; S did not merely recall a word, a phrase, or a face, but a whole range of different sensations and bodily affects:

To this day I can't escape from seeing colours when I hear sounds. What first strikes me is the colour of someone's voice. Then it fades off…for it does interfere. If, say, a person says something, I see the word; but should another person's voice break in, blurs appear. These creep into the syllables of the words and I can't make out what is being said.[25]

An interesting aside here is S's assertion that he cannot focus on what is being said if his synaesthesia is allowed to go unchecked; this perhaps explains why the human mind has seen fit to ensure that synaesthetic perception is unscrambled by cognitive processes.

S knew when a name correctly matched a face, for instance, because all of his senses told him so. Luria states that he did not remember the face *per se*, what he remembered was the bodily sensations the name produced; the same with Cytowic's 'Michael', who even cooked using his sense of touch rather than his eyes (Cytowic details how Michael, one evening at dinner, claimed that the chicken he was preparing was not yet spiky enough!)

Michael and S can be seen to represent, not some evolved sixth sense as nineteenth-century notions of synaesthesia might suggest, but (to use Cytowic's phrase) 'cognitive fossils' that allow us a glimpse of our own phylogenetic and ontogenetic past, a snapshot of what perception was like before the cortex categorises, organises, rationalises and generally constructs what most of us know as the world of perception. Some studies have suggested that synaesthesia is merely a part of normal neurological development, that babies up to about 4 months 'experience sensory input in an undifferentiated way (that) sounds trigger both auditory and visual and tactile experiences' and that it is 'a truly psychedelic state, and all natural – no illegal substances play a role'.[26] Using neuroimaging techniques, the brain patterning of young children were tested and the results suggested that, unlike most adults, infants experience the world synaesthetically, although of course it would be difficult to qualify this experience without speech.

Further studies have also stated the possibility that the universality of synaesthesia (both in terms of individual human development and in terms of species evolution) has contributed to the widespread use of metaphorical speech.[27] Poetry, religious symbolism, abstraction, art and scientific models could all be a product of the primal tendency to experience the world in a synaesthetic way – with all senses contributing to the perceptual soup of existence. Such a view of perception provides a radical break from the traditional biological notion of the senses in their specificity and in their number; it is difficult after all to note five senses when the delineation between them is so indistinct. However, we can also note that this represents yet another manifestation of the postmodern scopic regime, where not only is the hegemony of vision challenged but where the body (touch and taste in particular) is seen as being every bit as sentient as the mind. The synaesthetic links between vision and the other senses and vision and memory impact greatly upon our notion of what constitutes the process of cinema spectatorship; Cytowic's thesis that we might all be experiencing synaesthesia below the level of our consciousness means that, when we watch a film for instance, our minds can be having one experience (of the narrative, of character empathy, of political, sexual and ideological interpolation and so on) whereas our bodies and our limbic systems could be having another, altogether different experience, one that is rooted in our past, in our sensual memory and in synaesthesia, where visual inputs trigger gustatory or tactile sensations.

Mirror Neurons

The eminent neurobiologist Vilayanur Ramachandran called the discovery of mirror neurons 'the single most important "unreported"…story of the decade'.[28] In the same article, Ramachandran makes the claim that mirror neurons can solve many of the outstanding mysteries that occur in neuroscience and evolutionary biology: why, for instance, if the hominoid brain reached its full size about 250,000 years ago did it take over 150,000 years for tools, clothes, standardised dwellings and art to be produced? Why did the evolving human brain demand such a latency period? What prompted the huge leap forwards in human evolution once this latency period had come to an end? And where did the impetus for language come from?

Mirror neurons were first discovered in the ventral premotor area of the frontal lobes of monkeys, the area known as F5.[29] The neurons in this area largely govern the link between vision and movement especially 'walking, turning the head, bending the torso and moving the arms'.[30] However, as Rizzolatti, Fadiga, Gallese and Fogassi found, neurons that would fire when these activities were being conducted would also fire when the subject was watching these activities performed by another.[31] Further studies revealed that not only did the gestures and actions result in neurons being activated but that this depended, to a large extent, on context and intention: miming grasping without actually doing so, a picture of a hand or (in monkeys) a movie of a hand would not result in the same effect.[32] What is interesting and vital to an understanding of how mirror neurons can inform film theory is that, in humans, movies do produce results. In a study by Fogassi *et al*, films of hand actions were witnessed by a series of subjects and the resulting mirror neurons were activated; this suggests that for humans, at least, cinema is as real as life.[33]

As Rizzolatti and Craighero detail, there have been two major hypotheses put forward as to the functions of mirror neurons: firstly, that they aid imitation and the second is that they are the basic building blocks of understanding and knowledge formation; that to be human (or monkey) is inherently to copy.[34] Gallese suggests a term that is strikingly familiar in the context of the current thesis: 'embodied simulation'.[35] This concept not only reminds us of the kinds of developments made in film theory, phenomenology and psychoanalysis but once again challenges what we have identified as the removed processes of psychological empathy and identification. Gallese offers us a remarkable conceptual vision of how we orientate ourselves within the world:

> The mirror neuron system for action is activated both by transitive, object related and intransitive, communicative actions, regardless of the effectors performing them. When a given action is planned, its expected motor consequencers are forecast. This means what when we are going to execute a given action we can also predict its consequences. The action model enables this prediction.[36]

We must remember that this process is occurring on a neurobiological level, we may not even be aware that what we are responding to is governed by *what*, or more rightly *who*, we are looking at. Mirror neurons knit us into those around us without us being conscious of it, they allow us to understand other people not through abstract reasoning or categorical imperatives but because our bodies imitate those we are looking at. Our brains and bodies simulate that which is presented before us, creating a virtual copy that allows us to feel as others feel. Traditionally, it may be thought, that the body sweats, palpitates or becomes excited *through* fear at what it sees on the screen. Mirror neurons suggest that, in fact, this process should be understood in reverse – that we understand fear through the body, that it is the body and embodied simulation that is the primary experience of cinema.

Cytowic details a neurological activity that is allied to both synaesthesia and mirror neurons: the gustofacial reflex is centred in the neural structures of the brainstem and controls the body's reaction to tasted (and to an extent smelt) substances:

In the gustofacial reflex, different tastes produce fixed facial expressions (sweet = smile; bitter = disgust with tongue protrusion; sour = pursing of the lips).[37]

These reactions to various tastes and sensations are fixed and universal, they occur across cultures, across classes and, we could assume, across generations. As Cytowic states, this represents nothing less than a decision on the part of the individual about the nature of the substances they are consuming; it is an act of taste, of discernment and of discrimination. What is perhaps most interesting about this, as Steiner details, is that this same mechanism is displayed in anencephalic infants that is, babies born without a brain.[38] The body and brain stem make such discriminatory decisions without ever bothering the brain – or we could say the traditional notion of the self- at all. Our bodies become arbiters of what is good for us without our ever having to decide consciously.

Again, what we are building up here is a picture of the flesh as sentient, of the brain stem, skin, taste buds and eardrums as continually sense processing organs that undercut the monolithic constructs of the self. This molecular layer of consciousness constantly shifts and changes, existing within a state of becoming rather than being, sorting and organising inputs and connections and filtering out that which is not strictly needed for consciousness. If Cytowic is right, and the seat of synaesthesia is in the limbic system and not in the cortex, then the two modes can exist simultaneously: the limbic brain and the brain stem having one experience, the cognitive brain having another. We, as adult human beings, experience this often, when, for instance, we take a foul tasting medicine that makes our face screw up but our symptoms instantly and psychosomatically lessen, or when we persist with a bitter acquired taste such as coffee or olives revelling in the contradiction between the two modes of experience – the body's and the self's. Of course, these two modes should not be thought of as two distinct Cartesian entities nor even two sides of the same coin but, more rightly, as a Moebius strip where one leads into the other and where the dividing line between the two is difficult if not impossible to discern. The 'I' is formed somewhere along this Moebius strip and the self constructed through its folding and unfolding.

In his essay 'The Re-enchantment of the Concrete' neurobiologist Francisco J Varela makes the same point, only for him, the Moebius strip is an ever-shifting, rhizomatic series of networks:

There is considerable support for the view that brains are not logical machines, but highly cooperative, nonhomogeneous and distributed networks. The entire system resembles a patchwork of subnetworks assembled by a complicated history of tinkering, rather than an optimised system resulting from some clean unified design.[39]

Varela here reminds us of Deleuze and Merleau-Ponty; in fact, the latter forms a major part of Varela's image of the brain and the mind. For Varela, sight and mind can never be separated from embodiment and action, as he himself says:

Let me now explain how I mean to use the word 'embodied' by highlighting two points: first, cognition depends on the kinds of experience that come from having a body with various sensorimotor capacities; and second, these individual sensorimotor capacities are themselves embedded in a more encompassing biological and cultural context.[40]

So, for Varela, to think is inevitably to exist within a world of movement and, by extension, sensation. Visual perception of the world cannot be separated from embodied enactment of that same world. The brain and body form a rhizome not a tree and that rhizome forms another with the world around it.

§

I began this chapter with a discussion of the connections that exist between scientific knowledge and the wider social and cultural episteme. The biological body and its make up, far from being a never changing thing, exists within a network of discourses and metaphorical models that go to shape what we think of as our physical self. As we have seen by this brief survey of current neurological thinking regarding the senses and perception, the postmodern scopic regime and its main tenants have spread even to the biological sciences, as the all-encompassing primacy of sight is being challenged and questioned.

The fourth part of Robert Jutte's book, *A History of the Senses*, is called 'The Rediscovery of the Senses in the Twentieth Century'. In it, he examines many of the more recent developments in technology and cultural thinking regarding the body and its modes of perception:

According to an article in the *Stuttgarter Nachricjten* of 18 October 1999, we have now entered a 'haptic age'…The piece also noted other signs of the changing times: for instance, the stress on tenderness in sexual therapy, as well as the increasing demand for healers with 'magic hands' (animal magnetopaths, masseurs and chiropractors) and the supposedly growing number of adults in need of 'loving sex'.[41]

The haptic age, as Jutte details, is also commensurate with the olfactory age, with the rise in the manufacture and distribution of synthetic scents in both food production and cosmetics; the gustatory age with the rise in the popularity of television chefs, interest in food preparation and (due to changing economics) the availability of wine and other drinks and also the audio age, where iPods, in-car CD players and mobile phones deliver sound wherever one wants it, personally and with ease.

What is perhaps most interesting about this situation is that, more and more, theorists and historians such as Jutte are choosing to focus on senses other than sight in their work. In his introduction to the anthology of essays, *Empire of the Senses: The Sensual Culture Reader*, David Howes not only makes the same points we have been making here concerning the relationship between science and the wider cultural episteme:

> Cultural studies of the senses should…be cautious in their use of scientific data. Science cannot provide a touchstone of truth or a higher authority for cultural analysis. That is not to say that there is no 'truth' to science, but rather it is a culturally bonded truth.[42]

But he also makes the point that interest in this area has grown over the last twenty years or so and forms something of a 'sensual revolution'.[43] It is precisely this sensual revolution that I have termed the postmodern scopic regime, not because it does not deal with eyes or the processes of sight but because it recognises the contribution made to perceptual understanding by the body and its other senses, which is a point also made by Howes: 'Rather than attempting to "free" ideas from the knot of the senses, we should try to understand how meaning and senses are one.'

The notion that meaning and sense are one here is at the heart of the present book that will try, in the next section, to examine the way filmmakers play with their audiences' sensual memories, sensual experiences and (in the case of sound) their actual physical and embodied sensations. This way of looking at film touches upon emotion and cognition, for instance, such as the essays in Plantinga and Smith's 1999 anthology, *Passionate Views*, but, as I have already discussed, makes the distinction between embodiment as an index of the film's intentions and embodiment as a site or, we could even say, a tool of reception.[44]

Film is obviously a visual medium; again film theories of the postmodern scopic regime do not deny this – this would clearly be absurd – neither do they deny the existence of processes such as the suture, identification, or character empathy. Embodied film theories attempt to examine the embodied experience of film, the ways in which vision is undercut, enhanced and propped up by our memories, our sense knowledge, the processes of material understanding, the indices of our emotions, our subconscious relationship with colour, our embodied knowledge of space, other bodies, heights, textures, smells and so on. The postmodern scopic regime assumes that we cannot understand a world that we have not experienced physically, that even if we have not experienced a visual image directly we mediate understanding through knowledge we *do* have, constantly negotiating with the film's intentions and filling the void that exists between filmic presentation and our own understanding.

PART TWO: THE FILMS

4

ON HITCHCOCK

Everybody is supposed to be able to control the workings of his body – why? Our arms, our legs, our heads aren't completely ours; we don't make them. And couldn't ideas come into our limbs just like ideas live in our minds. Couldn't ideas live in nerve and muscle as well as in the brain?[1]

The first part of this book attempted to isolate and define the various tools of what I have called the postmodern scopic regime. This involved looking at a number of key areas of theory and relating them to changes in the way we think about the process of vision. Each of the areas I chose to look at had a specific relation to the area of spectatorship: Chapter 1 examined recent ideas of multi-modal film theory, Chapter 2 looked at changes in the conceptions of the self and its relationship to corporeality and the body and Chapter 3 looked at neuroscience and optics and how scientific discourses have, to a large extent, also posited a more synaesthetic, embodied visual sense that links specularity to the rest of the sensorium. I also began to suggest that what was emerging from this discussion was a different spectator, one that was not based solely on thought, critical distance and intellectual empathy but on bodily transitivism, mimesis, mirror neuron-based corporeal involvement and synaesthetic understanding. However, this thesis concerns itself with more than film theory in the abstract, it is more than a high level exposition of changing notions of sight. It is a practical exercise in how such ideas can be used by film critics and students alike and how they can form an approach that, not so much challenges the more traditional tools of cinema studies, but provides us with alternatives and differing perspectives.

One of the most resonant critiques to appear in Daniel Frampton's *Filmosophy* is that high-level film theory tends to lack the expository connection to its textual base, as he states:

> …as we head to more advanced analogies of film and mind the importance of examples, of the backing up of theories with illustrations, becomes at once crucial and sadly lacking.[2]

Ironically, this is also a statement one can make about Frampton's own book, which seems to talk of film and cinema as abstract concepts rather than specific instances of concrete media. Like those he criticises, Frampton often fails to view his theories *through* film or to suggest ways that film, as a specific medium, can inform the theoretical underpinnings of his work. Where films *are* cited as examples, it tends to be isolated scenes or frames rather than motifs, stylistic modes or entire sequences. What we end up with, as with many high level works of film and philosophy, is a work of film theory that has very little mention, let alone engagement, with films themselves. In this way, 'filmosophical' works tend to be illuminating in terms of philosophy but not so much in terms of cinema. Such works very rarely base their theories around in-depth filmic discussion and seldom concentrate on a specific director, genre or motif. To this end, the next section of this book will take an in-depth look at film and films as a whole, not only fleshing out (somewhat literally at times) the abstract theories we have been discussing so far but also adding a new dimension to our understanding of how film works.

The texts that form the basis of the discussion in Part Two are the films of Alfred Hitchcock. Hitchcock studies have grown rapidly since the publication of the first full scale book on his work by Chabrol and Rohmer in 1957 and even more so since the centenary of his birth in 1999.[3] There have been studies, articles and books on virtually every imaginable aspect of the director's oeuvre and life, from the music in his films to the dresses worn by his leading ladies, from his poster art to the relationship he had with Alma, his wife.[4] As Robert Kapsis states, Hitchcock has been used to highlight virtually every academic film theory from feminism to film art from Deleuzian film philosophy to, most famously perhaps, Žižekian/Lacanian psychoanalysis.[5]

Why then choose a subject already so seemingly oversubscribed? Why base an exposition of changing theories of cinema spectatorship on a director that has formed the basis of so many existing theories already? The answer to this can be broken down into three main areas, each of which not only help to illuminate (and to an extent defend) the use of Hitchcock here but also to highlight the methodological mechanisms of contemporary film theory and its objects.

Hitchcock as historical paradigm

Hitchcock was born on the cusp of the twentieth century on 13 August 1899 and many of his biographers posit this as an important psychological facet in his later life. John Russell Taylor points out that there was a geographic and demographic shift in this period surrounding the place of Hitchcock's birth, with the physical boundary line between Essex and London becoming evermore indistinct but the economic line evermore pronounced. The (now) London borough of Leytonstone (then a small Essex town) became a strange mixing place for migrant workers coming in from Essex and Suffolk, and the expanding middle classes going out from London. Hitchcock, as his many biographers point out, was a man on the edge of two centuries and in between two classes.[6] This liminality, this refusal to sit within accepted borders, will become a constant theme running throughout his work and throughout the commentaries upon it. Gilles Deleuze, for instance, suggests that Hitchcock represented a borderline between classical and modern cinema and, in this way, also between the Deleuzian movement-image and time-image.

> Inventing the mental image or the relation-image, Hitchcock makes use of it in order to close the set of action-images, and also of perception and affection-images…for this reason one might say that Hitchcock accomplishes and brings to completion the whole of the cinema by pushing the movement image to its limit.[7]

Strangely Victorian in his personal relationships and yet always eager to utilise new technology and cinematic ideas (the talkie, colour film, 3D, new moral and ethical codes and so on), Hitchcock's life represents a paradigm of post-First World War (narrative) cinema history – from his first beginnings with a film such as *The Pleasure Garden* (1925), through the rise and domination of the Hollywood studio system, and finally to the breakdown of the various decency codes and taboos with the 1972 English film *Frenzy*. The many awards and accolades he received in the last years of his life were testament to his position as an icon of cinema's own history, a fact that, as Donald Spoto suggests, Hitchcock was only too aware.

Hitchcock's career then can be characterised as one of change *and* consistency, offering to the critic at once a map of the progressive technology of cinema and a continuous aesthetic vision and directorial persona. Irrespective of one's view on his status as an auteur in the *Cahiers du Cinéma* tradition, Hitchcock's working methods remained startingly consistent throughout his life, shooting only the scenes and angles that had been previously storyboarded, for instance, or never actually viewing through the camera. Hitchcock's career then can be viewed as a kind of history of post-1920s English-speaking cinema but with the added advantage of offering a fairly consistent creative vision with which to form a ground.

With the advent of cheaply produced DVDs, Hitchcock studies have become easier. Previously, much of the difficulty in reading books such as Chabrol and Rohmer or even a text like Raymond Durgnat's *The Strange Case of Alfred Hitchcock* was that many of the earlier films were simply not available for study.[8] This position was made all the harder due to the fact that five of Hitchcock's greatest films – *Rope* (1948), *Rear Window* (1954), *The Man Who Knew Too Much* (1956), *The Trouble With Harry* (1955) and *Vertigo* (1957) - were not available for distribution until they were sold to Universal in 1983. The absence of description for the entries for *Easy Virtue* (1927) or *The Manxman* (1928) in Durgnat, for example, seems to suggest that the author was simply relying on earlier descriptions or outlines of the screenplays rather than the films themselves.[9] Today however only one of Hitchcock's recorded films, *The Mountain Eagle* (1926), is unavailable and this, as far as most critics are concerned, has disappeared entirely.

These two facts – the commensurability of Hitchcock's career and the vast majority of twentieth-century cinema and the recent availability of his films – make him an ideal subject for studying embodied film theory. As was previously stated, the notion that film can be experienced in an embodied sense goes back to the very beginnings of cinema, it makes sense then that, in order to fully develop this theme, we should not limit our study to those (more recent) films that deliberately deal with this area or forays into technologies such as virtual reality and IMAX cinema that provide an easy route into such notions.[10] Hitchcock offers us a relatively coherent and substantial body of work that not only covers a great deal of twentieth-century cinema but is also (now) readily available.

Hitchcock's Interest in Embodiment

One could be forgiven for making the assumption that there were two Hitchcocks: one constructed by Hitchcock himself and one constructed by the French auteur critics of the 1960s and 70s. Often, these two faces were not only separate from each other they were mutually exclusive. In an interview for *Movie* magazine for instance, Hitchcock clearly hints at the gulf between his own conceptions of his work and that of his younger, more earnest, commentators:

> Question: One feels of your later films that you have got much less interested in the mystery thriller element, much more interested in broadening things out.
>
> Hitchcock: Well, I think its natural tendency to be less superficial,

that's Truffaut's opinion – he's been examining all these films. And he feels that the American period is much stronger than the English period.[11]

This sly joke is typical of the Hitchcock that we receive from interviews and his own written work; the suggestion that Truffaut is better equipped to discuss the opinions of Hitchcock than the man himself is a humorous but ultimately telling insight into how the old master saw his young acolytes. Truffaut's celebrated book of interviews with Hitchcock reads at times like the two men are discussing different people: Truffaut the Catholic auteur and Hitchcock the filmmaker eager to please his public and his producer. The famous misheard phrase in the interview conducted by Claude Chabrol is another instance of just how wide the gulf was between the director's own self-image and that of the younger *Cahiers du Cinéma* critics:

> Some of my colleagues and I [Chabrol]…have discovered in your works a carefully hidden theme, and that is the search for God… In my somewhat flawed English I said 'Search of God'.
> He [Hitchcock] understands somewhat imperfectly and what he says is revealing.
> 'Search of good? Oh yes, yes; there is a search of good.'…
> But I set things straight.
> 'Not good: God himself'.
> He looks somewhat astonished, or rather surprised.
> 'God! A search of God? Maybe, but it is unconscious'.
> I attempt to justify my question, because I'm far from convinced. I want to get him to talk.
> 'You understand, your heroes are caught in a net of evil.'
> I say 'evil'. He corrects on his own:
> 'Devil, yes they are.'
> '…and they can escape only through avowal, through confession'.
> 'Sincere confession, yes; contrition'
> He adds with a disconcerting smile, 'But I am only aware of it after the fact.' These disclaimers are all the more disturbing since he makes it very clear that they are indeed dissimulations.[12]

This search for God will of course be at the heart of Chabrol's own book on Hitchcock some three years later, the search for *good* is a wholly different thing, one that is more recognisably populist in its artistic intentions. What is interesting in this interview is Chabrol's unwillingness to allow Hitchcock his own voice and his constant assertion of Hitchcock's place as an auteur and, more importantly, as an intellectual, despite the fact that Hitchcock himself is clearly uncomfortable with this mantle. We could simply put Hitchcock's reticence to see himself as an intellectual filmmaker down to his innate humility but it would be truer to assert that the French critics missed a great deal of what Hitchcock himself saw as important in his work: its ability to make money, to delight an audience and, ultimately, to thrill, chill and excite.

It is this last aspect of Hitchcock's work that makes him ideally suited to a study of the postmodern scopic regime. Time and time again throughout his own writing, Hitchcock hints at his intention to excite and move the bodies as well as the minds and characters of his audience; something that we have already described as the body as an index of the film and similar in concern to those intermediary postmodern scopic theories such as Linda Williams' 'body genres'. The posters for Hitchcock's films, for instance, offer their audiences thrills and chills of a particularly physical kind; the re-released *Rear Window*, for example, dared audiences to 'See it! If your nerves can stand it after *Psycho*!'; and the poster for *Torn Curtain* (1966) threatened to 'Tear you apart with suspense!' In Hitchcock's own writings and interviews, we are constantly presented with images of the bodily and its relation to suspense and fear; in an interview with Janet Maslin in 1972 he states that:

> To make you *feel the effect* of that strangulation, it's done in very close shots. The closeup of the man straining, his individual hands...what effect do you want to have on the audience? *Do you want to have the effect of scaring them, or making them feel the horror of it*?[13]

This desire to excite the bodies of his audiences is far removed from the assertions in Jean Douchet's famous set of essays for *Cahiers du Cinéma* entitled 'The Third Key of Hitchcock' wherein such feelings are described as 'vile and low'[14] and that such sensations must be overcome by the Hitchcockian key of intelligence. Once again, the *Cahiers du Cinéma* critics (and as a consequence a great deal of Hitchcock studies since) have missed the central motivation of Hitchcock's oeuvre. In some senses by 'taking Hitchcock seriously' they ignored the very reason many audiences went to his films in the first place.

The key to Hitchcock's intellectual positioning can be found in G.K. Chesterton's essay *A Defence of Penny Dreadfuls*; Chesterton, an important early influence on the young Hitchcock, declares that:

> One of the strangest examples of the degree to which ordinary life is

undervalued is the example of popular literature, the vast majority of which we contentedly describe as vulgar. The boy's novelette may be ignorant in a literary sense, which is only like saying that modern novel [sic] is ignorant in the chemical sense, or the economic sense, or the astronomical sense...[15]

To say that certain Hitchcock films only inspire 'vile and low' feelings (as Douchet does) is again like criticising them for being ignorant of chemistry or economics. It is the sensation that drives the films and the artistic vision; however these concepts do fit as neatly into the intellectual mandates of the auteur critics and removed cognition.

Hitchcock's distrust of the mediating processes of the visual is exemplified in his famous comment to Ernest Lehman on the set of *North by Northwest* (1959), when he says:

> Ernie, do you realize what we're doing in this picture? The audience is like a giant organ that you and I are playing. At the one moment we play this note on them and get this reaction, and then we play that chord and they react that way. And someday we won't even have to make a movie – there'll be electrodes planted in their brains, and we'll just press different buttons and they'll go 'oooh' and 'aaaah' and we'll frighten them and make them laugh. Won't that be wonderful?[16]

The image Hitchcock paints here of his ideal 'movie' is not one of vision and its relation to the self, it is not one of semiotic understanding, it is not one of psychologically determined empathy with characters or removed contemplation but of fleshy involvement, of sensation and a delight in the experience of movies and in the direct sensation of what movies do to us and through us.

Hitchcock Scholarship - The Vision and the Self

If there are signs in Hitchcock's own writing and interviews that he was interested in the embodied experience of his films, the vast majority of Hitchcock scholarship has, at best, ignored this and, at worst, attempted to expunge it altogether. The hitherto mentioned essay by Jean Douchet is a case in point: in the third section, Douchet outlines what he sees as the 'three realities' of the Hitchcock vision: the everyday world, the world of desire, and the intellectual world. For Douchet, it is the last of these that binds the other two together and allows the spectator to become the third term in the construction of the film's meaning. It is also the intellectual world that 'elevates' the spectator above the vile and low level of the body:

> [The intellectual world] is the main support beam of the Hitchockian oeuvre, the perpendicular which links the two parallel universes and thus allows them to communicate. It is on this beam that the filmmaker relies for all his films.[17]

The processes of thought, in Douchet's essay, are inextricably linked with the notion of seeing as he cites, firstly, the voyeurism of James Stewart in *Rear Window* and then Anthony Perkins in *Psycho* as exemplars of the Hitchockian spectator *within* the film. For Douchet, the space between the narrative and the audience's understanding is breached by the film's intellectual reality; it is this dimension that creates the conditions of empathy for the spectator, cut off physically as they are from the images they witness on screen. Where bodies *are* mentioned in Douchet, they are representations of bodies to be viewed – the body in the car, the body in the flat opposite and so on. The spectator, according to Douchet, exists as a visual and intellectual unit that communicates with the screen, completing the loop of understanding between its various levels of reality. This model does not of course consider the extent that the spectator's body and his or her embodied understanding might be informing and undercutting this process of intellectual communication despite Douchet himself using the language of embodiment at various stages throughout his essay. As we have seen, also, this model denies the thread in Hitchcock's own writing that attempts to distance himself from the intellectualising of his work and to value its material affects, again an example of the gulf that exists between critic and director.

The critical tropes of vision and the self in Hitchcock studies appear in many of the major perspectives: Laura Mulvey's influential essay 'Visual Pleasure and Narrative Cinema' makes heavy use of *Marnie* (1964), *Rear Window*, and *Vertigo* in its assertions on the primacy of vision in the cinematic experience in relation to feminist theory; George Toles' essay '"If thine eye offend…": Psycho and the Art of Infection' charts the similarities between Hitchcock and Bataille; and Slavoj Žižek's discussion of Lacanian psychoanalysis and Hitchcock in 'In My Bold Gaze My Ruin is Writ Large' relies heavily on the processes of vision and understanding despite the author making the crucial distinction between seeing and the Gaze.[18]

It is this over reliance on the image of vision, cognitive understanding and the self, twinned with the hint in Hitchcock's own writing that he was more concerned with unconscious, visceral emotion and bodily excitation that makes him an ideal subject for film theory of the postmodern scopic regime. The fact that Hitchcock has been (over) used so much in the area of psychoanalytic film theory makes him a prime candidate for a set of theoretical tools that suggests we should look at other areas of filmic understanding, areas that are perhaps less based in the constant fixed self and more in the subconscious processes of embodied experience.

The aim of the readings that follow is not to suggest that established methods of looking at film are wrong or that they have no currency in contemporary theory; the aim of these readings is to attempt an archaeological discovery of the many different layers of the filmic experience, layers that have hitherto remained untapped. The chapters that follow all centre around a specific bodily sense and will utilise a number of filmic examples, both from Hitchcock and other directors, in order to highlight the ways that films rely on embodied sensation for their meaning. I will also point out how this sensation relates to the narratalogical, conscious experience of the film and how one can undercut, support, or conflict with the other. Each chapter will end with an in-depth examination of a paradigmatic Hitchcock film that encapsulates the use of a specific sense and I will place my embodied reading alongside a more traditional canonical one to, firstly, show how the former differs and, secondly, show how the two methods of viewing film can work side by side.

Like the quotation from *The Hands of Mr Ottermole* that opened this chapter, the readings that follow attempt not so much to upturn the notion of thought and feeling but to redefine what they might mean; to suggest that thoughts and ideas could be centred in the limbs, trunk or organs of the body, to posit that filmic understanding could be linked to the flesh and bone rather than merely the eye and mind.

5

ON TASTE AND DIGESTION

The pleasures of the table belong to all times and all ages, to every country and every day; they go hand in hand with all our pleasures, outlast them, and remain to console us for their loss.[1]

This chapter focuses on how taste and digestion manifest themselves in films such as *To Catch a Thief* (1954), *Rich and Strange* (1932), and, most especially, *Frenzy*. As will become apparent, what this book is concerned with is examining how embodied theory can complement or provide an alternative to more conventional readings of popular cinema. In this way I look in some depth at Tania Modleski's reading of *Frenzy* in *The Women Who Knew Too Much*, and see how the body's reaction to the film differs from the mind's and the self's.

Taste is an ideal sense with which to start our examination of the embodied film theory and its relation to the processes inherent in understanding cinema. Obviously, taste is not utilised by the spectator in any concrete chemical manner when watching films, despite there being a whole wealth of associations and correlations between eating and the cinema, as James Lyons states in his essay 'What About the Popcorn? Food and the Film Watching Experience'; and yet, as we shall see, food, eating and digestion (or regurgitation) is surprising frequent in a great many of the images that we witness on screen.[2] Such images often have an instant impact on the bodies and minds of the viewer and have been used variously to sell products, to delight audiences, to suggest wider psychosocial states and to disgust and repel. Food is at once sensuous, sexual, and challenging, and the mouth an area both of intense privacy and distinct universality. Taste is at once shared and individuated; it unites whole cultures and yet changes over an individual's lifetime; it has a distinct evolutionary role and yet is so inextricably linked to the other senses that it has often been considered the lowliest of them all.

Oral activity often goes unnoticed in film whether it is the lighting and smoking of a cigarette, the casual eating of a meal, or the sipping of a Martini, but the specificity of film (as movement and time) makes the processes of eating and digestion curiously apt for cinematic representation. The question we shall be asking here is how do we understand such images and what function do they provide in terms of our experience of the film as a whole? Film theory of the postmodern scopic regime, as we shall see, attempts to move beyond the reliance on signification and signs and into more primary areas of human understanding; areas that are often subconscious but nonetheless affect our experience of viewing a film. Eating is a basic human activity that is both shared and personal, we are never free from the body's imperative to digest; even when no food has entered it, the body begins to digest itself, first the stored fat and then the muscle and soft tissue.[3] In the same way, we constantly taste the inside of our mouths and the air around us as we subconsciously monitor our own state of health and the make-up of our environment. We cannot divorce existence from digestion.

Where film critics have concentrated on food, it has tended to be almost exclusively treated as a metaphor or semiotic sign linked variously to gender, class, psychology and other elements of a character's persona. Often, food is twinned with the subtextual threads inherent in the film itself; Laurent Bouzereau, for instance, traces the links in Hitchcock between food and marriage, food and sex, and food and murder, a taxonomy that was taken up and explored in depth by Michael Walker.[4] Walker constructs convincing arguments for many of his observations: the link between Marion Crane's scant appetite and her sexual unease for instance in *Psycho* or the link between food and marriage in *Frenzy* and *Mr and Mrs Smith* (1941). He also expands this out into more speculative areas of character psychoanalysis: the hint of cannibalism in *Rope*, for example, or the vagina dentata of the lobster claws that Lisa prepares for L. B. in *Rear Window*. Walker however, fairly typically of Hitchcock critics, fails to recognise the embodied knowledge involved in our appreciation of images of food and eating, knowledge that perhaps only film theory of the postmodern scopic regime can offer. He says for instance referring to *Frenzy* that:

> Hitchcock is enjoying the effect of introducing the topic of murder into a conversation in such a way as to unsettle the appetite. But these are really no more than typical examples of his black humour.[5]

As we shall see with the in-depth reading of this and similar scenes in *Frenzy* below, the use of food in Hitchcock is anything but 'really no more than typical examples of black humour'; they are specifically designed, and serve, to disgust and revolt the audience and to disturb their physical equilibrium, an embodied reaction that provides a physical correlative to the conscious experience of the narrative (the body as an index of response) and one that is, in turn, based in synaesthetic knowledge and memory (the body as a site of reception). The failure to appreciate the importance of the body and the sensorium in the process of spectatorship can only arise from the privileging of vision above all the other senses; when one has discounted the importance of taste, smell or touch in film one is left to rely solely on metaphor or symbol to explain our relationship to images of eating or regurgitation.

Food in film, however, provides the first indication that our categorisation of the body as *either* a site of reception *or* an index of response is problematic, porous and open to question. As we shall discover, images of eating can be experienced, and thus read, in a number of related but distinct ways and this is so for many of the areas we are to look at in this part of the book. It is possible that, when presented with images of food and eating, the body can be used as *both* an index of response *and* as a site of reception. The sensation of nausea or disgust we might feel when presented with an unsavoury image of someone eating could be thought of as an index of the film (that is to say an *effect* of it) but one of the methods at least through which such disgust might arise is the synaesthetic use of taste and oral sensation which could be seen as the body as a site of reception or tool of understanding. Of course, the same image could also be read symbolically, as a point of identification, a narratological device and so on. Unpacking the multilayered richness of this model of spectatorship is at the heart of the present work.[6]

Taste and eating were famously important to Hitchcock. When he moved with his family to Los Angeles in 1940 the director regularly sent back to England and Europe for Dover sole, steak, and a particular brand of Swiss cider that he had acquired the taste for on his first shooting trip, forming a kind of gustatory umbilical cord that could never, despite the wealth of produce available in the USA, be broken. As Donald Spoto suggests, throughout most of his life, but especially in the latter years, food and drink for Hitchcock became substitutes for closeness, contact, and sexual union, exacerbated by almost a lifetime of celibacy and repression.[7] Food occurs throughout Hitchcock's *oeuvre*, often (as I have already stated) acting as a correlative for the relationships between characters or providing a fulcrum for the narrative. As Dick Stromgem details:

> By his own words and actions it is clear that food and drink provided Hitchcock with the security and defence against the unexpected and uninvited, against isolation as well as confrontation, and against a deprivation that soon became more social and aesthetic than physical.[8]

Food, in Hitchcock, and the processes of digestion and eating become quilting points for all of the various levels of the filmic experience cinema can offer, simultaneously providing the viewer with narrative information, characterisation, cultural symbolism and an embodied sensual affect that imbues specific scenes with a mood, a feeling or a physical correlative. Let us look at an example.

To Catch a Thief, for a great many critics, is a comedy of little worth. Spoto called it 'the product of a man on holiday'[9] and (strangely, anticipating this discussion of gustation) 'a creampuff of a movie'.[10] It is referred to only twice in Robin Wood's *Hitchcock's Films* and then only as an aside; even Hitchcock himself described the film once as nothing more than 'a lightweight story'.[11] For Raymond Durgnat, however, *To Catch a Thief*'s glossy exterior serves only to hide its darker heart, one that is concerned with exploring the links between marriage and theft, between retribution and guilt and, most of all, between pursuer and pursued.[12] A crucial scene in the film, the picnic between Francine and Robie, occurs almost exactly an hour into it and it is here that the relationship that will provide the focus for the rest of the narrative is cemented and here that the tropes that form the main themes of Durgant's argument are worked out.

After a fast paced drive through the mountainous landscape of the Riviera, escaping two policemen in a mysterious black car, Robie and Francine come to rest at the side of the road and picnic in front of a picturesque (but patently false) Mediterranean backdrop. Pursuit, as Durgnat correctly observes, is a key motif of the film and the sexually predatory Francine is as in control of her car as her emotions as she doles out beer and chicken from a basket and quips, 'Do you want a breast or a leg?', a question to which Robie can only answer, 'You make the choice'. We are obviously being made party to a seduction here but it is a seduction with a few notable anomalies: firstly, it is the woman who is doing the seducing and, secondly, this is very definitely a sexual, not a romantic, rite, one that occurs on a number of simultaneous levels – for both the characters and the audience. Symbolically, of course, this scene represents a sacrament with Francine as shaman; she not only asks Robie to feed upon her (not only does she offer him a leg and a breast but she literally becomes part of the meal towards the end of the scene as they kiss and her head rests in the picnic basket) but she also feeds upon him, her elevated position in the frame bearing witness to her status as high priestess.

This scene is notable for the method of eating it depicts and the sheer pleasure that each character takes in nibbling, licking, biting, tearing and swallowing the flesh of the greasy chicken that they both hold in their napkin-protected hands. There is surely some incongruity here: that two people, so smartly and expensively dressed, should be eating in such a precarious and careless manner; a manner that threatens, at any moment, to stain their clothes as well as their characters – but in many ways this is the point. Francine's choice of cold chicken on the bone, and more specifically the way it is eaten (held in the hand and ripped by the teeth) has symbolic value as a fertility rite where each character devours the flesh of the other and, in turn, offers themselves up to be eaten. There are countless examples of such fertility rites, consisting of the dismemberment and consumption of a human being or animal, in anthropological literature; in Sweden, for instance, the last wheat sheaf of the season is cut to make an effigy of a girl that all of the family then divide and eat; in Aztec culture, the god Huitzilopochti, every May and December, was broken up and eaten in effigy, an act that was accompanied by several ceremonies carried out by the temple virgins and the eligible young men and Levi Strauss tells us that, in French custom, it was common for the notions of cooking and marriage to be linked – a spinster or bachelor of too many years being placed atop an oven, presumably to warm them up.[13] The meaning of this symbolic layer, however, can only be grasped if we are first made aware of the embodied sensuality that underpins it; if we, as the spectator, understand the feel, taste, texture and smell of the food that the characters in the film each hold in their hands.

The embodied specificity of this scene can best be grasped if we compare it to an earlier lunch: the one between Robie and Hughson in the former's villa. Unlike the picnic, both participants here use cutlery, a fact that removes them (and ipso facto, the audience) physically from the food. The soup and quiche lorraine that they are both served is either never seen (as in the soup) or looks bland and unappetising (as in the quiche), despite Hughson's statements that 'the pastry is as light as air'; in fact, air is what they might as well be eating so uninterested are they in their gustatory experience. A close reading of the scene reveals that there is very little haptic activity here; the sounds of cutlery on plates, sounds of mastication, images of steam that allow us to gauge the temperature of the food, facial gestures of enjoyment and so on are all missing from a lunch that, although carried out in real time, lasts only two minutes, for two courses that are hardly eaten. Hughson at various times throughout the meal has his appetite interrupted by comments made by Robie (most noticeably about the cook's ability to strangle a German General), and the look of nausea on his face is, surely, transferred to the audience. We, as an audience, imbue some of this lack of sensuality. The lack of enjoyment we feel in our bodies during this scene is transferred to our experience of the character's relationship; we find their interaction as unappetising as the quiche, both of which are kept at arm's length for most of the time.

This is not so, however, with the scene between Francine and Robie; here it is the food that takes centre stage; here the chicken they eat is not only visible at all times but we can see it entering the characters' mouths and hear it in their words, as they talk with mouths full, busily biting and ripping with their teeth. Unlike his scene with Hughson, Robie stares intently at his food, hardly turning to look at Francine at all, as he concentrates on transferring his sexual feelings from the girl to what he is eating. I would assert that it is our embodied knowledge of food and the methods of consuming it that provides the audience with their fundamental experience of this scene. The dialogue, twinned with our own understanding of the sensuality of such a method of eating transforms this scene from a picnic into a seduction rite, and furthermore one that has a major importance for the rest of the film.[14] How much less erotic would this scene seem if the two ate with cutlery and plates, if the audience were not asked to draw upon their knowledge of the tactile feel of food both on fingers and on lips?[15] Merleau-Ponty's notion of the aesthesiological body (see Chapter 2) is useful in understanding the mechanisms here because, although 'completed by vision';[16] or rather, although instigated by vision, it is the limbic senses, taste, smell and proprioception that dominate here most especially through film's specific medium of movement in time.

One of the major keys to this scene is the extent to which each character displays what they eat to the camera, allowing the audience to share in their sensual pleasure. The saying 'we eat with our eyes' is a cliché that has its basis in fact and the link between what we see and what we taste has not only become an accepted part of food psychology but has entered in the field of food marketing and retail. As Gilman points out, the colour of our food has a marked impact on our willingness to taste it; colours such as blue that do not frequently appear in nature are less likely to appeal to our other senses (in the plural) and as such are not so often represented on the supermarket shelf or the restaurant menu.[17] The U.S. Food and Drug Administration (FDA) makes the connection between the visual and gustatory clear when it states:

> The color [sic] of food is an integral part of our culture and enjoyment of life. Who would deny the mouth-watering appeal of a deep-pink strawberry ice on a hot summer day or a golden Thanksgiving turkey garnished with fresh green parsley?

Even early civilizations such as the Romans recognized that people 'eat with their eyes' as well as their palates. Saffron and other spices were often used to provide a rich yellow color to various foods. Butter has been colored yellow as far back as the 1300's.[18]

We can say the same for other aspects of our food – its texture, its shape, its consistency and so on – all of which are primarily visual characteristics but all of which affect our desire to eat. Evidence gathered in the 1970s and 80s suggests that a specific area of the hypothalamus and substantia innominata (part of the basal forebrain) is given over to feeding *and* the visual recognition of food, in fact 11.8 per cent of the surveyed neurons in the population (764) area were thought to be given over to visual recognition and only 4.3 per cent to taste and mouth movements.[19] Rolls details:

> The responses of the neurons associated with the sight of food occurred as soon as the monkey saw the food, before the food was in his mouth, and occurred only to foods and not to non-food objects.[20]

This has a tremendous impact on our research here because it suggests, firstly, that we are all neurologically programmed to react to images of food in a different way as other objects and, secondly, that our gustatory knowledge is intrinsically linked to the visual. When we see food before us we become enmeshed in a transitivistic process of understanding that bypasses our conscious self and relies on the somatic links between brain and body. In the case of film, of course, we must be aware of declaring a simple Pavlovian response to this – we need not feel overtly hungry or begin to salivate when we see an image of food – but we do make sense of such an image, as an image of food, through different neurological mechanisms (ones that are linked to the processes of taste) than if we were to see, say, an image of an opulent fur rug that would appeal to our sense of touch. Images of food are inextricably tied to their place in what Merleau-Ponty has called 'the lived world' and it is through this that we understand them. I would assert that it is this, combined with (or even facilitated through), the displaying of the food in such a conspicuous manner in the above scene from *To Catch a Thief* that provides the necessary sensual knowledge for an appreciation of its symbolic meaning.

Based on our experience and understanding of them, different foodstuffs promote different emotional and sensual responses. In research carried out in the *Journal for Food Products Marketing* Diana Phillips suggests that:

Food products are different than other products. Consequently, consumers consume food for different reasons than they do other products. In many instances we consume food products not for what they do for us functionally, but for what they do for us experientially…we consume food because it makes us *feel* a certain way.[21]

The same could be said for images of food: we react to images of food on an emotional as well as an intellectual level, although of course we may not be aware of the former without specifically analysing the phenomenology of the experience. If we are presented with a scene in a film of people seated at a table eating, our emotional experience of that scene may be based just as much on our knowledge of the food they are consuming as the bonhomie (or otherwise) of the diners. Through various cinematic tools the audience understands the food as food rather than merely a visual image.[22] In this way, our embodied experience of taste and digestion is just as important in the experience of the film as our eyes and our sense of self.

Abjection and Rejection

Along with taste and digestion, one of the most notable uses of gustatory images in film is that of vomiting and indigestion. From the projectile vomiting in *The Exorcist* (1973) to the documentary regurgitation in *Super Size Me* (2004), the act of viewing someone being ill on the screen creates both punctuation for a scene and a shared physical experience between audience member and screen action. Vomiting is a much-underrated form of filmic expression and provides us with perhaps the clearest point at which the body becomes an index of response to a film. In scenes such as this we catch a glimpse of the specificity of film as a medium, especially one that works synaesthetically and through all sensual modalities at once.

As Levi Strauss details, vomiting is integral to many indigenous cultures. For the Bororo people, vomiting, like defecation, was a sign of easy passage through the body and so of health, both spiritual and physical; one of their myths tells of a young boy unable to speak because he cannot vomit up the burning fruit he has swallowed. Some of this same sense can be found in Thai Buddhist monasteries that offer purgative cures to those addicted to drugs both in Thailand and the West. Vomiting however can also be seen as a rejection of culture, as Levi Strauss also details:

> On the level of myth, the digestive process can be likened to a cultural procedure, and that consequently the reverse process – that is vomiting – corresponds to a regression from culture to nature.[23]

Hitchcock's light comedy *Rich and Strange* is one of the few of his films that deals with nausea and sickness. In three scenes throughout the film, the central characters experience firstly, sea sickness, then drunkenness and lastly, at the end of the film when they realise they have been fed the ship's cat aboard a Chinese junk, they experience a kind of stunned nausea that prompts them to momentarily gag. As John Ratey describes, we react biologically to another person's nausea in a remarkable feat of neurological empathy:

> The same area of the brain that responds to offensive tastes – the anterior insula – is also activated when one person sees another make a face showing disgust. This is a good example of how the brain combines senses to improve our chances for ongoing existence. In this case, the coupling of taste and vision allows us to perceive the disgust of another person eating, say, a rotten food, so we don't try to eat it ourselves. Even if we were to bring the food toward our mouth, the sight of it would prepare our taste system to perceive disgust.[24]

There is a direct link then between a visual image of someone vomiting or even experiencing nausea, its reception by the brain and then its manifestation as a biological event. In *Rich and Strange* we can again note a parity between the embodied experience and the narratological; the otherness of a strange culture is not only suggested semiotically, as Fred and Emily Hill, slowly visually explore the junk and its 'strange' inhabitants, but their discomfort is transferred to the audience via the arcane neurological mechanisms outlined by Ratey. It is interesting to note that the Hill's bouts of sickness and nausea only really start once they have left English shores and abate soon after they return. Hitchcock literally evokes in the audience a physical sense of unease towards images of cultural otherness.

This same sense of nausea is in engendered in one of Hitchcock's favourite episodes of *Alfred Hitchcock Presents*, *Lamb to the Slaughter* (1958) in which a character played by Barbara Bel Geddes kills her philandering husband with a frozen joint of meat only to later feed the roast to the investigating team thus destroying the evidence. The effect is both comic and strangely cannibalistic as one of the young policemen desires to eat 'this brown crispy stuff on the end here', the end that had only a few hours earlier been used to cave in the skull of the victim.

One question that we must address here is: what is the specificity of film – how does watching a film of someone vomiting or eating differ from witnessing that same scene in real life? The answer to this lies in what is not there rather than what is: film contains none of the thickness of real life, when we witness someone vomiting on screen, we have none of the smell, none of the feel of it, none of the taste if it were we ourselves who are vomiting; these are things that our brains and bodies need to flesh out – to fill in. Film, as a medium of movement and light, highlights the extent that our lives are lived multi-modally; that we depend upon a whole range of different sensual inputs, in fact so strong is our need for synaesthetic experience that we phantasmatically conjure it up when we are in the cinema seat.

Feeding Frenzy

Due, in a large part, to his personal interest in food there have been several studies that deal with Hitchcock's work and the gustatory; however, again, all of these works deal primarily with food as an image and as symbol rather than as a carrier of sensual meaning. Film theory of the postmodern scopic regime suggests that we can experience food on film as more than a symbol or point of psychological suture; it suggests that, through synaesthesia, cultural memory, embodied knowledge, haptic sensual understanding and other tools, we need to understand food's taste, smell and texture before we can ever make the semiological and narratological links suggested by traditional film theory. This opens up a whole new area of concern and challenges us to examine the full phenomenology of the filmic (as well the eating) experience

To this end, the next section of this chapter represents an in-depth reading of one of Hitchcock's most gustatory of films, *Frenzy*, using the tools we have outlined in the above section and earlier chapters of this book, in order to show how embodied film theory can both challenge and complement the traditional tools of cinema criticism. However, I intend to look at an established, canonical, work of criticism alongside my embodied reading and see how the one can either challenge or agree with the other.

Tania Modleski's reading of *Frenzy* in *The Women Who Knew Too Much* is remarkable for its willingness to tackle the full complexity of Hitchcock's relationship with women without resorting to blanket assertions of misogyny and sadism. Modleski begins her piece with the observation that *Frenzy* is inextricably linked to Hitchcock's earlier film *Blackmail* (1929) – both for instance, contain scenes of rape and violence towards women that have proved problematic to critics – *Blackmail* in terms of its narratological authenticity (Raymond Durgnant, especially, doubting that the attack takes place at all) and *Frenzy* in terms of the severity of the infamous scene in which Bob Rusk rapes and then strangles Brenda Blaney. Interestingly, *Blackmail* has also been singled out for its use of oral images and the importance placed on food in the narrative – many of the crucial scenes in the film occur around the dinner table or have food (or smoking) as a major element in them (the famous scene in which Alice hears only the word 'knife' for instance, occurs at the breakfast table; the blackmailer Crewe constantly demands oral gratification in return for silence, literally stopping up his mouth with cigars, breakfast and so on). *Frenzy*, however, is unequivocally about sex, death and food and the embodied demands it makes of its audience only heightens the discomfort and unease that forms a major part of watching it.

Modleski's essay, in some ways, attempts to address the question put forward by Robin Wood's earlier article 'The Fear of Spying: Can Hitchcock Be Saved for Feminism?'[25] Wood's essay is an unsatisfying mix of feminism and psychoanalysis neither of which coalesce into a unified critical vision; however, it was one of the first critical works to suggest that, despite its overall misogynistic tone, *Frenzy* itself is relatively sympathetic towards its female characters who are, by and large, the only morally decent ones in the film (aside, perhaps, from Inspector Oxford). Modleski, using Levi Strauss, Mary Douglas, and Julia Kristeva, reads *Frenzy* as a ritual of defilement, the simultaneous introjection and expulsion of all an engulfing femininity by a patriarchal world both attracted and repulsed by it:

> …it is possible to see in the film's brutality towards women still one more indication of the need expressed throughout Hitchcock's works to deny resemblance to – absorption by – the female, a need that for Levi Strauss lies at the inaugural moment of culture and of myth.[26]

This thread of Modleski's argument is interesting in that it twins, once and for all, two of the most noticeable aspects of Hitchcock's entire career: an ambiguous and difficult relationship with women and a fascination with eating. For Modleski, they are entirely commensurate (as they are for Levi Strauss) the one providing the impetus for the other – in Hitchcock (especially in *Frenzy*) as in many myths, the male symbolically devours the female to save himself from being devoured in turn. In this way woman is both food and excrement, both that which has to be introjected, made tame and incorporated through eating, and that which has to be expelled and abjected in order to maintain the purity of the gender. It is this 'fear of the devouring, voracious mother'[27] that drives the violence in *Frenzy*, the desperate need on the part of men to kill that which threatens to engulf them; and of course in Hitchcock we see this engulfing (m)other time and time again – Mrs Bates; Lydia Brenner in *The Birds* (1963); Madam Sebastian in *Notorious* (1946); Mrs Edgar in *Marnie*; Mrs Rusk, as well as ersatz mothers such as Lisa in *Rear Window* and of course Brenda Blaney.

The opening scene of *Frenzy*, with its depiction of an English politician announcing his intention to eradicate 'the waste products of our society which for so long have poisoned our rivers', is rapidly interrupted by the nude body of a woman floating in the Thames, strangled by a necktie. As Modleski writes:

> The corpse of a woman is a figure of extreme pollution…the feeling is very much [in *Frenzy*] one of violating the ultimate taboo, of being placed into close contact with the most 'impure' of 'impure animals': the carcass of a decaying female.[28]

Throughout *Frenzy*, we are constantly presented with the abject of the abject, the dead body of a woman, and this is also linked with food – Rusk's eating of the apple before he kills Brenda Blaney, the potatoes that surround the dead body of Babs Milligan, the snapping of the breadsticks by Mrs Oxford that remind us of the dead fingers of Babs and so on. For Modleski, however, *Frenzy* is a film with ambiguous psychosexual overtones, on the one hand revelling in the destruction and defilement of the female body, on the other being disgusted at what one character calls 'the lusts of men' – simultaneously degrading and sympathising with its female characters. The world of *Frenzy*, as Leslie Brill details, is one where 'not many princes and princesses meet, marry and live happily ever after'.[29] But this is due, in a large part, to the evil inherent in men not women – a fact that constantly subtends Hitchcock's vision.

Modleski's essay, then, treats images of food and eating as being symbolic of deeper psychosexual and psychocultural tendencies – of man's need to destroy (devour) and to eject that which threatens to engulf him (what Modleski calls woman as 'edible commodity' and 'inedible pollutant'). She points out that Hitchcock constantly juxtaposes images of eating and images of death forging the link between the two in the mind of the viewer throughout the entire film.

It is apparent from this brief summary of Modleski's thesis that she makes no use of the kind of embodied tools of understanding that we have outlined in the preceding chapters. Her argument rests on the classical film theory methods of symbol, ideological analysis and spectatorship qua pure vision; thus, asserting and maintaining the links between what the audience sees and how they think. But how do we understand the physical implications of scenes such as the one between Bob Rusk and Brenda Blaney or the infamous mealtime scenarios between Mr and Mrs Oxford at the dinner table through our extended sensorium? What is the true phenomenology of scenes such as this? What processes do we, as feeling, sensing beings, go through in order to understand images that have an embodied specificity? And how do we understand non-visual information such as taste in a medium where they are not physically presented to us?

Frenzy, as we have established, is a film about food; more than this it is a film about the taste, texture, and smell of food, and about the emotions and sensations that it evokes. For Hitchcock, filming it represented a form of sensual homecoming, the fruit and vegetable market of Bob Rusk being almost identical to that worked by his father over seventy years earlier. Spoto details that much of the early impetus for Hitchcock filming in London was in order to capture the rapidly changing Covent Garden produce market before it disappeared forever and this is clearly reflected in the degree to which the director revelled in not only its sights but its sounds, smells and kinaesthetic excitement. At times, the direction is almost documentary-like as Hitchcock films through boxes of fruit and vegetables, inviting the audience to use its haptic sense to flesh out what it must be like to stand, literally, in the middle of the boxes. In an early scene, where Blaney walks through the Covent Garden market to meet Bob Rusk, Hitchcock's camera adopts what could be thought of as a 'free indirect discourse' that is neither wholly subjective nor objective but rests somewhere in between, seemingly adopting the gaze of the fruit that litters the screen.[30] In this scene Blaney seems to emerge from the produce itself, framed as he is by the bright greens and oranges of the market.

Frenzy is replete with not only images but with references to all manner of oral activity: the first time we see Dick Blaney he is drinking whiskey in The Globe pub: on our initial meeting with Bob Rusk he is eating an apple; Rusk then offers to placate Blaney through an offer of grapes; Brenda Blaney feeds her husband at her club; Inspector Oxford tells Sergeant Spearman that he 'is looking positively glutinous with self-approbation', and so on; in fact, all though the film the gustatory is never far from the characters' or the audience's mind. The character of Bob Rusk neatly fulfils the definition of the oral sadist outlined by Karl Abraham in his paper *Oral Eroticism and Character*:

> [An important notion] is the connecting of sadistic instinctual elements with the manifestation of the libido flowing form the various erotogenic zones…In our psycho-analysis we are able to trace

phenomena of very intense craving and effort back to the primary oral stage. It need hardly be said that we do not exclude other sources of impulse as factors in those phenomena. But the desires derived from that earliest stage are still free from the tendency to destroy the object.[31]

When Rusk is not eating he is drinking and when he is not drinking he is picking at his teeth either with his tiepin or his fingernail. Through such activity his mouth becomes a focal point for the viewer who has no choice but to be drawn to it; at various times Hitchcock films right into Rusk's open mouth revealing a set of uneven faintly yellowing teeth surrounded by sweating lips. What arises from such a technique is Rusk's mouth appearing as, what Deleuze and Guattari might call an organ-without-a-body, an eating, kissing, licking, biting machine that is no longer attached to a brain or a social conscience. This is different from the vagina dentata and different again from the phallus; it is an unstoppable consuming organ that only has a vestigal role in communication (Rusk speaks in clichés and short sentences) and has instead been left to satisfy its desire for consumption. However, Rusk's full oral nature is brought to the fore twenty-five minutes into the film when he attacks, rapes and strangles Brenda Blaney.

The rape scene is perhaps one of the most infamous in the whole of Hitchcock's *oeuvre* but it is also one of the most involved. Unlike the similar scene in *Psycho* that allows the audience some moral distance by stylising the violence, the viewer here is placed firmly within the action; we are made constantly aware of the sheer biology and corporeality of this intense situation. The scene opens with Rusk entering Brenda Blaney's office, tellingly at lunchtime, shutting the door behind him and idly talking. As he flicks through the filing cabinet the tension mounts until it reaches a climax as he asserts his intentions by biting into the apple that had hitherto been Brenda's meal. Rusk's mastication here is intentionally loud, we hear the sound of the apple being churned around in his mouth, wet with saliva, saliva that will in a moment be on the skin of his victim. As Rusk kisses Brenda forcefully on the lips, there is a cut to a close two shot that isolates the physicality of the attack, again it is the mouth that we are made to focus on here, Rusk's hovering menacingly over Brenda's skin; asking the audience to not only experience some of the claustrophobia of their proximity but to smell the apple on his breath and to taste his mouth on ours.

Later on in this same scene we witness again the haptically-suggested feel and taste of Rusk's mouth as we experience his voice so closely miked that we can hear the movement of his tongue as he speaks. I would assert that we draw on our own understanding of oral closeness, in scenes like this, to flesh out the images that we see on the screen and it is this that gives them its particular horror. As the rape progresses we, like Brenda, become bodily disengaged; as she begins to chant the 91st Psalm (and he begins to chant the word 'lovely') the action becomes less one of physicality and more of meditation. Like Brenda, the audience suspends their physical selves for a moment in order to avoid the full corporeal horror of the situation. The embodiment of the earlier images becomes stilled and what we receive are perfect examples of what Deleuze called affection-images (we shall examine these further in the next chapter) whereby perceptions (both visual, haptic and sensual) extend not into action but into feeling and emotion. The close-ups of both characters' faces (the close-up itself paradigmatic of the affection-image in Deleuze) become inextricably tied to the underlying embodied experience *and*, through this, the emotion that Hitchcock aims to instil in his audience.

The notion of mirror neurons becomes key to an understanding of our relationship to the images in this scene. Typically, it has been thought, this scene places the audience in the position of Bob Rusk, chiefly because it is from his point of view that many of the shots are framed. Even when Rusk himself is in shot, it is quite obviously his subjectivity we are experiencing – in the close up two shot at the beginning of this scene for instance, we see all of Brenda's face but only the side of Rusk's. This is undoubtedly why so many critics have found this scene problematic in terms of its ethical position, causing William Pechter, for one, to comment that the director had 'exploited the new permissiveness to satisfy the audience's taste which he had heretofore subverted but not satisfied with sensationally horrific detail'.[32] Mirror neurons, however, suggest that we engage bodily not with whosoever eyes we are looking through but whose face we are looking at.

This places the audience's sympathy here not with Rusk but with Brenda; it is her face we see throughout many of the shots in this scene and therefore her experience we share. It is her skin that we feel through, her nose we smell with, and her mouth we taste with. The rape scene then, far from merely revelling in what Robin Wood saw as the 'tensions personal to Hitchcock (and) to our culture'[33] asks us to feel what it is like to be a victim in a society beset with dominating and predatory males. It forces us to confront the sheer physicality of rape by neurologically suggesting what a rapist's mouth feels like on our skin, what it tastes like when he kisses us and what it feels like when he ties the ligature around our neck and pulls until our tongue becomes too large for our mouth. This scene, one of the earliest major ones in the film, sets up what is a crucial underlying emotion throughout the rest of the narrative – disgust. As we have seen above, we use our sense of taste, smell and touch in this scene as a tool for understanding its significance and through neurological connectivity are made to feel some of the revulsion and disgust that Brenda feels upon being forced to endure a rape.

There are three murders in *Frenzy* and three scenes where eating becomes the focal point for the audience, all of which feature Inspector Oxford.[34] These scenes (that roughly divide the film into three distinct Acts) have both an internal 'rhyme', in the sense that Raymond Bellour employs in his study of *The Birds*, and a syntagmatic meaning, in that they provide an ever-increasing sense of bodily disgust at the very points in the film where Hitchcock is withdrawing from the visual. So, let us take each of these scenes individually.[35]

0:55:38 – Inspector Oxford eats breakfast in his office
Appearing at the half-way point, this scene is unique in the film in that it depicts someone simply enjoying the experience of eating food. We are presented with a series of shots that lovingly detail the make-up and consumption of a full English breakfast, complete with bread, butter and tea. Inspector Oxford compares this staple of English cuisine to the *café complait* of 'a cup of coffee half an inch deep in floating bits of boiled milk and a sweet bun full of air'. We are made aware of the sheer gustatory pleasure of Oxford by the manner of his eating – he constantly cuts, spears, breaks, shovels and chews the food, whilst talking to Sergeant Spearman about his wife's insistence on gourmet cooking, obviously enjoying every mouthful. As we have discovered, the processes inherent in the communication of this pleasure (using notions such as haptic vision and mirror neurons) can be viewed, not so much as one of identification, but of sheer transitivisitc enjoyment. We draw upon our own embodied senses to understand the pleasure in this scene, a pleasure that is enhanced through our synaesthetic appreciation of images of food and drink.

The excess of bodily enjoyment that pervades this scene is a key to its syntagmatic importance within the film coming soon after the physical discomfort of the rape of Brenda Blaney but before the nauseating meals that Mrs Oxford serves. This is a rare moment of gustatory pleasure for both the Inspector and the audience, something that, as eighteenth-century gastronomic author Jean Anthelme Brillat-Savarin suggests, promotes 'an indefinable and peculiar sensation of well-being, arising out of an instinctive awareness that through what we are eating we are repairing our losses and prolonging our existence'[36] The image of the breakfast here is more than a symbol (of Englishness, of early mornings, of tradition), it provides a sense of physical, corporeal well being that stands in contrast to the discomfort of the previous rape scene; a scene that, as we have discussed, was explicitly designed to cause a sense of bodily ill-ease and disgust. We have, in other words, what could be thought of as a bodily mirroring, with one scene providing the opposing rhyme for another.

1:03:30 – Inspector Oxford eats soup de poisson

Whereas the above scene could be thought of as the ending of Act One, the next scene we have of Inspector Oxford can be thought of as beginning Act Two. Again this scene has importance both in terms of the images contained within it and in terms of its structural context. After previously explaining that his wife is undertaking a course in gourmet cooking, Inspector Oxford arrives home to find a home cooked meal placed before him. Unlike his breakfast, however, the *soup de poisson* that Mrs Oxford has prepared for him is far from appetising. Many of the critics who have looked at this scene have read it as purely an example of Hitchcock's playful humour; Leslie Brill, for example describes it as the 'comic subplot',[37] and Donald Spoto states that their 'later scenes are hilarious, among the most comical sequences in the Hitchcock catalog'.[38] However, as far as the audience's sense of taste and revulsion are concerned this is far from a comic scenario.

What we are presented with is an image that is obviously designed to nauseate and disgust us, the lid of the tureen that holds the fish soup is lifted and we are shown a frothy brown liquid that has various recognisable parts of fish and other marine animals floating in it. Hitchcock then cuts to the disgusted face of Oxford whose ill-ease we consequently feel as his wife lovingly spoons squid, fish heads and soup into a bowl ready for him to eat. We are then presented with one of the very few subjective point-of-view shots in the whole film as Inspector Oxford gingerly lifts an emaciated fish head onto a spoon but then drops it back into the plate obviously nauseated. Tellingly, the only other scenes that feature POV shots are those where Rusk is either strangling Brenda Blaney or searching frantically for the tiepin in the back of the potato truck, somehow twinning the two activities (eating and killing) in the mind of the audience.

It is our sense of taste and texture that provides the undercurrent of disgust in this scene, the fish that Oxford lifts out of the bowl has a sickening consistency to it that synaesthetically suggests a fatty, glutinous taste and the soup itself is muddy and cloudy. Hitchcock's close up of the bowl and the spoon that lifts the soup reveals subtle micro-movements that haptically evoke the nauseating taste and texture of the featured food; this is a distinct example of what we termed, at the beginning of this chapter, food conveyed through filmic specificity, such micro-movements would not, of course, be possible in a medium such as the photograph or painting.

The disgust on the face of Oxford is matched only by that same sense in the stomachs and tastebuds of the audience. We understand the images in this scene through our embodied senses, fleshing out the sight of the soup with our knowledge of how it must taste like, feel like and smell like and this, in turn, nauseates us and makes us feel constantly ill at ease. We can note straightaway that we are presented with a vastly different scene than the one between Robie and Francine or Robie and Hughson, a difference that is based primarily on embodied understanding.

What is crucial to an understanding of how Hitchcock manipulates the bodies as well as the minds of his audiences is the fact that this scene comes just after the killing of Babs Milligan, a killing that we are not permitted to see. Where, in Act One, we were disgusted by the vision of murder and palliated by food, in Act Two, we are disgusted by the image of food precisely because we were denied being made witness to murder. This notion goes right to the heart of the postmodern scopic regime; the whole sensorium is appealed to when vision is no longer relied on or needed as a method of exchange between image and spectator. Eating gradually begins to take the place of homicide, not in terms of its symbolism but as a carrier of embodied meaning.

1:35:30 – Inspector Oxford eats pied du porc

The embodied disgust facilitated through Hitchcock's manipulation of our experience of the taste and texture of food climaxes with Oxford's last supper, *pied du porc*; and in this scene the director brings together many of the tools of gustatory understanding that we have looked at so far. As the familiar cloche is lifted we are presented with the sight of two anaemic-looking pig's feet in a rather insipid sauce that Mrs Oxford tells us is the same as 'the French use for tripe'. This is a world away from the hearty steak and baked potato that she assumes her husband wants to eat, and the look on his face bears witness to this. As Mr and Mrs Oxford talk of the corpse of Babs Milligan, the inspector attempts to cut into the pig's foot with little success – it is bony, fatty, full of gristle and is unyielding to his knife and fork. The look of the meal is less one of meat and more one of dead flesh as it slides about the plate in its own juices. Inspector Oxford places a piece of the foot into his mouth and the disgust he feels is instantly palpable, it is gristle and bone, he tries to chew but his teeth only scrape along the hard surface and pick at the fatty gristle that he pulls out of his lips with a rubbery elasticity. Oxford talks to his wife with a piece of the pig's foot firmly lodged in the side of his cheek, allowing the audience to fully appreciate its hardness and its indigestible nature.

This scene, however, takes on a more sinister tone through the subject matter of the couple's conversation. It is obvious that not only is Hitchcock relying on our sense of taste and texture to make sense of this scene he is also manipulating our social taboos. This is the closest we come in *Frenzy* to an overt reference to cannibalism, something that is not only suggested throughout but that appears in other works (*Lamb to the Slaughter*, *Rope* and so on). As the couple talk of the snapping of Babs Milligan's fingers, Mrs Oxford absent-mindedly snaps and eats a breadstick, twinning in the mind of the audience once and for all the taste of her cooking and the taste of human flesh. Again, Hitchcock is playing with the tensions that exist between the body's experience and the mind's; we are made to feel disgust in our stomachs and mouths as well as through our sense of social convention.

The mirror to this scene, the embodied rhyme which forms its counterpoint, is the murder of the unnamed blond woman who is found in Rusk's bed at the end of the film.[39] Again, we see that the disgust felt by the audience is in inverse proportion to the amount of information we are afforded concerning the murder of a woman; this time we are not even aware of it happening until after the fact. Hitchcock manages to make us feel revolted and disgusted about a murder without even showing it, what Adam Lowenstein refers to as the 'inadequacy of the showing/suggesting binary that continues to organise Hitchcock's critical reputation'.[40]

It is in this way that our embodied reading of the film – the body as both a tool of understanding and an index of response – can be compared with Tania Modleski's feminist reading. For Modleski, the underlying sense of *Frenzy* was of ambiguity, of fascination *and* revulsion on the part of the director and ergo the audience. We can see that this is largely supported by the body's experience of the film that, at various times, plays upon our relationship to different forms of food and drink in order to either soften the blow of a violent attack (Brenda Blaney) or to suggest disgust and revulsion where no visual images are available or needed. The body's experience of *Frenzy* reflects very much what Modleski details is a major facet of the film: that it both reveals and condemns the 'lusts of men', lusts that are both of and for the flesh.

This chapter has attempted to assert the importance of taste to films like *Frenzy* and others. I am positing the notion that the body here, especially the stomach and the taste buds, have just as much a hand in the construction of what it means to understand *Frenzy* as the brain or the mind. This is a subtle but vital difference from the conventional tools of film theory;

the body is not conscious in the same way that the brain is; therefore, the processes of signification and cognitive identification fail to describe the processes it goes through. It is altogether more fluid, more visceral, more immediate and more evanescent. As I have attempted to assert, the distinction between the use of the body as a tool of reception and as an index of a film offers us a valuable way into embodied spectatorship, one that not only characterises and classifies existing theory but that offers a crucial framework for developing new avenues of study in the future. Taste is a sense that is inextricably linked to sight; it gives us at once a cultural and a personal identity, but it is also a proximal sense, eradicating the boundaries between subject and object, relying on closeness and the intermingling of bodies. Taste provides a counter narrative to many films but especially those created by Hitchcock.

6

ON SMELL

Smell is a potent wizard that transports us across thousands of miles and all the years we have lived.[1]

In the last chapter we looked at ways in which taste can inform the cinematic experience but perhaps more importantly we began to see how embodied film criticism can work in a practical sense, how its tools and methods can be used to look at films that do not necessarily deal primarily with embodied images and how it can inform mainstream cinema. To continue with this process, this chapter now turns to smell and to how images of olfaction can provide us with extra sensual images. Again, I begin by briefly looking at the importance of smell to the human being as well as tracing threads in various film theory that has dealt with it. Understandably, these are not so numerous as those dealing with taste and eating but they are there if one digs deep enough for them, or perhaps even if one follows one's nose long enough. I end this chapter with an in-depth discussion of the 1943 film *Shadow of a Doubt*. I contend that a knowledge of how Hitchcock arranges the smellscapes of the two main characters, Uncle Charlie and Charlie, provides a vital key into his larger philosophical, cultural and psychological mandate and that this can only be understood fully if one utilises certain tools of the postmodern scopic regime.

In their now classic work *Aroma,* Classen, Howes and Synnot describe smell as *the* postmodern sense.[2] For them, perfumes, odours and aromas are not only nomadic in nature in that they roam freely, invading private and public spaces without contest, but, in a world where synthetic perfumes are preferred in scientific tests to their natural counterparts, they can be seen as an almost perfect example of the Baudrillardian simulacra; where the synthetic is literally invested with more desire than the real thing. As Classen, Howes and Synnot state, modern aroma has become real in much the same way that Coca Cola is advertised as 'The Real Thing', which is to say realistically synthetic.

It is a short step from synthetically creating aroma to synaesthetically creating it. In fact, these two can be seen as merely steps along the same path of virtuality. Synthetically created smells constantly rely on synaesthesia to flesh out their meaning and to add extra-sensory value to the univocity of a single sensual experience. Perfumes that are geared towards consumers have names that attempt not only to entice them to buy but to centre them in a world of meaning and experience by more than the primary sensual input. Luca Turin lists some of these names: Vanilla Musk, Alabaster, Aqua Allegoria, Eden, Freedom and countless others all attest to the links between smell and colour, smell and taste, smell and touch, and smell and sight.[3] A perfume such as Dark Vanilla by Coty barely needs to be physically smelt at all to be experienced; it relies at once on synthetic and synaesthetic creation – being born out of the virtuality of the laboratory but existing in the simulacrum of linguistic correspondence and multi-sensual knowledge. Synthetically created smells then rely heavily on the multi-modal nature of our sense appreciation, a process that works, as we shall see, in reverse with sight and sound triggering mimetic and transitivistic experiences of smell. The cinema is also both synthetic and synaesthetic; the images we see on screen are as synthetic as the perfume we spray onto our skin – they are distillations of a reality that is too complex for representation – however in order to be understood they need to be re-framed by the spectator within the synaesthetic experience of their own lives.

Smell is linked to all manner of socio-economic and socio-political discourses; its place as the postmodern sense is not only based on its chemical characteristics but also on the degree to which modernity attempted to expunge and repress it; the modern city with its glass-fronted facades, steel buildings and underground sewers being a kind of physical manifestation of the desire to eradicate the annoyance of the proximal senses, smell being chief among them.[4] Recently, it has been seen as a way of undercutting the hegemony of the dominant discourse – the smells of Indian and South East Asian restaurants that regularly add spice to the olfactory experience of the English town and cityscape being an ideal example of how the molecular forces of immigration challenge the molar constructs of race, class, and national identity. Largey and Watson detail that, traditionally, the male of the city (especially those in the UK and the USA) would strive to be odourless, free even from the perfumes used by women or more sexually suspect men and even today terms used for men's fragrances very often eschew their olfactory nature and point, instead, to their practical, utilitarian uses: after shave, splash on lotion, cologne, and so on. The modern man, like the modern city, deodorises, removing all traces of what was once wild and *unmanageable*, what was primitive.[5]

It was perhaps this image, of the deodorised bourgeois Westerner, that was at the root of Hitchcock's own mistrust of smell. Out of all the senses, smell is the one that is directly featured least in his work; whereas taste and touch are used for their own sake, sometimes providing *the* primary sensual experience of a film, smell is left, as it very often is, to subtend the main sensual narrative and to exist on the borders of the attentive imagination, as Hegel stated in his *Lectures on Aesthetics* the nose is rarely considered to be 'an organ or artistic enjoyment'.[6] Blaney in *Frenzy* sleeps with the old men of the Salvation Army hostel and retains some of their smell that he immediately tries to dry clean off; Marnie is told by Mark that she has the smell of horses about her and a dog enthusiastically sniffs the arm of Stevie as he sits holding a can of explosives on a tram in the London rush hour in *Sabotage* (1937) but, by and large, Hitchcock does not make overt mention of olfaction, allowing its natural tendency to make itself felt; as we shall see, this happens surprisingly often.

Smell, then, does have a place within film and film appreciation – not in the synthetic creation of substitute aromas with gimmicky technologies such as Odorama and Smell O Vision in films such as *The Scent of Mystery* (1960) or John Waters' *Polyester* (1981) – but in the synaesthetic and haptic appreciation of lived sensual experience that provides the embodied ground for the brain and the mind. Smell is inextricably linked to memory and, through this, to our sense of space, place, and identity; but it is also constantly in flux, existing in a continual becoming that avoids being tied to specific meaning and thus to semiological processes. Smell is, by its very nature, tied to the other senses but it is also an extremely powerful aide-memoir and it is this that makes it interesting for a study of the postmodern scopic regime. Tools such as Laura Marks' conception of mimesis, olfactory haptics, synaesthesia, the Deleuzian affection-image, and so on, allow us to examine how smell manifests itself in a medium that does not present it chemically and again this will be twinned with examples drawn from Hitchcock and, towards the end of the chapter, placed in relation to an existing study of his work.

Marks-ist Film Theory – Philosophising Smell

Laura Marks is one of the only film theorists to have studied the reception of smell images in cinema. Her work represents an attempt to not only understand how vision can be supported by the proximal senses but how they can become the primary sensual experience when the hegemonic specular processes break down or are challenged by different sensorial regimes. For

Marks, smell is a mimetic sense, it uncovers a 'continuum between the actuality of the world and the production of signs about that world'[7] In order for it to be registered, smell needs to be physically absorbed into the body and then inculcated into a whole range of largely unconscious sense-making frameworks that not only register its meaning but centre it within a network of time and space through memory. Marks cites C. S. Pierce's notion of 'Firstness' – that which is experienced by the body and does not exist in relation to anything else – to describe the immediacy of smell and its biological reception. As we shall see later on in this chapter, Firstness was also used by Deleuze in his affection-image, a concept that Marks also employs to look at embodied film spectatorship. Marks, however, asserts that smell can be drawn on by a cinema audience to make sense of certain images despite its obviously chemically receptive processes. She suggests that smell can be conveyed in film through three different ways: firstly through identification with a character on screen engaging in smelling or sniffing, secondly through synaesthetic appeal to other senses such as sound and movement and, lastly, through haptic appreciation of close up images and images of touch; because smell is a proximal sense, the closer we get to an image, the more likely we are to be asked to draw upon our olfactory memory to fully appreciate it. These categories are a useful entry point into our evaluation of the workings of olfactory cinema and so I would like, at this point, to look at them one at a time.

Identification

As was discussed in relation to taste, the notion of mirror neurons and the suggestion that they tie us inextricably to the world that we inhabit calls into question the usual processes of cinematic identification; smelling, with its distinctive yet subtle facial movements is an intentional act bound inextricably to the chemical processes that it serves. It also has phylogenetic and ontogenetic meaning as Freud outlined in *Civilisation and Its Discontents*; and so, like eating, we respond on an instinctual level to watching images of others enjoying or being repulsed by the odours they smell.[8] As neurobiology has suggested, the process of interpreting such images maybe more mimetic than even Marks herself has suggested, we do not so much read other people's faces as mimetically experience what we know to be the underlying affect of their expressions. Our brains register such images as if we had experienced the sensation ourselves.

In *Frenzy*, for instance, we understand the smell of Blaney's jacket through the expression on Babs' face as she recoils in horror at its musty smell and in one of Hitchcock's earliest films, the silent melodrama starring

Ivor Novello, *Downhill* (1927), we are presented with the familiar image of the connoisseur smelling a cigar: his eyes stare off into the distance, closing the visual in order to concentrate on the act of olfaction, the cigar is drawn slowly under the nose and the aroma inhaled with a deep breath, the image is one of pure olfactory enjoyment. In fact, Archie's position of connoisseur is underlined at this point through the sheer skill and pleasure with which he handles and savours the smell of his cigar, as the same act carried out inexpertly by Roddy reveals only his own amateurishness.

In another of Hitchcock's early films, *Champagne* (1928), we are again presented with an image of olfaction but this time it has distinctly phylogenetic links: the scene features the central character of The Girl and her father. Forced into cooking for the first time through a perceived poverty, The Girl produces a plate of unappetising looking food that her father sniffs at suspiciously before politely declining.[9] As Diane Ackerman details, we often smell something before we taste it, not only to get our saliva glands working in readiness to eat but to safely test if a food stuff is edible or not.[10] Watching a scene like this from a film as early as *Champagne*, where time, and the original low fidelity nature of the film stock have bleached the image to merely a collection of blurry greys, we rely heavily on the recognition of bodily movements to understand the subtle nuances of a character's emotions and feelings; we are left in no doubt as to how the father feels about his daughter's cooking, not perhaps through recognition of signs but through knowledge of our own bodily processes and reactions. The importance of mirror neurons in this scene can be seen in Iacoboni, *et al*, who state that:

> Action recognition…has a special status with respect to recognition. . . Action implies a goal and an agent. Consequently, action recognition implies the recognition of a goal, and, from another perspective of an agent's intentions. John sees Mary grasping an apple. By seeing her hand moving toward the apple, he recognises what she is doing ('that's a grasp'), but also that she *wants* to grasp the apple, that is her immediate, stimulus linked intention or goal.[11]

In scenes such as this not only do we understand the bodily movements themselves (the bending forward towards the plate, the tilting of the head, the recoiling and the screwing up of the face) but we also grasp some of the intention, the context of the situation and its larger consequence. Notice how, because of its specificity as movement and time, this process can *only* be of relevance to film, film studies and theory concerned with other moving images.

Sound

Marks suggests that a smell can also be conveyed using contingent senses via synaesthesia. As we saw in Chapter Three, we must not confuse the popular and the clinical senses of synaesthesia; what Marks is referring to here is the multi-modal appreciation of senses rooted in our lived holistic experience not the spontaneous registering of one sense on another that characterises clinical definitions. One of the clearest examples of this occurs in the 1930 production of *Juno and the Paycock* when Hitchcock films, in stark close-up, the sausages Boyle (Edward Chapman) cooks up on the stove after returning from the public house. The sound of their sizzling is clearly audible over the crackle of the audio, adding to our sense of how they might smell, as the fat and smoke that we can see coming from them permeates the room and so too the camera frame. Merleau-Ponty describes some of the processes of appreciating such images in his essay 'The Film and the New Psychology':

> Cezanne said that one could see the velvetiness, the hardness, the softness, and even the odour of objects. My perception is therefore not a sum of visual, tactile and audible givens: I perceive in a total way with my whole being; I grasp a unique structure of the thing, a unique way of being, which speaks to all my senses at once.[12]

For Merleau-Ponty, not only was the cinema reflective of epistemic changes in thought, it also exemplified contemporary movements in psychology through its attempt to create a Gestalt reality of sound, audio and embodied understanding. This 'unique way of being' extends into how we make use of re-perceived images such as those presented to us in film and cinema – something that forms the basis of Vivian Sobchack's work *The Address of the Eye*. The sound and look of Captain Boyle's sausages cooking in the pan may consist merely of audio-visual representations but we cannot help but receive them in a way that chimes with all of our senses at once.

Close-olfactory haptics

Smell's place as a proximal sense is perhaps at the heart of why it is also considered one of the lowliest. In order for us to be able to smell something, its tiny particles must literally be taken into our bodies as the air borne molecules pass through the nostrils and are filtered by tiny hairs that grow out of the nose. This air then passes over the olfactory receptors situated at the upper portion of the nasal cavity and, once in the area of the nasal receptors, the particles held within it are dissolved in a mucus layer and the process of smell recognition begins. It stands to reason that the closer we get to a source of smell the stronger and more pronounced it gets until it engulfs us and becomes unbearable.

It is precisely the link between proximity and olfaction that Marks cites as forming the basis of olfactory haptics. Marks' point is that, when vision and audition fail to provide the necessary information needed to understand an image we draw on other senses to do this for us – when an image is degraded or provides no recognisable visual cues, for instance, we are more likely to rely on smell, touch and taste to flesh out its meaning:

> By resisting control of vision, for example being blurry, haptic images encourage the 'viewer' to get close to the image and explore it through all of the senses, including touch, smell and taste.[13]

I would assert that not only is this the case but that this can be extended into film language and to the choices a director makes in terms of shot selection and framing. The close-up encourages the viewer to extend their sensorium and to draw on the proximal senses that might otherwise be kept at bay by the distancing effect of the medium and long shot; an example of this occurs in *The Birds* when Mrs Brenner finds the dead body of her neighbour in his bedroom. As Žižek correctly states, the interesting aspect about the camera work in this scene is that it 'gives us an inversion of the process we expect',[14] where normally we would imagine the camera to linger firstly upon the man's legs and then track slowly up his body where it would come to rest on his face, allowing our eyes to fully meet his empty gaze, here instead Hitchcock makes this journey in two very quick jump cuts that elide distinct visual recognition and leave the audience with merely a memory trace of what they have seen. Žižek attributes this startling set of images to an eradication of '"the time [needed] for understanding", the pause needed to "digest", to integrate the brute perception of the object',[15] and it is exactly this that we can see forming the basis of olfactory haptics, where vision is elided (not through a blurry image this time but though jump cuts that bring us closer to an object too quickly) and we are asked to draw upon other senses – the smell of death, of blood, of rotting corpses, of wild animals and so on – for the scene's impact. The shot mirrors the dizzying effect of being drawn too near the corpse and being engulfed by its smell.

Marks centres her analysis around intercultural and diasporic filmmakers residing, mainly, in Europe and America. It is the experience of being in another's culture and furthermore one that places such high onus on vision and distanciation, she asserts, that drives the desire to appeal to proximity and embodied knowledge. Denied access to the dominant culture, immigrant filmmakers and artists seek to uncover ways of undercutting traditional forms of representation by appealing to senses that encourage us to use our own sensual memory and embodied experience.

For Marks, the appeal to smell is one of the chief ways that intercultural and diasporic identity can be established and memories of cultures other than the West can be proliferated and celebrated. One of the films that works especially well with these notions is Black Audio Film Collective's *Mysteries of July* (1990) a work that deals with the disproportionably large numbers of young black males to die in police custody in Britain in the 1980s. Marks describes the way in which the filmmakers rely on haptic images and olfaction to suggest a social and psychological mourning that is somehow beyond the visual, resting more in the area of the instinctual or the affective:

> *Mysteries of July* enacts an elaborate ritual of mourning. Candles and satin, which reflects their light in pools of intense colour. Mourners walk slowly, in silence, carrying candles. In a scene of grief and rage, these colours, textures, and imagined smells take on an intensity that cannot be expressed verbally or visually.[16]

The filming of senses other than sight becomes a political as well as an aesthetic act, one that attempts to work against the distance created by the visual recognition privileged by Western ontology. The image of incense proves to be both a point of non-specular sensual involvement and at the same time evokes the supra-rational discourse of spirituality and ceremonial mourning. The twinning of intercultural memory with embodied sensation and affect is nothing new. Helen Gilbert[17] suggests, for instance, how certain types of dance in Australian Aboriginal plays enact a specific type of cultural memory that dialogue and narrative could never achieve. Interestingly, Gilbert also details how traditional notions of theatre criticism often pass off dance and embodiment as little more than spectacle 'thereby eliding its signifying practices with aesthetic (read normative) standards of judgement',[18] something that we have asserted is also the case with embodiment and film theory.

Of course, we must be aware here of simply appropriating the counter-hegemonic discourse of embodied experience as it relates to race and/or gender. Hitchcock, as a filmmaker, was nothing if not bourgeois and socially conservative. In his films, where black or Asian characters do appear (*The Ring* (1927), *The Man Who Knew Too Much*, *Murder!* (1930)) they are often, at best, un-noticeable, at worst stereotypical. In *The Ring*, the white carnival goers take turns to dunk a smiling black carnival worker into a tub of water by throwing balls at a target; in *Murder!*, Handel Fane is both transsexual and mixed race, each of which testifying to his position as existing outside of traditional notions of morality; and in *Lifeboat* (1944), arguably Hitchcock's only sympathetic black character, Joe, is greeted by Tallulah Bankhead with 'Its' Charcoal!' When we attempt to use critical tools and ideas taken from intercultural and diasporic cinema to look at Hitchcock, and other mainstream Western directors, it is with a certain degree of mindfulness that what we are dealing with is not a straight application of ideas but a process of uncovering deeply buried sensual involvement, involvement that has never been asserted does not exist in white Pan-European aesthetics simply that has been suppressed or repressed by other, more pervasive, ideologies.

Laura Marks' discussion of Ngozi Onwurah's film, *And Still I Rise*, highlights the degree to which embodiment is both problematic and celebrated in post-colonial and intercultural studies. Onwurah's film aims to explore the traditionally held view that black women, especially, are seen as synonymous with sensuality and embodiment; the representation of their sexuality in popular culture, for instance, residing somewhere between fascination and fear. However, as Marks asserts, the film also presents a celebration of black female sexuality that is itself embodied and sensual:

> Rather than demur that there is no difference (between white and black sexuality), most of her interlocuters take pride in black female embodiment…This is Onwurah's strategic move to reclaim the black female body from the legacy of enslavement.[19]

The crucial aspect to such thinking is that multimodal sensual appreciation can provide a counter hegemonic alternative to traditional Anglo-American specularity, but that sometimes this means negotiating with traditionally held stereotypes and preconceptions.

One of Hitchcock's most sensual films, *The Pleasure Garden*, concerns itself with exactly these issues: sensuality, cultural otherness, embodiment and inter-racial sexuality. Interestingly it is also his most smoke filled film, with character after character not only smoking cigars, cigarettes and pipes but allowing the smoke to twirl sensuously out of their mouths and noses, filling the frame with an eerie soft focus that is reminiscent of the incense that fills the mourning scenes in *Mysteries of July*. In one scene, Mr Hamilton, the owner of The Pleasure Garden nightclub, is even filmed smoking a cigar in front of a sign that declares 'Smoking Prohibited'. The smoke in *The Pleasure Garden* exemplifies how Marks' notion of olfactory haptics can work in a mainstream film by interrupting and dissipating the outlines of the images on screen and by asking the audience to use smell to fill out the sensual picture. Smoke in this film, like *Mysteries of July*, is not only important for what it signifies but for the function it serves in terms of the acuity of the visual field. As Raymond Durgnat suggests, *The Pleasure Garden* could perhaps be considered one of the director's least Hitchcockian films, a fact that is perhaps unsurprising considering it was his first feature, coming a full twelve months before *The Lodger* (1926). One of the most noticeable differences between this and his many subsequent works is the level of sensuality Hitchcock affords himself and his audience, as lesbianism, exoticism, exhibitionism and openly sensual body contact provides the erotic undercurrent to a narrative concerned with moral ambiguity and indeterminateness. The removed visual philosopher of *Rear Window* is little in evidence in this film that is as much about the body as the mind.

The Pleasure Garden is suffused with images of fragrance and aroma, many of which serve to underline the movement of the central narrative – not only are the early scenes filled with cigar and cigarette smoke, providing tobacco-scented air and a sense of immorality to the interior of the club itself. In the latter stages of the film we are shown an earthly tropical paradise complete with fragrant plants and flowers that represent an altogether different olfactory experience. Levet's native lover played by Nita Naldi is not only symbolic of non-western sensuality but of how this is enforced by all of the senses; Naldi's hair, for instance, is adorned with flowers, a fairly typical, but highly successful, example of primitive perfumery, making her not only a tactile, auditory and visual object (in Levet's eyes) but an olfactory one as well. The extent that Naldi's character exists beyond the bounds of Western specular logic is exemplified in the scene where she reappears as an apparition, literally deconstructing the visual categories of presence and absence and existing more as a cloud of smoke than flesh, smoke of course not only being a central motif in the picture as a whole but a word that shares chemical characteristics and an etymological link with perfume. Ultimately, we could assert, *The Pleasure Garden* concerns itself with the dangers of such sensual engulfment especially as it relates to olfaction, this same sense of course can be found in texts such as Gauguin's *Intimate Journals* that details the experiences of the Westerner abroad, as Gauguin writes:

> One thing, however, annoys me in the Marquesans, and that is their exaggerated taste for perfumes. The shopkeepers sell them a frightful perfumery made of musk and patchouli. When they are gathered together in church, all these perfumes become insupportable.[20]

Smell and Memory

Due in part to its relationship to the limbic system, smell has an important place in the storing and retrieval of memory. Proust, in the short story 'Another Memory' suggests that smell is every bit as evocative as taste when it comes to the instant recall of time and place. The story details a brief and fleeting olfactory experience that leaves the narrator with a myriad of sensual and sensuous memories:

> In my humdrum life I was exalted one day by perfumes exhaled by a world that had been so bland. They were the troubling heralds of love. Suddenly love itself had come, with its roses and flutes, sculpting, papering, closing, perfuming everything around it…love went away and the perfumes, from the shattered flacons, were exhaled with a purer intensity. The scent of a weakened drop still impregnates my life.[21]

Proust here points to a fundamental aspect of olfactory memory: that it may lose its chemical power but never loses its embodied meaning; it may fade but it never relinquishes its connection to the original experience. Hirsch argues that olfactory memories are especially effective in the recall of a whole scenario or mood and can aid in the remembrance of specific emotional states and psychological contexts.[22] Refugees from Cambodia, for instance, have been detailed as experiencing a severe form of olfactory triggered panic attack when, for instance, the sulphurous smell of a car's exhaust fumes suggests the odour of a gunshot or certain biological odours reminded them of the scores of dead bodies that littered the Cambodian countryside. One such antidote to these experiences was to carry a menthol inhaler that patients would sniff if they could feel an attack was imminent.[23]

The key aspect to olfactory memory however is not, as Toller, Hotson and Kendal-Reed state, its retention and recall but its holistic and embodied nature – smell memory is memory that is linked inextricably to our emotions and to the experiential nature of the initial situational impetus.[24] The neurophysiology of smell acts as a kind of anatomical correlative to the ways in which it works in most people's everyday experience, some impulses from the olfactory nerves travel to the thalamus, the translating function for the cerebral cortex, but most go straight to the limbic system, the animal part of the brain that we have identified as being crucial in areas such as embodiment and synaesthesia. This means that we both think and feel smells at the same time, the relationship between the two actions is not, as it is in all of the other senses, either exclusive or sequential. When we recall smells, also, we do so by recourse to their holistic experience, mimetically creating what could be thought of as the conditions for understanding rather than understanding itself.

Smell memories can transport us back through time and can elide space, engendering in us the feelings we felt when we were first presented with it. Smells can also be evoked through visuality, and vice versa, and have both a semiological and a subconscious meaning. This meaning is both personal to individuals and pertinent to whole cultures and generations. The themes of embodiment, recollection, cultural identity and Hitchcock are all present in David Martin-Jones' 2006 work, *Deleuze, Cinema and National Identity*, that not only attempts to use Deleuze's sometimes elitist film theory to look at mainstream cinema but also makes the connection between individuated diegetic memory and national identity. Although Martin-Jones does not extend his discussion into spectator practices and cinema reception (dealing only with character memory) his practice of asserting the link between the bodily postures and sensations of characters and the larger socio-political mandates of the filmmaker is interesting for our thesis here. Like Laura Marks' discussion of *Mysteries of July*, Martin-Jones examines the ways in which embodied memory and understanding can provide the basis for a discussion of national and cultural identity through its relationship to time, drawing on *Vertigo*, for instance, he describes the socio-political subtext that not only forms the ground of the narrative but is literally written into the very way the characters move and how they experience their own bodies:

> *Vertigo* is a movement-image that foregrounds how Bhabha's time lag in the national narrative is reterritorialised by a performance of national identity in the present. This realigning of history is effected by creating a match with a certain image from the past. The perceptual need for this action to be repeated is seen in the reappearance of the necklace.[25]

Using both Bergson and Deleuze, Martin-Jones asserts that bodily triggered memory images in films such as *Vertigo* can serve as indicators of national identity; the portrayal of time being in close relation to the surrounding socio-political ethos. In *Vertigo*, Scottie's attempt to recreate a version of the present in which the racial and cultural tropes of post-colonial subjugation in the form of Carlotta is expunged through economic transformation mirrors, says Martin-Jones, America's desire to appear culturally accepting in the Cold War era, where US exports become more and more tied to its place as a world leader. What is crucial here, for the embodied thesis, is that, in this and other films, such memory-images are inextricably tied to the body postures and sensations of the characters themselves.

Following on from Martin-Jones, I would assert that this also works for the embodied experience of the audience. Not only are the bodies and senses of the characters inextricably linked to time, memory and diegesis but those of the audience too, as senses such as smell become inextricably caught in a network of meaning that lies beneath the conscious experience of the film. As previously stated, smell's connection to the limbic system makes it an ideal carrier of subconscious, body knowledge that is felt and sensed without consciously thought. By drawing on their own sensual memory directors attempt to create images that resonate with their audiences and underline the narrative movement of their work.

The Foul and the Fragrant – Polluting Forces in Shadow of a Doubt
One of Hitchcock's most personal films, *Shadow of a Doubt*, is a clear example of how multi-modal reception and national identity can support each other in mainstream cinema. *Shadow of a Doubt* has been seen as not only a work dealing with aspects of national identity but also with personal memory and has often been considered a watershed in the director's career and life. Directed in 1943, at the high point of US involvement in World War II, it has been described as Hitchcock's first truly American picture, one that noticeably leaves behind the Englishness of *Rebecca* (1940) or *Suspicion* (1941) and, as Robin Wood details, was also popular with audiences and critics alike.

Commensurate with the mandates of this embodied film theory, I would now like to examine the presentation of olfactory images in *Shadow of a Doubt* and relate them to a more canonical example of Hitchcock criticism. In doing this, I will make use of a number of critical tools that we have identified already (olfactory haptics, smell as it relates to cultural identity, synaesthesia and so on), but I would also like to add one more: the smellscape. The notion of the smellscape is increasingly being used in anthropology and sociology to describe not only a spatial but a temporal organisation of smells and olfactory experiences. The smellscape, broadly linked of course to the landscape or cityscape, is a method of grouping spatially or temporally contiguous smells together so that they can form meaningful relations - a map of smells that stretches across time and space. Smellscapes tend to be more individuated than landscapes; they are not only spatio-temporally based but concerned with racial and cultural identity, they can be self affirming and exclusive but they are always telling, being as they are the contingent product of lives lived.[26] Smellscapes orientate us in our lives, both in terms of the present and in terms of our past – they are like olfactory maps that not only tell us where we are but also hint at where we have come from.

As we shall see, the smellscape does not have to be experienced directly, that is chemically, to actually be present, in fact many of the images we see on screen arise and derive their power from being linked to the larger web of meaning that is the smellscape – the sea, for instance, does not consist merely of one smell (salty air, for instance) but a whole range of sensations (olfactory and otherwise) that add up to a unified but ever changing whole. This in turn gains meaning for us both culturally (the liminality of the coast, historical images of the sea and so on) and psychologically (individuated memories concerning childhood, holidays). The smellscape is the totality of these and is, of course inextricably linked to other senses such as sight and touch.[27] *Shadow of a Doubt*, I will assert, presents to a large extent a comparison and at some stages a clashing and overlapping of different smellscapes, one polluting, the other cleansing, that mirrors what Robin Wood sees as the underlying ideological agenda of Hitchcock during this period.

Wood's essay on *Shadow of a Doubt*, 'Ideology, Genre, Auteur', in *Hitchcock's Films: Revisited*, follows on from comments he makes in the introduction to the same book where he asserts the importance of the dialectic in the film.[28] Wood, like many critics before and since, stresses the degree to which doubling is constantly used as both a visual and a philosophical trope throughout.[29] Donald Spoto lists some of the binaries that litter the screenplay:

> The structural element at work in *Shadow of a Doubt* that expresses [a] division in Hitchcock's spirit is the almost infinite accumulation of doubles: the two Charlies; two detectives in the East pursuing Uncle Charlie, then two in the West; two criminals sought; two women with eyeglasses; two dinner sequences; two amateur sleuths engaged in two conversations about killing; two young children; two older siblings; two railway-station sequences; two sequences outside a church; two doctors; two double brandies served at the 'Till Two bar by a waitress who has worked there for two weeks; two attempts to kill the girl before the final scene; two scenes in a garage, one declaration of love and one attempt at murder – and so on, almost past counting.[30]

For Wood, the repetition of the binary, or perhaps even the duality, is reflective of Hitchcock's political mandate at the time: the defence of small town

America against the sickness of crime and inherent internal evil. The Newtons represent (as mentioned in the film itself) a typical American family that maybe flawed and unstable but ultimately serves a purpose – to proliferate a safe and essentially 'good' humanitarian ideology. As Wood correctly observes, unlike a film like David Lynch's *Blue Velvet* (1986) that itself takes small town America as its starting point, the notions of goodness and innocence in *Shadow of a Doubt* are never brought into question; Hitchcock allows his audience to believe whole heartedly in the binary of good and evil just as young Charlie does. At the end of the film the sense is not so much of good triumphing over evil but of the binary being revealed, a fall from grace in the true biblical sense of the term.

It is easy to see how Wood's account of *Shadow of a Doubt* could be used to situate the film within the socio-political context of World War II; exemplified by Hitchcock's two propaganda shorts for the British Government, *Bon Voyage* (1944) and *Aventure Malgache* (1944), and the 1942 film *Saboteur*, what seemed to concern him most during this time politically was the notion of the enemy within that threatens the status quo and the sanctity of family values.[31] However, as Wood suggests, Uncle Charlie (as both outsider and internal agent) threatens the safety of the family, not by destroying it but by polluting it:

> The small town (still rooted in the agrarian dream, in ideals of the virgin land as garden of innocence) and the united happy family are regarded as the real sound heart of American civilization; the ideological project is to acknowledge the existence of sickness and evil but preserve the family from their contamination.[32]

The two worlds that are personified in young Charlie and her uncle are not so much a duality then, or even a dialectic, but competing Manicheistic intensities that can infiltrate and work into each other, changing and contaminating, transforming and polluting each other, like smoke mingling with clean air.

This last point is of course central to the role of smell and olfaction in the film. Along with the other binaries, *Shadow of a Doubt* represents the playing out of a coming together of two different smellscapes based both in place and in time and this, again, has resonance with Hitchcock's socio-political mandate. The first hint we get of this occurs in the film's very opening scenes: the celebrated opening montage reveals not only a cityscape but a smellscape, with its waterside docks, its cars rusting in the city, its crowded tenement streets full of people, its gas works that dominate the skyline, its hot sweaty rooms and, lastly, of course, its cigar smoke. Robin Wood correctly observes that Uncle Charlie is the only character to smoke throughout the film (aside from Mr Newton who smokes a 'fatherly' pipe – very often unlit) and yet his only explanation of this is the somewhat clichéd recourse to the Freudian phallic symbol:

> Uncle Charlie is one of the supreme embodiments of the key Hitchcock figure: ambiguously devil and lost soul…from his first appearance, Charlie is associated consistently with a cigar (its phallic connotations evident from the outset in the scene with the landlady) and repeated shown with a wreath of smoke curling around his head…[33]

It is hoped that this chapter has shown that, using embodied critical theory, a cigar can (to use the often quoted Freudian statement) be just a cigar but it is no less important for that. Charlie's cigar is the ultimate vehicle for his role as pollutant in the fragrant small town smellscape that will follow. At times, Charlie's cigar acts (like those in *The Pleasure Garden* and the incense in *Mysteries of July*) to disrupt visual acuity and to give a pure sensual image. In one scene for instance, Uncle Charlie sits in bed smoking, he blows a smoke ring and a cloud of cigar fumes completely obscure his face asking the audience, as Laura Marks states, to draw on their knowledge of smell for understanding. In the Till Two club, both Charlies are wreathed in the smoke that hangs in the air so much that those in the background are greyed and blurry in the kind of haptic fuzziness that Laura Marks reserves for VHS films that have been degraded over the years; again, because our vision is impaired here, our sense of what the club must smell like is used to flesh out the experience.

In contrast to the smellscape of Uncle Charlie and the city, we have that of young Charlie and the small town. The smells that constitute this olfactory picture are, on the surface, as wholesome and all-American as the town itself: it is the apple blossom that constantly seems to line every street and to form a major part of the framing for Hitchcock's camera; it is the home baking of Mrs Newton (the cake she bakes for the magazine, the meals she cooks for her family), it is the grass that is on the ground and, most importantly perhaps the roses that not only stand in Young Charlie's room but are printed on the wallpaper.[34] This is obviously an entirely different smellscape to that of Uncle Charlie; it is free, fragrant, airy and good.

Interestingly, as Hirsch details, many of the fragrances in Young Charlie's smellscape appear in the nostalgic olfactory recollections of those born in the 1920s and 30s. Based on interviews with 1,000 shoppers in Chicago,

Hirsch's research found that there were distinct divisions between those born before 1940 and those after – the former group remembered smells consisting of roses, grass, hay, tweed and sea air and those born after tended to remember more artificial smells such as parent's cologne, Play Doh (in the 1950s and 60s) and plastic, suntan oil, felt tip pens and chlorine (in the 1960s and 70s). The smellscape inhabited by young Charlie then is highly redolent not only of a place (small town America) but of a time, a kind of golden time of childhood innocence that may even never have existed at all.

Ultimately, however, the importance of smellscapes in *Shadow of a Doubt* does not rest with the notion of two distinct olfactory maps but with the notion of pollution. Throughout the film, what we witness is the gradual contamination of young Charlie's smellscape by her uncle's, bit by sooty bit, his blackened and acrid smoke threatens her rose scented fragrance, something that comes to a head in the final scenes where she is trapped in the garage, choking on car exhaust fumes. This point is exemplified in three keys scenes that I shall now go through one at a time.

00:16:52 - Uncle Charlie's Arrival

Hitchcock here frames the arrival of Uncle Charlie's train through the boughs of a fragrant apple tree bedecked with blossom. William Rothman, in his minute analysis of Hitchcock, *The Murderous Gaze* fails to mention the arrival of the train at all, choosing instead to skip to the scene of the two Charlies meeting on the station. However, we can see that, for us, the arrival of the train has huge importance. One of the most obvious things about this scene is the extent that the characters in the foreground (Mr Newton and the two children) are dwarfed by the huge plume of black smoke that billows out of the train's smokestack, almost obscuring the whiteness of the small town American sky. As the train gets ever closer, the viewer is presented with an increasingly black screen as well as the synaesthetic audio cues of a train approaching a station and slowing down. This is a sign, in *Shadow of a Doubt*, that the two smellscapes are intermingling, that the smoke of Uncle Charlie's world (the city, crime, cynicism, money, etc.) is impinging and transforming the fresh air of the Newtons'.

We draw upon our knowledge of similar scents to give meaning to scenes such as this but this may happen below our level of conscious thought. One does not need to have experienced the smell of a steam locomotive to understand the black, acrid, choking smell of its smoke; the knowledge of smoke *per se* is enough to allow us to experience some of the scene's embodied meaning. As the train gets nearer the station, the smoke takes on the look of ink in water, as its dark plumes literally mingle with the sky in a sombre a foreshadowing of what is to come. Symbolically, the train and its smoke momentarily blots out the trees that stand to the left and right of the track as the visual images mirror the perceived olfactory experience of the smoke covering up the fragrance of the apple blossom.

This scene is interesting in that it seems to sum up many of the issues of dealing with smell in the cinema. As an audience we, quite obviously, can not actually smell the smoke that we see on screen, the images themselves are, quite patently, visual; however, we do need to draw on our other senses here in order to fully appreciate the roundness of scenes like this; they become in other words what I have termed 'tools of understanding' – faculties that allow us to understand the wholeness of an image.

00:19:14 – Uncle Charlie, Emmy and the Bedroom

As was previously stated, *Shadow of a Doubt* was Hitchcock's most personal film. Not only was it a kind of hymn to an innocent past, but many of its characters mirror Hitchcock's own life, most notably of course, the name of his recently deceased mother Emma and Mrs Newton. As Uncle Charlie meets his sister, Emmy, for the first time in years they face each other amid the trees of Santa Rosa in what, we have seen, as a typical framing device; the fragrant trees providing the counterpoint to Uncle Charlie's role as polluting force. Here, each shot is framed by the trees in the background, ensuring that the audience is constantly reminded that what we are dealing with here is a smellscape that is both natural and fragrant. We are a world away from the foul smelling dumps, the slow moving river and the smoke of the big city; instead, the olfactory landscape here consists of the fruit trees, grass and fresh air of the Californian summer that seems, until Charlie arrives, more a state of mind than a season. This sense of olfactory nostalgia is mirrored in the conversation between Charlie and Emmy where the former exclaims:

> Charlie: Emma, don't move…standing there you don't look like Emma Newton. You look like Emma Spencer Oakley of 46 Burnham Street, Saint Paul Minnesota. The prettiest girl on the block!

Hitchcock places us within a kind of Edenic present that is at once forever the past, and the natural images and their associated smells reminds us of the interviews carried out by Hirsch. The construction of this smellscape, that is part nostalgia, part geography continues in young Charlie's room when we are presented with another item on Hirsch's list – roses. Aside from those printed on the walls of the room, there is a large vase full of roses seated on the dresser, Uncle Charlie picks one and roughly breaks the stem to place it in his buttonhole, as he does so he holds it tantalisingly close to his nose, inviting the audience, as Laura Marks suggests, to share in the olfactory experience of this breath of scented air. Crucially, he is not smoking here, the smellscape of the Newtons' (through the image of the rose) has infiltrated Uncle Charlie – the two worlds are fully intermingled.

01:32:58 – The Attempted Murder of Young Charlie

Probably the most obvious example of the polluting force within *Shadow of a Doubt* is the sequence in which Uncle Charlie attempts to murder young Charlie by locking her in a garage with a car's engine running. It is this sequence that forces the latter to readjust her view of her uncle and, ultimately, the relationship between good and evil that underlines the film's narrative and socio-political mandates.

In this sequence Hitchcock utilises many of the filmic tools that we have looked at already. The thick black smoke from the car exhaust creates a blurry, indistinct visual field that is hard to penetrate; we see the occasional hand, steering wheel, a car's front bumper but that is all, everything else is shrouded in mist and smoke. Speaking of haptics in *The Skin of the Film*, Laura Marks states that, 'While optical perception privileges the representational power of the image, haptic perception privileges the material presence of the image',[35] and this is surly some of the sense we derive from this sequence: robbed of the chance to interrogate the images as instances of parts of a recognisable narrative, we are asked merely to experience the claustrophobia, the confusion and, above all, the choking smell of young Charlie's situation. It is no coincidence that in the moments where we need to visually interact with the images without recourse to our sense of smell (such as the crucial shots of young Charlie's hand reaching for the non-existent car keys) the smoke mysteriously disappears. Hitchcock, as Marks suggests, is asking us merely to experience the materiality of the image here, rather than engage in the process of visual recognition.

This sequence does, however, have a meaning within the film. This, I would assert, is the point at which the polluting force of Uncle Charlie reaches its high point, all the way through, the two worlds have been gently infiltrating each other, the smoke from the city train for instance mixing with the fresh air of the Californian sky and the fragrant rose from the Newtons' house being attached to Uncle Charlie's buttonhole. The sensual experience of the sequence in the garage however is that of pollution and contamination, the thick black smoke has finally engulfed the innocence of young Charlie and we, as the audience, are made to feel some of that. The smellscape of the city has not only collided with that of the small town but has polluted it to such an extent it threatens its very existence. Here we can see how the body, most particularly the nose and olfactory apparatus, is used as both a site of reception – in that we draw upon our sense of smell and its related memories to understand the image – and a tool of understanding, in that we made to feel nauseous and choked.

As we can see, this embodied reading of *Shadow of a Doubt* mirrors Wood's ideological reading; both present the coming together of two worlds – one, in Wood's account, concerned with ideology and character, the other, mine, concerned with the various smells that are represented throughout the film. Again, the interesting aspect for us here is the degree that one critical stance can support the other; our bodies (noses, lungs, skin etc) have one experience and our minds another.

It should not be thought that smell plays as important a role in the cinema of Alfred Hitchcock as taste or, as we shall see, sound. There are, however, examples of recent mainstream films where smell is featured as the primary point of sensual contact for the audience; Tom Twyker's *Perfume* (2006), for instance, is an obvious example of just how far we use our sense of smell when confronted with certain images. Films like John Waters' *Polyester* and Jack Cardiff's *Scent of Mystery* are interesting examples of films that began as gimmicky experiments in olfactory cinema (Waters' film, for example, was viewed with a scratch and sniff card) but can be viewed today as exemplifying synaesthetic cinema because they must be experienced outside of the initial olfactory technology. It is surprising that a film like *Polyester* loses very little of its quirky scatological humour when we are presented with the images only, devoid of the chemically produced smell card – a testament, perhaps, to the degree to which we use this sense when viewing visual images.

7

ON HEARING

> The consequence for film is that sound, much more than the image can become an insidious means of affective and semantic manipulation. On the one hand, sound works on us directly, physiologically…On the other, sound has an influence on perception.[1]

Hearing, as a sense, obviously has a privileged place within embodied film theory largely because, unlike smell, touch and taste, we are actually presented with its physical objects all the time: soundwaves and their movement through air. However, as many commentators on film sound have suggested, it has often been seen as the poor relation of visuals by the vast majority of film theorists.[2] Kaja Silverman states as much in an early passage from *The Acoustic Mirror*:

> The soundtrack has had a curious theoretical history. Notoriously passed over in favour of the image, it has nonetheless consistently figured as what Marianne Moore would call the 'real toad' in cinema's imaginary garden, somehow conjuring belief long after the *visual vraisemblable* has curled and faded.[3]

Silverman here points to what has become a truism of film theory and filmmaking: that sound is often seen as somehow grounding the evanescence of the visuals within an everyday reality; what Stanley Cavell has termed 'a world of immediate conviction'.[4] In Chaplin's *Modern Times* (1936), for instance, sound is often used as a signifier for a banal and quotidian reality that undercuts the romance of silence: the sound of the work klaxon forces the workers to begin their mind numbing toil, the Salestalk Transcription Company's gramophone record provides an eerie disembodied voice that seems to mirror the inhumanity of the factory, and, finally, Chaplin's own curiously disingenuous tones once and for all put pay to the mystique of the little tramp by making absurd sounds tumble from his lips.

Sound is both ever present and often ignored. We are never free from the imperative to hear, for even if we are immersed in complete silence we are, in Murray Schaffer's words condemned to listen to the sounds of our own body as it declares its presence in a world of sonic identity – gurgling, beating, creaking and groaning.[5] In the cinema, it is sound, not the visuals, that blocks out the world beyond the theatre, sound track music acts as both a carrier of emotional meaning and provides a kind of background hum that covers up the unwelcome noises of those around. The importance of this is particularly noticeable when it is absent such as in a film like Antonioni's *Blow Up* (1966) whose silence forces the audience to not only confront the sonic gaps in the film but the rustling, gurgling, chewing, slurping and fidgeting of one's neighbours.

This chapter proposes the following questions: what is this physical engagement with sound and how is it related to film theory of the postmodern scopic regime? How is sound experienced corporeally rather than translated intellectually? How is sound linked to the lived body and how does this alter our involvement with it? How does sound serve to underline or undercut the narrative elements of the film and what is the relationship between sight and hearing in the cinema? Sound in film *has* had a history of critical engagement; Mary Ann Doane, for instance, talks about the embodied presence of the voice in film; however, what concerns Doane, as with many writers on film sound, is projected sound rather than received sound.[6] Doane's conceptual body is the body on the screen rather than the body in the audience; when we start to think in terms of hearing instead of speaking, the perceptual frameworks and intellectual arguments become altered. This chapter looks at how sound is received and interpreted by the body and ears of the audience member and explores how this can be manipulated by the filmmaker to, again, offer more subconscious and subcognitive routes into the filmic experience. This chapter, then, does not look at areas such as language, musical semiotics, the tone of sounds (in terms of their symbolic or mythic value) or sound as a carrier of meaning generally; what it is interested in is how film directors, and of course Hitchcock specifically, use sound to instil in their audiences a particular corporeal experience, whether that be based on an emotion such as frustration or through more direct means.

Once again, the underlying framework to this chapter is centred around the binary of the body as an index of response and the body as a site of reception. This figure is particularly important with sound because our ears elide the necessity for sight altogether. Touch, taste, and smell, are all, obviously, mediated by vision and, as we have stated already, serve to bridge certain gaps in our perceptual understanding, however sound and hearing can also usurp our perceptual understanding, providing a layer of meaning that sight can never access and a set of perceptual registers that can both complement and counterpoint the visual elements. An essay by Pudovkin, originally published in 1929, on the nature of asynchronous sound, outlines what he thought should be the role of sound within the cinema.[7] For Pudovkin, the relationship of sound and vision can be summed up by the physical image of the frame and sound strip on the celluloid itself, distinct and yet linked by the larger assemblage of 'the film'. The relationship between audition and vision is, then, 'realized by an interplay of meanings which results…in a more exact rendering of nature than its superficial copying'.[8] This is in essence what I have been arguing for throughout this book: that it is in the interplay of sensual experience that the true meaning of the film can be found, not in the privileging of any one sense over the other. My only departure from Pudovkin is that he is concerned with sound as a carrier of semiotic meaning (the sound of the countryside opposed to the town, etc.), whereas I am concerned with sound as a facilitator or progenitor of corporeal sensation.

The Ears of the Skin: The Body as an Acoustic Site

David Sonnenschein's *Sound Design* is one of the few film studies texts that deals specifically with the physical reception of sound, or what Sonnenschein calls, 'sound energy transformation'. [9] When a film's soundtrack (whether it be language, sound effects or music) is viewed not only as carrier of meaning but as a flow of physical energy we need to draw up different critical tools to examine it, ones that factor in how our bodies might receive sound in a physical more direct way and how this process changes and transforms itself throughout the duration of the film. Sonnenschein details for instance how the body's experience of different frequencies can be utilised by the sound designer:

> Sound can affect our body temperature, blood circulation, pulse rate, breathing and sweating. Loud music with a strong beat can raise body heat, while soft, floating, or detached, abstract music can lower it. This phenomenon can be used in sound design to accentuate or counterpoint a scene with, for example, a cold winter day or a searing rocky desert.[10]

Is this not exactly what we have characterised as the body as a site of reception? Sonnenschein is suggesting here that sound can have a primary effect on the body unmediated by any sense of subjective identification; the heart beats faster when we hear certain kinds of music not only because we are made scared, nervous, or anxious through generic or cultural codes (i.e. the body working an index of certain emotional or psychological conditions) but through processes of biological and neurological reception. In fact, we could assert that we feel scared, nervous or anxious precisely because our bodies are receiving and registering such non-cognitive information. In other words, our bodies here are working in a way that is exactly opposite to many notions of film theory that assume our heart beats faster because we experience the emotional content of a film rather than our bodies receiving corporeal stimulation in the form of sound waves.

We can look at how bodies become a receptive site for sound waves in two linked but separate ways: the pitch of the sound which is measured in Hertz (Hz) and the level or intensity of sound which is measured in decibels. The human ear can detect sounds in the region of 20 to 18000 Hz and is comfortable dealing with an intensity of sound in the range of 0 to 120 decibels.[11] Anything below or above 20 to 18000 Hz (sub or ultrasonic sound) will not be heard as sound but can have marked physiological effects on anyone within range and can cause cardiovascular disease, stress and a host of other non-aural complaints. In certain cases, then, the ear becomes only one way that we receive sonic information, as our bodies become literally a kind of skin for the reception of sonic waves.

We receive sound waves in a way that is roughly topographical, the lower the frequency the lower down in the body we feel it. As Sonnenschein states, a tone of around 65 Hz will resonate in the lower back, pelvis, thighs and legs, 65 Hz is roughly the frequency of electrical hum or a low C on a keyboard. Timpanis, bass drums, bass guitars, and other low register instruments affect 'sexual, digestive and deep seated emotional centres'[12] such as the solar plexus. As the frequencies rise, so do their receptive sites on the body, until we experience the highs of violins and female screams in the shoulders, neck, and scalp. As Anna Powell says in relation to horror films:

> Sound waves, as well as light waves, travel through us and work strongly on the sensorium, bypassing the cerebral cortex and mainlining into our central nervous system.[13]

Infrasound, which is sound beyond or below the levels of human hearing, has been used in a number of experimental musical works such as Evgenia Chudinovich's collaboration *Infrasonic* (2003), which fused contemporary music with psychological and acoustic research to produce results that the audience not only heard but also felt.[14] The first concert of 'soundless music' was staged at the Purcell Room in London in 2003; the audience was not only presented with a number of infrasonic performances, such as an audio-visual work by Ravi Deepres, works by Roddy Skeaping and Howard Skempton and Hayden Parsey, but also filled out questionnaires about how they were affected during the concert. Despite not representing a rigorous scientific test, Angliss, O' Keefe Lord and Wiseman's study details some interesting correlations between infra - or low-scale sound and unusual bodily experiences: many audience members reported an increased heart rate, headaches, tingling sensations and nausea and, just as Sonnenschein suggests, many also stated that they felt cold during the performances.[15] 61 per cent of those polled stated that they felt some form of unusual physiological experience after a recital of Dutch composer Ton Bruynel's piece *Toccare* originally composed in 1986.

Such studies, although contestable, do indeed highlight the theoretical proposition that sound has the ability to affect us in physiological ways. As Ferguson, Davis, and Lovell state, the levels of the cinematic soundtrack very rarely reach the decibel levels needed to cause pain in the listener although according to Ferguson, Davis, and Lovell, the average intensity level of Hollywood films such as *Saving Private Ryan* (1998), *Lethal Weapon 4* (1998) and *Armageddon* (1998) sometimes reached 90dB, this was never at the sustained levels that would be needed to cause damage to the ear.[16] The notion that we are affected physically by the many and varied ways a film can transmit sound is an interesting and a reasonably secure one. In this way, the ears of the skin provide us with the ground for an emotional response, not the other way round; it is this that represents the initial sensation out of which the empathetic and thus narratological elements are formed.

Sonic Relations: The Body as an Index of Audition

Given that there has been scholarly work carried out on the importance of the body in music and the importance of the soundtrack in film, it is perhaps surprising that there has never been the suggestion that the body plays a major role in the experience of the sounds emanating from the cinema's loudspeakers.[17] We have seen how the body can be thought of as a site of reception for various sounds but it can also be thought of as an index of the various psychological states, emotions and processes of secondary identification that continually grips an audience when it is watching a film. Like all of the areas we have looked at so far in this book, the body as an index of audition is subtly and yet vitally different from the body as a site of sonic reception.

Imagine, for instance, a loud scream close to an ear; we could suggest that this represents a number of different layers of experience for the person unlucky enough to be hearing it. Firstly, as we have suggested already, there is the initial reception by the body and the ear; this can best be thought of as a physiological experience, if Sonnenschein is right, we would receive such a pitch at the top of the neck and the back of the head as well as through the auditory channels of the ears. We would then, perhaps, associate this sound with various social and cultural codes we might be familiar with (the distress of others, someone in pain, someone afraid and so on) which would then instil in the listener a bodily reaction of their own – they might feel nauseous, for instance, their heart rate might increase, they might start to sweat or feel faint themselves and so on. Only then, perhaps, would the listener 'understand' the initial stress that caused the scream in the first place, not through the psychological processes usually cited in film theory but through a form of corporeal mimesis and transitivism.

Kate van Orden, in her essay, 'Descartes on Musical Training and the Body' highlights how music, sound and the body were linked even in that exemplar of cognition, Rene Descartes:

> Music drew Descartes's attention not only outward to the stars, but inward as well, to the hidden parts of the body and the gray matter of its soul, for the senses he enjoined in his study mediated between the outer and the inner worlds. The senses operated as conduits for stimulation, and their effects on the inside of the body required a deepening mathesis that could include the physics of the internal microcosm.[18]

Again, here van Orden uses a set of conceptual images that we have identified as being commensurate with theories of the postmodern scopic regime: intermodal fluency, synaesthesia, the senses as a conduit for corporeal knowledge and so on, all emanating from a thinker typically thought of as negating the importance of corporeal experience. Sound is a carrier of both abstract ideas and bodily emotions; both a major constituent of language and a way of undercutting its hegemonic position, sound is of, and greatly affects, the body.

One of the ways that the body becomes an index of sound is through its removal; the coming of the sound film was not only concerned with noise but with its absence and the talkie not only released the expressive use of the voice but the use of silence. Adam Mars Jones' article, 'Quiet, Please', bemoans the trend in modern cinema to overuse music in the soundtrack and to saturate the ear of the audience with, sometimes inappropriate and unsympathetic sounds.[19] However, what Jones calls silence is really only the absence of music – true silence in film very rarely happens and when it does it often brings with it an eerie tension that provides a counterpoint to the rest of the filmic experience. In *Frenzy*, for instance, Hitchcock uses silence in two contextually different ways that each result in the same rise in tension for the audience: the first instance occurs as Babs Milligan exits the Globe pub, suddenly the world becomes quiet, the noise of the street is dimmed and, after a second or two, all we hear is the sonorous voice of Bob Rusk as he appears behind her.[20] Not only does the surrounding silence focus our attention on Rusk's voice in this scene but we are sonically displaced; Rusk is deliberately closely miked so that we feel his voice on our skin; Sullivan tells us that in the dubbing notes to *Frenzy*, Hitchcock picks out this scene for special attention:

> Silence in the pub as Babs storms out, command Hitchcock's dubbing notes: "Drop all sounds – traffic and everything. And bring it up again when the camera tracks to the two head shot of Rusk and Babs so we get the effect when his voice is heard behind her big head…This is dramatic licence, but I think it is necessary to get the fullest effect out of Rusk's sudden appearance.[21]

The 'fullest effect' Hitchcock talks of here refers, we could assume, to the tension and shock of Bab's encounter with Rusk, tension and shock that registers on the body and that relies, in the main, on aural rather than visual engagement. The second use of silence in *Frenzy* comes at the moment of most tension, in the scene where Blaney is wrongly sentenced in the court. The closing of a door by a waiting policeman severs our sonic involvement with the action and, again, Hitchcock incites tension and nervousness in his audience by removing their access to a cogent soundtrack. For almost 18 seconds (an age in modern cinematic terms) the audience is presented with visuals only, filmed through the glass door of court building number one; we are fully aware of the verdict because we can see the reaction of Blaney in the dock but the tension of the scene is highlighted and made all the more visceral by the silence that hangs heavily over it.

Silence, under these circumstances, becomes more than a mere absence that denotes lack; it becomes what Deleuze might have termed a sonsign, 'a pure sensory image'[22] that signals the collapse of the sensory motor process and seeks other paths to filmic involvement. The pure sonic image acts upon the audience member in a different way to the sensory motor linkage of the movement-image, in Deleuze's words, it represents an escape from the world of clichés and, commensurate with Hitchcock's position as existing between the two regimes of images for Deleuze, in his films it disrupts the flow of the narrative and provides nothing but a moment of pure sensory intensity. The silences in *Frenzy* have very little semiotic or narratological value which is perhaps why neither of these scenes are dealt with much in Hitchcock literature, but they do have a vital role to play in the flow of the film's sensory intensity and even interrupt, as Deleuze suggests, the visual aspects of viewership. Sonsigns (and their related concepts opsigns and tactisigns) invite us to experience a film in a more sensual, molecular way, divorced from the more molar constructs of meaning, interpretation and interrogation.

Perhaps one of the clearest examples of Hitchcock's use of the sonsign occurs in his earliest sound film, *Blackmail*. The famous scene occurs at the breakfast table after the murder of Crewe, a philandering artist, by Alice White the daughter of a tobacconist. As a nosey neighbour (unaware of Alice's guilt) discusses the murder in front of her and her family, Hitchcock isolates the word 'knife' from the tirade of sentences that the neighbour sallies forth. The effect is disturbing for both Alice and the audience as we enter a kind of shared, guilt-inspired reverie brought on by the hypnotic sound of the neighbour's voice. Raymond Durgnat is right when he comments upon the scene:

> How simple, sharp, exact is that distortion of sound: 'mumble mumble, knife! Mumble mumble knife!' not only the sudden jerk and squawk of phrase within the syllabic fuzz of faintness, but the whole sensory gestalt achieves a perceptual rightness which distinguishes from the touchingly earnest formalism of the avant-garde and authentic stream of consciousness.[23]

Durgnat here recognises the pure sonic nature of the scene, a scene that should not be reduced to simple syntagmatic meaning related to the underlying guilt of Alice. As Truffaut observes, the scene is the auditory equivalent of the many visual tricks and innovations that characterised Hitchcock's early, expressionist inspired, work. [24] This scene is a brief interstice in what is an otherwise (in Deleuzian terms) movement-image based film, as we are asked to stop for a moment and revel in the vaguely hypnotic repetition of sound. Although perhaps an embryonic example, the knife scene in *Blackmail* could be thought of as a sonsign in the same sense that Godard employed 40 years later.

Screams in the Shower – Psycho-analysis

The shower scene in *Psycho* is one of the few single scenes in cinema to have had an entire study dedicated to it and the visuals at least have been minutely documented, studied and interrogated.[25] Hermann's musical score has also been looked at in some depth mainly in terms of its surprising use of harmony, the mirroring of orchestral sounds with the visual elements and the ironic history behind its inclusion in the first place.[26] What has not been looked at however is the specific way in which Hitchcock's sound designers, William Russell and Waldon O. Watson, create a series of interwoven sounds that are every bit as terrifying, disturbing and artificial as the visuals that have been so minutely studied.

The soundtrack to the shower scene in *Psycho* lasts for approximately 25 seconds, from the moment Norman pulls back the curtain to Marion Crane's last breath which is clearly audible under the glissando chords of Bernard Hermann's score. On close inspection, the soundtrack to this famous scene is perhaps more complicated and contrived than many might imagine and its construction revealed as a sonic montage of various sounds and various voices, one of which is clearly not Janet Leigh's. The soundtrack itself consists of five main sounds: the sound of strings in the non-diegetic 'music', the sound of running water from the shower, a female voice, the sound of stabbing and the sound of the shower curtain being opened. All of the sounds are of a high frequency, Janet Leigh's scream for instance registers a peak of 1334 Hz and the highest note of the violins in the score, E, also register around that area (E in the second octave representing 1320 Hz). If Sonnenschein is right, and we feel such heights of pitch in the back of our necks and the top of our heads, we experience the twinge of recognition in this area just as Marion Crane feels the knife in hers![27]

We can compare this embodied method of studying the soundtrack with the method employed in a text like Giannetti's *Understanding Movies*. For Giannetti, the high-pitched notes of the violins represent the 'sound effects of shrill bird noises'[28] and are used to characterise Norman Bates throughout the film. However, as Prendergast suggests, this is not only a misinterpretation of the narrative (the audience are asked to assume the figure is Mrs Bates not Norman at this point) but it is most probably an incorrect assumption: neither Hitchcock nor Hermann ever mention wishing to create a sonic theme for Norman during this scene and, besides, the 'sound effects' Giannetti talks of are not effects at all but notes on a violin; their importance lies not in what they sound like but with what they are – sonic stabs in the receptive flesh of the audience member.[29] The real effect of the soundtrack on the listener/viewer surely must consist in its appeal to the body rather than the imagination or the intellect.

The scene is as shocking aurally as it is visually, perhaps, even more so, even if we ignore the connotations of the sounds themselves (the psychological impact of hearing a woman's dying screams, the symbolic sounds of the violins and other noises). Unlike the visuals, the soundtrack is unambiguous, there are no cut-aways, no tricks of montage, sounds of stabbing unequivocally invite us to corporeally involve ourselves in the murder of the woman and, for the ear, the knife always hits home. The soundtrack not only complements the visuals, it compensates for their censored lack; if Hitchcock was forced to be creative in his editing to avoid ever seeing the knife hitting the flesh, in the soundtrack we hear the wet thud of steel repeatedly slicing the skin and we are left in no doubt as to what is happening.

Examination of the score that accompanies the shower sequence (section IV, The Murder) reveals that the body's experience of its pitch equates roughly to the arc of movement within the frames, in a way that is surprisingly similar to that envisioned by Eisenstein in his essay 'Synchronization of the Senses' although Eisenstein of course refers only to the 'imagery perception of the music'[30] rather than its physiological reception. The movement of the scene, in the sense that Eisenstein uses in his pictorial diagrams, is ever downward – at the opening of the shower curtain we are looking upwards towards Norman's raised arm, it is at this point that the high Es are played on the violins. As the scene progresses we descend, both in terms of visuals and in terms of sounds (with their obvious physical correlations), until the F of the bass note in the 16th bar. We have gone from the highest note in the sequence to the lowest in the same time Marion Crane goes from standing upright in the shower to lying face down in the bath, her head resting on the lowest point in the room. The lows of the cellos at the end of the vignette are matched by the slowing and finally stopping of Marion Crane's breaths as we are taken still further downward down the vortex of the plug hole and out of the scene. In this sequence, to use Eisenstein's phrase (although with reference to a different text of course) 'the montage elements touch literally every sense, except perhaps that of taste…the sense of touch…the sense of smell…the sense of sight…the sense of hearing…the sense of movement… [and pure emotion, or drama]',[31] as Hitchcock, his sound designers, and Bernard Hermann, create a 'vertical montage' of visuals and soundtrack that, through the physical reception of sound is, almost literally, written on the body of the audience.

Craig Sinclair's essay 'Audition: Making Sense of/in the Cinema' highlights what is a vital role of sound and hearing in breaking the hegemony of the visual within film theory. For Sinclair, the soundtrack of a film is not only *as* important as the visuals, it is in some ways more so, because it brings into question the usual practices of what he terms 'the WASPatriarchal viewer',[32] and more importantly the gendered perspective that underlines it. Sinclair uses the term cinema 'experiencer' instead of 'spectator' or 'viewer' in order to avoid the linguistic trap of scopic hegemony and suggests that the soundtrack can undercut the male gaze of the camera by providing a sensuous, feminine space that offers a more polysemic experience of narrative and character. Discussing Laura Mulvey's seminal essay 'Narrative Pleasure and Visual Cinema', Sinclair states that:

> Audition serves to undermine the very hegemony that Mulvey posits in the visuals and in doing so appeals to 'other' elements of the audience from those who merely gaze at the screen.[33]

The soundtrack not only asks us to use different registers of understanding, these registers can undercut the hegemony of the primarily male gaze; by eliding the need for a single perspective and the monovocal interrogation that usually follows from this, sound engulfs us in a sensual experience that is often associated with those outside of the dominant discourse.[34]

A corollary to Sinclair's argument is that sound in cinema also challenges the positioning of the spectator (or experiencer), whilst vision distances them, keeping them outside the frame of the screen no matter how hard the director tries to draw us in. Despite efforts in 3D, the visual elements of cinema are always doomed to exist on a flat plane, in two dimensions; we are never anything else but a stranger to the images that flicker across the screen.[35] Sound, however, knows no such boundaries; as Michel Chion demonstrates in his *Audiovision,* the soundtrack may seem to emanate from and be centred on the screen; but this is, of course, not the case; it extends beyond the bounds of its apparatus and invades the space of the listener, as we have seen literally affecting the body (flesh, hairs, bones) of the audience member. It is this proximate quality that, according to Sinclair, provides links between a study of the soundtrack and the feminist philosophy of a thinker such as Irigaray who uses touch, closeness and sensuality as mechanisms of undermining the distance of patriarchal modernity.

Sinclair's view that sound presents a more feminised sensual experience is debatable but it does sometimes result in perceptual paradoxes that undercut the usual practices of perspectivalist visual ontology.[36] One particularly striking example occurs in Peter Medak's film, *Let Him Have It* (1991), when Derek Bentley, the lead character is filmed inside a garden shed filled with valve radios. As Bentley turns on the radios one by one, the Dolby surround sound imitates the aural placing of the various sets as they are turned on, creating, to the ears of the audience, the sense that they are in the shed itself, listening through Bentley's ears. We experience here a kind of split perception, where we are simultaneously outside the frame and inside as well. Visually we can only ever be outside the perceptual field of the film but aurally we can experience exactly what it is like to be inside the screen itself. The archetypal image of visual perspective, Alberti's 'perceptual pyramid'[37] is enclosed in a constantly shifting, molecular field, that, not so much challenges (as Sinclair suggests) as complicates it, and we are asked to exist in a kind of multi-modal anamorphosis that means we hover between viewing position and listening position. The visual sense is so privileged in the cinema and in film studies that this split is very seldom even noticed by the viewer who undergoes what we could think of as a *méconnaissance* brought about by the symbolic register of cinema itself. Technologies such as 5.1 surround-sound aim to mirror reality but instead create a new experience that could never be reflected in real life where we occupy two (or perhaps even numerous) perceptual positions simultaneously.

'Not Just Any Kind of Silence': The Sound of the Birds

Of all Hitchcock's films, *The Birds* is the one whose soundtrack has generated the most critical work.[38] It is sonically remarkable in a number of ways, not least of all because it features no music. Instead, the aural soundscape consists of a network of recorded and electronically generated sounds that constantly vie for the listener's attention. As Jack Sullivan points out, this revelling in the aural is also present in Du Maurier's original story that is, itself, full of the tapping, squawking, cawing and flapping of the birds that terrorise her Cornish fishing village.[39] Sullivan's other point, that the electronically created sounds of the birds represent a form of alternative music, seems less convincing, because the whistles and caws that, at times, almost literally assault the ears of the audience member serve not to 'soothe the savage beast', but to irritate, terrorise, and generally disturb the equilibrium of the narrative and *ipso facto* the spectator.[40] The sounds of the birds exist as a sonsign rather than music, coming between the viewer and the film rather than facilitating or adding to its visual aspects. As we shall see, in *The Birds*, Hitchcock manages to achieve what could be thought of as a vertical montage of suspense, where each element of the film contributes to the overall embodied effect. Equating the sounds of the birds with music seems to denigrate their role as a carrier of the film's emotion; they do not attempt to mimic another sound or art form, they are what they are – pure sound waves that travel through air affecting the audience member on a number of different corporeal levels. Hitchcock was obviously at pains to stress this point by creating them electronically rather simply recording them from nature, completely removing their real world referent.

Elisabeth Weis' two articles on sound in *The Birds* (the essay 'The Evolution of Hitchcock's Aural Style and Sound in *The Birds*' and Chapter 8 of her book *The Silent Scream*) illuminate quite succinctly the effectiveness of the soundtrack created by Oscar Sala, Remi Gassmann, and Bernard Herrmann. For Weis, the sonic elements of the film do not, as most soundtracks do, complement the visuals but instead usurp their primacy, occasionally exposing the inherent impotence of visual representation and its relation to terror and horror:

> By the time of *The Birds*, screeches are even more important than visual techniques at terrorising the audience during the attacks. Indeed bird sound sometimes replace visuals altogether. Moreover, Hitchcock carefully manipulates the sound track so that birds can convey terror even when they are silent or just making the occasional caw.[41]

Weis sees the soundtrack to *The Birds* as representing somewhat of a climax to Hitchcock's burgeoning desire to directly affect the audience member without the mediation of narrative or character. She highlights the degree that his three previous films, *Vertigo*, *North by Northwest* and *Psycho* each contained scenes that were specifically designed to appeal to the spectator directly (the dizziness in *Vertigo*, the drunkenness in *North by Northwest*, the screeches in *Psycho*) and Weis sees the sound of the birds as representative of Hitchcock's move away from films based on the mechanisms of empathy, identification and psychological sympathy and into works that encourage 'a more direct audience involvement'.[42]

Such ideas are at home in this discussion of what we have termed the postmodern scopic regime that suggests filmmakers use non-visual senses to encourage a mimetic rather than an empathetic response. As we have seen, part of the contingent outcome of film theory's privileging of vision above all other senses, is a commensurate privileging of the kinds of tropes that Weis claims Hitchcock's later career tried to move away from. In *The Birds* (as in other films), Hitchcock succeeds in negotiating between the different senses so that each can be used to either complement or contrast with another; as Weis states, Penelope Houston's argument that the strength of the soundtrack in *The Birds* is to compensate for the weakness of the visuals fails to recognise the extent that differential sensual involvement was always a key feature of his work and became more so toward the end of his working life, as we have already seen with films such as *Frenzy* and *Shadow of a Doubt*.[43]

If each Hitchcock film has a specific character (*Psycho* as Gothic horror, *Lifeboat* as political disquisition, *Shadow of a Doubt* as tone poem) then *The Birds* is surly the filmic equivalent of an abstract expressionist painting; the real lives and motivations of the characters, as Weis details, are secondary to the direct appeal to sensual involvement on the part of the audience. It is in some ways a narrative film that forgoes its narrative realism to seek other artistic aims and it is on these that its success or failure rests. The birds are not, as Robin Wood stated, 'a concrete embodiment of the arbitrary and unpredictable';[44] neither are they symbols of the decline in moral and social responsibility they are instead pure movement, colour and sound that instil fear, tension and horror into the audience – abstracted bodily affects that exist outside of any one individual character and therefore outside of the usual remits of the theory that attempts to frame them.[45] *The Birds* therefore should not be considered a film necessarily concerned with Oedipal familiarity, social apocalypse or any other content based aesthetic but with the translation of form into mimesis, a form of cinematic fairground ride that fulfilled Hitchcock's infamous desire to plug straight into the brains of the audience and play them like an organ.

There are eight attacks or effects of attacks shown in *The Birds*: the first (0:20:15) features Melanie on the motorboat in Bodega Bay; the second (0:52:03) occurs at the children's party; the third (0:54:30) in Mitch's house after the solitary bird falls down the chimney; the fourth (0:59: 27) at Farmer Dan's house; the fifth (1:11:08) outside the school; the sixth (1:25:39) after the 'bird's eye view of the town burning; the seventh (1:40:00) in Mitch's house again, this time after he has boarded up the window; and lastly, the attack on Melanie in the attic of Mitch's house (1:47:00). We could of course add a further one here and refer to the end of the film, as the birds menacingly observe the Brenners and Melanie 'drive' away in their car. It is Elizabeth Weis' point that each of these scenes represent a split between the emotions of suspense and surprise; visual cues create suspense, she asserts, whereas sound creates surprise, each attack can therefore be characterised by the relative degree to which it depends on either sight or sound for its impact.

Viewing all of the scenes together, however, we can also add that each presents the audience with a different yet emotionally similar embodied experience, appealing in the main to four senses: sight, sound, touch and movement. However, I would also add smell to this in one of the scenes at least. Hitchcock creates what could be thought of as an orchestral variation on a theme by replaying the same scene over and over again from a different sensual angle, exploring the many ways in which an audience can be affected by a film. The entire latter half of the film can, I would assert, be thought of as an exercise in multi-modal difference, sometimes complementing, sometimes undercutting the value of vision in the cinematic experience. In this, Weis is only partially right in her assertion that 'there are two sets of variables that he seems to be manipulating in relation to the different sound effects: whether the birds are introduced first aurally and visually or whether the birds are ominously noisy or ominously silent'.[46] Whereas this is certainly true, a more embodied reading can undercover another facet of the film: that each replayed scene is characteristic of a different embodied sense that has become detached from the characters and is allowed to be completed by the audience; let us now look at each of these scenes in turn.

Attack One:

Coming around half an hour into the film, we are introduced gently to the embodied tropes that will, later on, become the mainstay of the film's experience. Melanie is in the boat, after just depositing the lovebirds in Mitch's living room; she has almost made it to dry land when a single gull swoops out of the sky and pecks her forehead leaving it bloodied and scratched. In *The Silent Scream* Weis states that 'The gull enters the frame well before Hitchcock adds the sound of wings or the bird screech.'[47] However, close analysis of the scene reveals that this is not the case: at 0:25:17 we see a cut away shot of the gull complete with flapping wings and screech, we then see the frame that Weis is referring to (the close up of Melanie in the boat framed against the hills and lake) then at 0:25:18 the gull simultaneously screeches, flaps its wings and attacks Melanie who clutches her head. This is the only scene in the sequence where visuals and soundtrack are in accord i.e. where they are synchronised to a great degree. Although other scenes will present sound and vision coming together, it is also the only scene where fear of the birds is mediated by the direct involvement of one recognisable character – Hitchcock uses synchronous sound here for perhaps the last time to picture a bird attack; from now on, his motive is to make us feel the attacks on us rather than on a character.

Attack Two:

The second attack occurs at Kathy's birthday party, interestingly, just as the children are about to play *blind* man's buff. It is this scene that first introduces what will be a constant theme throughout the rest of the film: the synaesthetic interplay of the senses, almost all of the power of the bird's attack here comes from the sounds that emanate from the soundtrack, as vision is partially (although not completely) abandoned in favour of abstract sounds and movement. Watching the scene without sound reveals the stark nature of the special effects, with only one or two birds at most appearing in the frame at anyone time – it is the soundtrack that is full of birds, the sonic frame that resonates with their screeching and cawing. This scene also introduces the role of proximity in the creation of terror; in reality the amount of birds that are shown, their size and their distance would not ordinarily result in the audible flapping of wings that literally packs the soundscape. As Gianluca Sergi states, sound creates a reality that is beyond the sensual boundaries of normal experience, the soundtrack elevates the audience member into what he terms a 'superlistener'[48] that privileges the reception of sound over the reality of the visuals.

Michel Chion details how sound can affect our temporal appreciation, how the 'ear analyses, processes, and synthesizes faster than the eye'.[49] In this scene, we see how sound can also change our understanding of space, the birds (either imagined or non-existent) in this scene seem close enough to touch our skin despite the fact that they are framed against an expanse of sky and the wide vista of Bodega Bay. The images of the children feeling the closeness of the birds are nothing compared to the synthetic sounds of their flapping and screeching, that provide us with a synaesthetic bridge between the senses of sound and touch.

Attack Three:

This sense is continued but to a much greater extent in the next attack that takes place in the living room of the Brenner house. This is the first of two scenes that take place here but each has a distinct character and an overriding sensual experience. What we experience here is the abstract terror of engulfing movement twinned with a commensurately abstracted soundtrack. As Weis correctly states, by this point Hitchcock has abandoned altogether the pretence of character empathy and we are presented instead with an almost expressionist montage of sound and vision that at times resembles the avant-garde film work of artists such as Stan Brakhage. This scene is a counterpart to the previous, for here we are presented with movement within an enclosed space; the link between touch and sound then becomes ever more apparent as we are presented with what Laura Marks calls 'haptic sound'; that is, sound not meant to be interrogatory, not intended to be semiotic, but instead designed merely to be experienced and to be internalised. Vision and sound work in unison in this scene and so too appreciation of kinetic motion, but our empathy with the characters is reduced as they are hidden behind a veil of strangely two dimensional birds – a product no doubt of the limited special effect technology. The birds cease being distinct individuated threats and become instead a mass of movement and colour that come closer to notions of the sublime than contemporary theories of horror.

Attack Four:

If attack three concerned itself with the coming together of sound and vision, attack four, the aftermath of the carnage at Farmer Dan's farm concerns itself with sight and smell. For the first time in the film, sound is elided in favour of vision and it is a stark vision that, as Žižek suggests in *Looking Awry*, forces us to confront the Real of horror. Tellingly, of course, there is no sound at all here but as we saw in the chapter on smell, we are still presented with a multi-modal experience as sight is matched with smell (of death, of blood of feathers and so on) to flesh out the experience and to add a particular character to the scene.

As Hitchcock himself stated to Truffaut, the silence in this scene is intended as a counterpoint to the sounds that follow:

> F. T. When Jessica Tandy discovers the farmer's body, she opens her mouth as if to scream, but we hear nothing. Wasn't that done to emphasize the sound track at this point?
>
> A. H. The soundtrack was vital just there; we had the sound of her footsteps running down the passage, with almost an echo…we were really experimenting there by taking real sounds and then stylizing them so that we derived more drama from them than we normally would.[50]

This is a clear indication that, for Hitchcock, it was the sound that carried the embodied meaning in *The Birds*, not the visuals.

Attack Five:

In the fifth attack, that takes place outside the school, we see a combination and escalation of all of the multi-modal tropes we have witnessed so far. Sound and vision here combine, but so too does touch and movement.

Not only does Hitchcock frame the faces of the running children so tightly they are obscured by the flapping crows, but their screams melt in with the cawing of the birds until what we are presented with is a mélange of natural and synthesised sound that can be nothing but a Deleuzian sonsign. It loses much of its referential value and becomes instead a kind of pure sound of terror. As the children run we can see their faces but it is not this, I would argue, that causes us to flinch, instead it is the abstracted sense of fear and engulfment that we experience upon being party to the haptic images and the complementary soundtrack.

Attack Six:

Again, Hitchcock looks to movement for embodied specificity in this scene; however, unlike the others, this time we are presented with movement both inside and outside of an enclosed space. However we are presented with another, non-visual sense, here – weight – as gull after gull collides with the window of the telephone box that Melanie hides herself in. As Aristotle tells us, the appreciation of mass, like odour or taste, is not one that can be facilitated visually, in order to understand it we need to draw on our synaesthetic knowledge, our knowledge of heaviness and of density. It is this that Hitchcock plays with in this scene when first he pictures the birds light as air in the over head shot of the burning coastal town and then as they smash into the glass of the phone booth. Hitchcock twins sound in this scene with touch (or more rightly with the appreciation of mass) to communicate the madness of the birds and the fragility of the flesh that they swoop down upon, as the by now, familiar thrum of the bird's wings is matched by the thud of their bodies on the glass.

Attack Seven:

Attack seven is the most interesting of all because it is here that Hitchcock finally realises what he has been leading up to for the whole of the film: the complete cessation of visual terror in favour of one that is borne only through the soundtrack. Irrespective of what the birds signify, in this scene they reach the ultimate in abstraction – complete (or at least virtually complete) visual effacement. Holed up in the Brenners' living room, the windows barred, all we are made witness to is the sounds of the birds as they fly into the windows, break them and sacrifice themselves, all amid a torrent of noise. Viewing the scene with the sound missing reveals a surprising truth about the film as a whole, as each character, obviously in fear (apart the isolated moment where a bird *is* shown) looks skyward in a kind of religious horror that could easily signify the witnessing of an apocalypse.

Watching without sound also highlights Chion's point that sound is inextricably linked to our appreciation of temporality and temporalization, what he calls 'the added value' of the soundtrack. Not only does this scene seem longer in silence (especially the section before the attack) but individual actions seem protracted and awkward without the binding element of sound. Without this too, cuts and edits in the film that might otherwise be missed (such as the barely noticeable cut where Mitch exists the hallway only to come back instantly with a hammer and nails) become immediately apparent. At moments like these, sound is revealed as the glue that papers over the cracks in the visuals.

Attack Eight:

The eighth and final attack occurs in the attic of the Brenner house and has been seen as a final triumph of visuals over sound. Hitchcock himself stated that it was his intention in this scene to present the birds as silent assassins, far beyond the need to screech and caw. However, of course, this scene is far from silent. Using what we have called 'haptic sounds', Hitchcock creates the sense of closeness like no other scene; it is the birds' wings flapping that we are aware of most here and we understand this through recourse, not to vision, but to touch and skin sensitivity. I am suggesting that we do not so much empathise with Melanie here as mimetically involve ourselves with her situation. We have come full circle, the first attack centred on Melanie and depended, to a very large extent, on empathy and identification, by the time Hitchcock has played out all his embodied variations (sight and sound together, sound and internal space, sound and external space, sound and movement, sight and smell, sound alone) we can appreciate the abstract nature of the fear that plagues the film; again the meaning of the birds is not in what they represent but what they are – pure sound, pure movement and pure terror.

The final scene of the film is crucial to understanding what role sound plays in it; as Hitchcock said, the silence that pervades these images is not merely an absence of sound, it is what he calls 'not just any kind of silence… an electronic silence, a sort of monotonous low hum that might suggest the sound of the sea in the distance'.[51] From the high frequencies of the birds' screeches we are left with the low, almost subsonic, frequencies of an electronic hum that we would, according to Sonnenschein, feel in our emotional centres – the solar plexus, the back and the belly. Our mimetic terror continues, and the last emotion we are left with is an unspecific unease, a feeling that all is not well, that the story has not ended.

Our sense of hearing, then, not only allows us access to auditory information; that is, information that is based in the semiotic nature of sound, but also embodied sensation. The effect of the sounds of the birds remain with the audience long after it has filed out of the cinema and into the street, long after the actual sound of the screeches have faded with the curtain closes. Only when we relate the usual sensual faculties of cinema to the rest of the body and its sensorium do we begin to understand the full thickness of the experience. Sound envelopes us; it affects all of us; it agitates the small hairs on our bodies; it hurts us if it is too loud; it frustrates us if it is too low and we have to strain to hear it. Sound can be beautiful and it can be painful – it can carry meaning in the form of language and symbol but it can also go beyond words. This chapter has looked, not at how sound can be interpreted, but at how it can be experienced; as we have seen, however, this is, in itself, a form of knowledge, one that extends beyond the usual definitions of cognition and understanding.

8

ON TOUCHING

Our world touches itself, can be touched, is touch; our world *is in touch*.[1]

The preceding chapter examined how hearing affects the body of the cinema viewer. As was stated, sound, unlike taste and smell, is actually physically present in the theatre; therefore, its effects are perhaps more easily imagined. Touch is also present; the specific feel of the velour of the cinema seat and the closeness of one's neighbour can be seen as vital to the cinema experience but it is also one that is perhaps doomed to the past, as DVDs and home viewing become more prevalent. Again, however, this chapter does not look at the physical and real aspects of touch in the cinema experience but touch as a virtuality drawn on by a sensorium that is related to the real world but not necessarily part of it. This chapter looks firstly at how touch has been dealt with in critical work and its emerging importance in film and cultural theory; it then moves on to look at how closeness is used in Hitchcock (and by extension all films); and then concludes with a detailed exposition of *Rear Window*, a film that has traditionally been seen as highly metafictional and no less so for film theory of the postmodern scopic regime.

Touching denotes closeness; it is the first sense we develop and arguably the last one we lose. There is no moment in our lives where we are not touching or being touched; by clothes, by our own hair, by the furniture we sit on it, by the keyboards we work on, by our loved ones and occasionally by our adversaries. Touch is inevitably an embodied sense that cannot be localised in any one part; it is instead a continuously shifting experience that spreads itself over the skin, forming an interface with the environment close by us – touch is the only sense that is common to virtually every human being and every animal ever to have existed. It is because of this that touch (and its main sensory organ, the skin) has been the subject of increasing interest in the cultural and anthropological sciences in recent years: Ashley Montague's seminal text *Touching: The Human Significance of Skin*[2] charts not only the biological necessity of touch but its role in attachment theory, sexuality and its manifestation in different cultures throughout the world;

Jacques Derrida's *On Touching – Jean-Luc Nancy* is an archaeology of touch that examines its traces through European thought; Claudia Benthien's *Skin: On the Cultural Border Between Self and the World*, as the subtitle suggests, is an attempt to chart the role of the skin and touch through cultural and artistic artefacts, from its place in language to its manifestation in avant-garde art and more populist forms of self expression like piercing and tattooing and Steven Connor's *The Book of Skin* charts similar territory but concerns itself with different aspects of the experience of having a skin – its colour, its smell, its removal (with respect to flaying), and so on.[3]

Touch and the skin has also, as we shall look at during this chapter, been used in film theory: Laura Marks' two books *The Skin of the Film* and *Touch*, as the titles suggest, examine in detail the importance the skin and touch have in the process of understanding films and other visual media. Tarja Lane's article for the *New Review of Film and Television Studies*, 'Cinema as Second Skin', looks at the role of skin as a perceptual ground with reference to the films *Silence of the Lambs* (1991) and *The Ring* (1998) and Vivian Sobchack's essay 'What My Fingers Knew' paints, in evocative detail, the experience of her skin and fingers when presented with images from the opening of the film *The Piano* (1993). There is already a reasonable history, then, of what we could think of as tactile film theory that serves to undercut the primacy of sight and provide in-roads into the postmodern scopic regime.

One of the difficulties touch and skin present when dealing with our notions of embodied film theory is that the classifications of theories that assume touch to be an index of the film and theories that assume it to be a means of perception are difficult to discern, not through any lack of clarity on the part of the theories themselves but through skin's liminal character. If the hairs on one's arm stand up because of the cold – is that the skin responding to temperature or perceiving it? If my skin crawls because I see a nest of rats scurrying over a victim on screen – is that my body reacting to sight or is it the way I interpret sight? The dividing line is not clear. Touch is also the sense upon which all others are based, hearing is nothing more than the feel of hairs on sensitive membranes, sight nothing more than ideated light waves acting upon nerves, taste, the passing of food over certain areas of the mouth and lips and smell, the touching of minute chemical particles on receptive areas of the nasal passages. The skin provides the physical material for all sensual organs, as Montague details:

> The whole body is covered by skin. Even the transparent cornea of the eye is overlain by a layer of modified skin. The skin turns inward to line the orifices such as the mouth, nostrils, and anal canal. In the

evolution of the senses the sense of touch was undoubtedly the first to come into being. Touch is the parent of our eyes, ears, nose and mouth.[4]

Touch tells us not only about texture but about temperature, weight, density, distance, sharpness, physical make up, and so on. In this it orientates us totally in the world.

Strangers and Stranglers: The Art of Murder
There are two important kinds of murder in Hitchcock: the faraway and sudden and the close and tortuous. Each of these represents a different sensual experience for the viewer and each also, as we shall see, makes use of a different scopic register. The faraway and sudden, such as the shootings in *The Man Who Knew Too Much* (1934), are clean, precise and serve mainly as a narrative event – the removed nature of the crime mirroring the experience of the audience member who perceives events from a distance, both scopically and emotionally. In *Sabotage*, the killing of Stevie is infamously quick and clinical, the audience does not have the time to become fully physically embroiled into the action, so much so that we are kept outside of the bus at some distance when the moment of death actually occurs, all we are presented with are its contingent effects (the smoke, the noise, the violence). Despite Hitchcock famously admitting his mistake in killing Stevie (the boy's death is made little of), we are asked to feel none of his pain, very little of his physical presence; instead it is intended, to a great extent, as a narratological device, propelling the film from the second to the third act.

At the end of *The Lady Vanishes* (1938), the shootout produces bodies but no corpses, we are kept from the reality of death by distance and by weaponry – the gun allowing us to remove ourselves from the actuality of death, and when it does occur it is quick, clean and (for the audience member at least) painless. It is difficult, for instance, to feel a connection to those shot from a distance in siege of the original *The Man Who Knew Too Much*; their bodies are merely falling objects that hardly affect us at all; they cease to become conduits for embodied sensual involvement and exist instead as signs of some narrative element (the need for the hero to win through, the need to resolve the moral tension and so on).

The killing of Mr Caypor in *Secret Agent* (1936) is perhaps an exemplar of the first kind of Hitchcock murder. Lured to the top of the Langenthal Alps by The General, Caypor is pushed off to his death, setting the narrative in motion and allowing us valuable insight into the character of The General. What makes the scene interesting is that we are presented with the details of the murder through an optical (and we could suggest meta-cinematic device) – a telescope – which removes the viewer from the scene both in terms of embodied involvement and, ultimately, empathetic mimesis but allows us visual access into the diegesis. As Murray Pomerance suggests:

> …we can esteem the compositional use of depth of field and lens in the mountain murder of *Secret Agent* – the regard for lenses and settings, for the distance as the proximal, for the enormous contained in the momentary, smacks of Mahlerian orchestration. And, always, Hitchcock's twisting, provocative, often hilarious, yet always sensitive thought is like Wittgenstein's.[5]

The close and tortuous murders in Hitchcock, however, promote an altogether different sense for the viewer: the attack on L. B. Jeffries in *Rear Window*, the strangulation of Brenda Blaney in *Frenzy*, the garrotting of David Kentley in *Rope*, the killing of Verloc in *Sabotage*, the shooting of Juanita de Cordoba in *Topaz* (1969), and, perhaps the best example of all, the killing of Gromek in *Torn Curtain*, all attest to the ugliness, the slowness and the sheer difficulty of death at close quarters, as the audience is made to feel some of the pain of death and some of the physical exertion of killing in equal measure. The sense of killing here becomes something more than visual; the distance created by the usual processes of cinema is broken down and proximity is engendered. The images become tempered with a haptic quality that relies (as we have suggested in earlier chapters) on smell and taste but also on touch, on closeness.

Robin Wood discussing the killing of Gromek states:

> At the moment when we learn the truth, our whole relationship to the film changes, we seize gratefully on Michael as a hero; here is someone we can completely identify with. It is this involvement with a character, hence with a course of action, that makes the killing of Gromek the most disturbing murder in the whole of Hitchcock. The murder of Marion Crane shocked us, certainly; but at least we were taken by surprise, and had never *wanted* it. But here, as soon as Gromek reveals his presence, we say 'He will have to be killed'…we are implicated, we are killing Gromek – and Hitchcock spares us no discomfort for our complicity.[6]

Wood, unknowingly perhaps, points to exactly what we have been highlighting here: that the role of touch and proximity is, firstly, knitting the audience into the mimetic processes of the film and, secondly, through this engendering some form of physical discomfort (touch as both a means of perceptual reception and as an index of response). Taken as an increasingly proximal process of sensual involvement, the murders of Caypor, Marion Crane and Gromek – the distance, the middle distant (with knife not hand) and the close (with hand) – represent a shifting use of the senses, where a purely optical vision gives way to one imbued with haptic and tactile qualities. Whereas the optical experience facilitates removed contemplation of the visual experience, the tactile register provides an altogether more embodied site of reception.

We see this division of optic and haptic in the work of, among others, Alois Riegl, Wilhelm Worringer, Adolf von Hildebrand and, of course, Walter Benjamin. In his essay 'The Work of Art in the Age of Mechanical Reproduction', Benjamin alludes to the kinds of scopic regime changes we have been discussing in this book; he states for instance that: 'Just as the entire mode of existence of human collectives change over long historical periods, so too does their mode of perception.'[7]

The changing mode of perception, for Benjamin was linked inherently to the destruction of the aura, a destruction that was linked with the desire for images that presented themselves ever closer, as Margaret Iverson states in her book on Riegl:

> In Benjamin's celebrated essay 'The Work of Art in the Age of Mechanical Reproduction' (first published 1936), he gave a highly original inflection to the categories of haptic and optic perception. His well-known observation of the decay of the aura surrounding works of art in modern times announces a new mode of perception or a new way of appropriating the objects of sense that seeks to overcome distance. He noted the desire of the contemporary masses to bring things 'closer' spatially and humanly.[8]

Here we see, in theory, the point that we have highlighted in Hitchcock: the notion that to bring something closer, to make it proximal, inevitably challenges the removed contemplation of the optic-cognitive processes; little wonder that, for Benjamin at least, the rise of arts such as cinema meant a challenge to the usual processes of vision – of seeing and being seen. Bringing things closer spatially inevitably entails utilising other senses and the memories that arise from them; in the murder of Gromek for instance, as Wood correctly identifies, the removed Kantian observer has been completely engulfed by what Bernard Berenson called 'tactile values', the relating of visual images to the knowledge and experience of the flesh and the skin; this in turn undercuts the usual processes by which we are knitted into an empathetic narrative as we ourselves recognise some of the physicality and tactility of a murder. As I have suggested, this is in stark contrast to the quick and clean assassinations of some of Hitchcock's murders, something that Hitchcock highlighted in an interview with the American Film Institute:

> Barroom brawls in Westerns are always a bore for me, because one man hits the other, the table collapses and he falls back over the bar. If they would only do a few big close ups here and there, it would be much more exciting, instead of looking at it from a distance.[9]

Tactile Values and Haptic Vision

There is a theoretical link between nineteenth and early twentieth-century art critics such as Alois Riegl, Adolf van Hildebrand, and Bernard Berenson, and recent works by film theorists such as Laura Marks and Vivian Sobchack. In each, vision exists not only as a method of delineating shape, colour, light, and spatial relationships but, twinned with touch, in discerning texture, movement, three dimensional form and even kinetic energy. In such theory, vision is not so much undercut as expanded upon; the chief demarcation occurs not between sight and the other senses but between pure optics and a sight imbued with elements of other sensual knowledge, mainly touch. The introduction of the tactile into the visual arguably brings into question two of the major cornerstones of Western biological reasoning: the autonomy of the senses and the Cartesian duality. When the brain's perceptive faculties are inextricably linked to the body and its feelings we have to rethink the categories of thought, perception and sensation.

Two of Bernard Berenson's major works, *Aesthetics and History* and *The Florentine Painters of the Renaissance*, deal extensively with the concepts of tactile values and ideated sensations.[10] The picture Berenson paints of the ontogenetic evolution of the visual sense is surprisingly postmodern for a text written in the last throes of the nineteenth century (*The Florentine Painters of the Renaissance* was originally published in 1896):

> Psychology has ascertained that sight alone gives us no accurate sense of the third dimension. In our infancy, long before we are conscious of the process, the sense of touch, helped on by muscular sensations of movement, teaches us to appreciate depth, the third dimension, both in objects and in space.

> In the same unconscious years we learn to make of touch, of the third dimension, the test of reality. The child is still dimly aware of the intimate connection between touch and the third dimension. He cannot persuade himself of the unreality of Looking-Glass Land until he has touched the back of the mirror.[11]

Here we see Berenson pre-empting the Lacanian figure of the child gazing into the mirror, caught in some pre-mature reverie and fascinated by the visual. However, rather than entry into the symbolic register, for Berenson it belies a more tactile, physical realm. We cannot, he suggests, divorce our visual understanding of images from our phenomenological experience of the depth, the roundness, the texture and the touch of the world – a world that provides both ground and source for vision. However, Berenson goes further than this, for him, it is precisely the experience of three dimensions that distinguishes art from the symbol. The symbol, must be interpreted, it is flat, not of this world, but the art work must resonate with the worldness of an object, it must present not only form and line but properties that transcend the usual sensible objects of vision, as he says in *Aesthetics and History*:

> Tactile values occur in representations of solid objects when communicated, not as mere reproductions (no matter how veracious), but in a way that stirs the imagination to feel their bulk, heft their weight, realise their potential resistance, span their distance from us, and encourage us, always imaginatively, to come into close touch with, to grasp, to embrace, or to walk around them.[12]

Could such an idea be used to understand our reactions to certain images in film? Despite the camera's indexical nature, could lighting, *mise-en-scéne*, special effects and post-production be seen as a way of elevating certain cinematic images above that of 'mere reproduction' and would the key to understanding this be based, not in sight, but in touch? In Hitchcock, we could think of such scenes as the close up of the glass of milk in *Suspicion*, the money in *Psycho*, the knife in *Blackmail*, the body in *The Trouble with Harry*, the many instances in *Dial M for Murder* (1954) (due to the 3D nature of the release), and others; all are examples where certain objects, certain images of objects, become separated from the chain of visual representation and demand instead a more tactile sense. Deleuze hinted at this in his notion of the *demark* but failed to fully appreciate the multi-sensual nature of the term that 'leaps out of the web' and thus reveals the world to be something other than it seemed.[13]

Sometimes, as in the end of *Psycho* as the car is pulled out of the swap, Hitchcock asks us only to witness and engage with the tactile sensuality of an image (viscosity in the case of the swamp, smoothness in the case of the sensual material in the gold dress of *To Catch a Thief*, roughness in the skin of the shrunken head in *Under Capricorn* (1949), the weight and the density of a corpse in *The Trouble with Harry* and so on). Critics have attempted to attach symbolic values to such images (William Rothman for instance and his assertions of the primeval swamp out of which Marion Crane is born), but, by and large, these seem strained and secondary to what it is primarily an invitation to share in a sensual tactile experience, something that, as we have seen, was considered by Berenson, to be *the* distinctive character of an art work.

Laura Marks traces the term 'haptic' vision and its specific manifestation back to Alois Riegl and his work on Egyptian and Roman art. This term was also taken up by Deleuze and Guattari in their work *A Thousand Plateaus* where they link it to the perceptual processes associated with nomadic art – carpet making, metal working, small items of portable sculpture – where the link between what the eye sees and how the hand feels is not completely severed as it is with most western notions of seeing. For Deleuze and Guattari, haptic vision challenges the distinct boundary between object and subject, providing new avenues of visuality and links between how we see and how we feel.

Laura Marks uses the notion of haptic vision in a very specific sense. For her, the term refers to the portion of sight that is given over, not to the determination of specific images, but to the appreciation of texture, of surficity and of movement. Haptics here relate the sense of sight to the rest of the sensorium; in order to understand what we have seen we must evoke in ourselves the physical sensation of touching or feeling. As she says in her book *Touch: Sensuous Theory and Multisensory Media*:

> Haptic vision appeals to a viewer who perceives with all the senses. It involves thinking with your skin, or giving as much significance to the physical presence of an other as to the mental operations of symbolisation.[14]

Haptic vision invites the eye to pass over the image without the need to interrogate it or to determine specifics. Imagine looking upon the ocean or into a blazing fire; our eyes here shed some of their normal use value and instead take on the role of fingers, exploring shapes and surfaces. The experience of such perception is indeterminately sensual, offering a vague sensation rather than specific information. It is also, asserts Marks, more synaesthetic than optical vision, connecting sight with our other senses such as touch in a form that elides conscious evaluation. Haptic images in the cinema are to be experienced rather than analysed.

Haptic vision very often goes hand in hand with optical perception. Many filmmakers play with the borders of these two ways of seeing. In Fassbinder's *The Bitter Tears of Petra Von Kant* (1972), for instance, the opening shot allows the camera to linger over the opulence of the fur rug in the lead character's bedroom. Our eyes take on the role of hands as the camera examines the soft furnishings and we are asked merely to understand what this means sensually rather than examine it semiotically. However, like many directors, Fassbinder quickly twins this with a close-up of a face so that the optical nature of the eye – its role as an interrogator – is restored.

Haptic images need not be tied to the director's original purpose; Marks points to the haptic nature of certain grainy images in experimental films such as those recorded on pixelvision cameras, a technology that recorded images on audio tape and so produced highly pixelated results. This notion extends, she asserts, into the degradation of film and video through time; as the clarity of the images decay, so optical interrogation becomes less important. In Hitchcock's early films such as *The Pleasure Garden*, *Number 17* (1932) and *Champagne* the washed out crackle of the images becomes as much an experience of the film as the narrative, our eyes become less a means to interrogate the specificity of the images and more like fingers, feeling the grain of the film. In an era of high definition digital image reproduction, the haptic quality of early celluloid film is likely to be interrogated more rather than less as we become more sensitive to image decay; the viewing experience of early Hitchcock is inextricably bound up with that which we cannot see and with the sense that, in the cinema, the eye is denied as much as it is pandered to, as Marks states:

> The main sources of haptic visuality in video include the constitution of the image from a signal, video's low contrast ratio, the possibilities of electronic and digital manipulation, and video decay.[15]

The haptic experience of the materiality of film is a constantly changing one that varies from person to person and from reproduction to reproduction. The aura of originality may indeed be missing in the production of film but the patina of age certainly makes itself felt on the slowly degrading picture something that, as Marks suggests, interrupts our optic relationship to it.

Cinesthesia

As well manifesting itself in haptic vision, the importance of touch in the cinema extends into the area of synaesthetic reception. As we saw in the chapter dedicated to neuroscience, recent thinking on how the brain works (and by extension its neurological processes) has begun to challenge the fundamentally frameworks neuroscience has, to a very large extent, often relied upon. Not only is there a physical continuum between the brain and the body (the brainstem reaching far down into the body's core through the spinal column), but, as writers such as Antonio Damasio have demonstrated, the concept of 'feeling', of bodily emotion is inextricably connected to that of thinking – the body thinks every bit as much as the brain. As we also saw, recent theories regarding synaesthesia, most notably from neuroscientist Richard Cytowic, have suggested that, on a limbic level far below the level of consciousness, we all process sensual information in the same way: synaesthetically, only then to compartmentalise different sensual information through recourse to autonomous perceptions. Consciousness, in other words, is nothing more than a sensual filter.

Vivian Sobchack uses this as a basis with which to talk about the experience of cinema in her essay 'What my Fingers Knew' (see Chapter 1 for a fuller discussion). In this essay, touch and tactile information (mainly of the rain and the wind in the opening scenes of *The Piano*) become the main sensual focus rather than sight and hearing. Her term 'cinesthesia' is a useful one not only because it combines the notion of cinema spectatorship with notions such as synaesthesia but because it also suggests paying attention to the more sub-cognitive processes in film spectatorship, what we could think of as the limbic experience but what we have also characterised many times throughout this thesis as the body's experience. For Sobchack, the 'feeling' she receives from a film like *The Piano*, however vague is an important element of the filmic experience, every bit as important as the sense of character, narrative or *mise-en-scene*, as she states:

> A phenomenology of the cinesthetic subject having and making sense of the movies reveals to us the chiasmatic function of the lived body as both carnal and conscious, sensible and sentient – and how it is we can apprehend the sense of the screen both figuratively and literally. That is, the lived body transparently provides the primary chiasmatic premises that connect and unite the senses as both carnally conscious and meaningful…[16]

The cinesthetic subject then is one who is inextricably linked to the images on screen, not through empathy or identification but through lived sensual experience.

Sobchack's description of the opening scenes of *The Piano* match distinctly the opening of Hitchcock's *Jamaica Inn* (1939), a film that has been criticised as being un-Hitchcockian, mainly, we could assert, because of its subject matter and the construction of its plot. Raymond Durgnat classified it as little more than a potboiler, Graham Greene called it a 'bogus costume piece'[17] and even Hitchcock himself was apologetic about the film when speaking to Truffaut. *Jamaica Inn* has often been seen as film swiftly constructed before the director went on to Hollywood and better things. The film, although flawed narratologically and in terms of its casting, is an ideal example of the importance of the 'feel' of a film. The opening shots of the storming ocean followed by the desolation of the windy moor, are major sensual tropes that underline the isolation of the central figures. Coldness and wetness are the opening figures in a drama that will depend, for its effectiveness, on a pervading sense of moral and existential detachment, a sense that is echoed in *The Piano*.

As Sobchack details, this is much more than the use of certain images to suggest an atmosphere. 'Feeling' in a film like *Jamaica Inn* relates both to the general sense of the images and the way that we understand those images, our skin has knowledge of wetness and coldness and it is this information we draw on to understand such images; it is the body's knowledge that grasps what Merleau-Ponty calls 'the unity of an object'. Merleau-Ponty describes the relationship between lived sensible information and synaesthesia:

> The senses intercommunicate by opening on to the structure of the thing. One sees the hardness and brittleness of glass, and when, with a tinkling sound, it breaks, the sound is conveyed by the visible glass… In the same way I hear the hardness and unevenness of cobbles in the rattle of a carriage, and we speak appropriately of a 'soft', 'dull' or 'sharp' sound.[18]

It is precisely this intercommunication between the senses that, I would suggest, underlines some of the appeal of a film such as *Jamaica Inn* that proved to be hugely popular despite still being fatally flawed. *Jamaica Inn* is as much about the skin and touch, as it is about the eyes and the mind and in this it is highly successful, as the many cinemagoers that saw it upon its release testified to. Viewing a film as a material experience as well as a cognitive one expands its critical possibilities as well as allowing us to understand the popularity of some films that do not meet with critical approval. Narrative film may offer visual pleasure but it also offers corporeal pleasure as many of the theorists in this thesis have suggested.

The Kiss, Closeness and Caress
The screen kiss has a long history. The first instance of it is generally thought to be the Edison short *The Irwin-Rice Kiss* produced in 1896 and even at this early stage cinema's ability to capture the erotic was clearly in evidence. The physical closeness of May Irwin and John Rice is the first thing one notices about watching the film, as they bill and coo in a way that underlines their bawdy sexuality; what we are presented with is not so much a kiss (although this does occur to some extent towards the end of the film) but a series of nibbles, touches, silent mouth movements and caresses that can mean nothing other than a seduction and capitulation – although we are never quite sure who is doing which.

We can view the screen kiss in Deleuzian terms: as well as the sonsign, Deleuze mentions in *Cinema 2: The Time-image*, the *tactisign*, the 'pure sensory image' that is based not in sight but in touch. For Deleuze, the tactisign especially, constituted both the ending of the sensori-motor structure of the movement-image and the formation of a new regime: the time-image. It is the affective power of touch that signals the failure of the traditional aesthetic and ontological linkage of classical Hollywood cinema, the point at which the action-image breaks down and falls apart. Even in the most action-based of Hollywood films, the kiss is seldom considered to be a moment of narrative or character development; hardly ever can it be read in terms of the sensori-motor schema of the movement-image. Mostly it is an invitation to revel in the sensuality of closeness, to feel (in Deleuze's Bergsonian terms) the duration of time and the sensation of the skin.

Nowhere is this point more obvious than in *Notorious*, a film that contains three main kissing scenes, the most tender of which occurs in the middle of the film, as Devlin and Alicia talk on the balcony. Unlike the later kiss between the two in Sebastian's wine cellar (which is arguably designed to propel the narrative), this scene is a brief sensual respite in what is a fraught narrative. Commensurate with the time-image and its reflection of duration, the scene is shot in one continuous take that only comes to a close as Devlin exits the room. Whereas the scene does have certain narratological functions (highlighting the relationship between Devlin and Alicia, the building of tension and so on) the camera's closeness belies the intentions of Hitchcock to stress the sheer physicality of the two performers and to engage the audience in the tactile sensation, the tactisign, which is their lovemaking.

One other aspect of Deleuze's tactisign that has relevance to the screen kiss is his insistence that it is a 'pure sensory image'; that it somehow occurs below the levels of conscious cinematic involvement and exists instead on some deeper, more corporeal realm. Identification in scenes such as those from *Notorious* need not, we could suggest, be limited to the gender one belongs to or the sexuality one chooses; in the Irwin-Rice Kiss we need not identify along gender lines to feel the scratchiness of John Rice's moustaches upon our skin; as Deleuze suggests, the tactile sensation becomes detached from the subjective and becomes a pure feeling – an image of touch. The kiss in Hitchcock, when it is the product of true feeling, is always an invitation to feel closeness rather than arousal despite his leading ladies often presenting a highly sexualised persona.

As Tarja Laine suggests, the skin in film 'structures our perception beyond the outside/inside division, locating us as touching and being touched in the cinematic experience'. [19] As our skin registers its understanding of the closeness that we witness on screen, as the hairs on our bodies react to the sensual memory of touch, we are literally re-touched by the film, the site of reception extending all over our bodies creating a carnal understanding that, as Sobchack claims, can sometimes occur before the eyes can even discern an image:

> As cinesthetic subjects…we possess an embodied intelligence that opens our eyes far beyond their discrete capacity for vision, opens the film far beyond its visible containment by the screen, and opens language to a reflective knowledge of its carnal origins and limits.[20]

A consideration of touch in the filmic experience not only erases the division between inside and outside, but between the spectator and the film; we simultaneously touch and are touched by cinema as we make use of our sensual memories to flesh out the meanings behind images. As Ashley Montague states, 'touch is the basis of sociality; it is the primary method of connecting to the world; those suffering from autism or schizophrenia find it difficult to allow others to get close to them and such conditions are often thought to stem, in part at least, from tactile neglect in early childhood'.[21]

Our ability to empathise, to understand another's feelings, character and motivations, to engage with another's reality is inextricably linked to our knowledge of our own skin.

Rear Window – The Distant and the Close

Rear Window has always been regarded as being concerned with metafictional discourse and with scopic interrogation; moreover, Hitchcock's own assertion that it is his most cinematic work has often been interpreted (only partly correctly I will suggest here) as meaning that it deals with the inextricable links between these two. Stefan Sharff's *The Art of Looking in Hitchcock's Rear Window* is an exemplar of the kind of cinema theory that has been devoted to it since Jean Douchet's *Hitch and his Public,* the work that first noticed the importance of visuality (of seeing and being seen) in Hitchcock's work in general, but especially in *Rear Window*.[22] Sharff's book is a scene-by-scene examination of how characters in *Rear Window* exchange glances and gazes and how this sutures the viewer into the diegesis, as he says:

> The epicentre of the film is the notion of looking, observing and seeing across from the gazer, across from someone, 'across…' The window of protagonist L. B. Jeffries (James Stewart) is across from the other windows around the inner courtyard…Jeffries is the principal 'seer', while we (the viewers) see him seeing – as well as what he sees.[23]

Sharff is indeed correct in his assertions: *Rear Window* is undeniably concerned with the 'art of looking', but, as we have seen, in more recent years, the art of looking itself has become a contested field; no longer the simple act we once though it was. The canonical point that Jeffries represents some form of pure scopic voyeur because of his lack of mobility is diluted when we consider the synaesthetic nature of vision under the postmodern scopic regime. Unlike many critics' assertions, Jeffries' inability to walk does not preclude him from using his body as a site of reception or an index of response, in exactly the same way as the viewer in the cinema seat.[24] In fact, as we shall see, this is exactly what, I will argue, the film is concerned with.

In this sense, I would agree with most critics that *Rear Window* is metafictional and that it deals with cinematic processes. However, I would disagree that it is thus solely concerned with vision and looking. Due to its metafictional nature, the reading that follows not only discusses the relationship the viewer has with the images on screen (as most of the readings in this book have done) but segues also into the area of textual and symbolic criticism, taking Jeffries as symbolic of the cinema viewer and showing how, in this film more than any other, Hitchcock combines empathy and identification with mimesis and embodied affect.

Rear Window's relationship to looking is complex and multi-faceted; it is not a simple case of stating that it either does or does not deal primarily with vision. As Durgnat[25] details, contained within the celebration of looking in the film is a critique of it; often the denouement of the film has been interpreted as a form of divine punishment for sins transgressed: Thorwald becomes a form of avenging angel for all those who have been spied upon by Jeffries and Jeffries himself, in the final scenes, has become a castigated and castrated shadow of his former self – symbolically facing away from the window with his eyes closed. In these scenes, it is Lisa who retains her true self despite outward appearances (although, as Modleski has asserted, *Rear Window* has a difficult relationship with gender).

One of the clearest examples of critical work that deals with this complex paradox is Robert Stam and Roberta Pearson's essay 'Hitchcock's *Rear Window*: Reflexivity and the Critique of Voyeurism' first published in 1983. Stam and Pearson set out their own aims as:

> [examining] *Rear Window* not only as a reflexive film-about-film but also as multitrack inquiry concerning the cinematic apparatus, the positioning of the spectator in that apparatus, and the sexual, moral, and even political implications of that positioning.[26]

It will be immediately apparent from this that Stam and Pearson's approach heralds mainly from a fairly established area of film studies: the apparatus theory of Baudry, Metz and Comolli. Stam and Pearson assume *Rear Window* to be a film essentially concerned with seeing and visuality; but what makes their essay useful to us here is their observation that it not only critiques vision but does so through manipulation of its audience as well as through its narrative – the apparatus itself has become both the object and the subject of enunciation, as they state:

> The critique of voyeurism in *Rear Window* is not elaborated only through narrative structure and thematic motifs; it is realised through the manipulation of the precise code most relevant to that critique – the code of point of view. And this manipulation is far more rigorous and subtle than most critics have acknowledged.[27]

By highlighting the voyeuristic aspects of the apparatus (at one point for instance Jeffries makes the point that his own voyeurism is legitimized because others have the right to view him if they wish), Hitchcock makes the process of viewing commensurate with that which is being viewed. Stam and Pearson conclude with the fundamental point that has formed the basis of this book:

Rear Window poses the question that so preoccupies contemporary film theory and analysis: the question of the place of the desiring subject within the cinematic apparatus. This theory and analysis shifts interest from the question, 'What does the text mean?' to 'What do we want from the text?' 'What is it you want from me?. . . Tell me what you want!' Thorwald says to Jeffries, and his question, ostensibly addressed to the protagonist, might as well have been addressed to us.[28]

This stance, however interesting and useful to us here, ignores the fundamental point of film theory of the postmodern scopic regime and the limbic processes that form its base. Using such theory we can add another dimension to Stam and Pearson's litany of questions: embodied film theory also asks, 'What does the film do *to* us?' and 'How do we receive it?' When we have expanded the receptive processes of cinema, the way we perceive filmic images becomes as much a question for critical debate as what they might mean or how they might be constructed. In other words: our body's experience becomes a form of knowledge not hitherto considered.

Viewed as a series of embodied encounters (on the part of the both Jeffries and the audience), we can see that the perceptual trope at the heart of *Rear Window* is one of closeness and distance and of the ever decreasing gap between the two. As we have already stated, like the cinema viewer, Jeffries is forced to use his body as a site of reception and an index of that which he sees. As he looks around the courtyard at the apartments opposite, he uses his sense of hearing (music, voices, the sound of the morning alarm and so on), his sense of taste (the food of Miss Lonelyhearts, the breakfast of Miss Torso), his sense of smell (the flowers of Thorwald and the smell of the hot bodies) and his sense of touch (the weight of the newly wed bride as she is carried over the threshold, the weight of the newly killed wife as she is carried away in the suitcase bound for all parts of the city). Jeffries draws upon his body's knowledge in order to understand what is going on around him; he not only sees, he experiences, transitivistically.

We can clearly see him using his body as an index of that which he sees in the scenes in which Lisa crosses over to Thorwald's apartment. He ceases being the removed observer of traditional criticism as his body is made to sweat, his heart is made to beat, his skin is made to crawl and his muscles made to constrict in excitement and terror at what might be about to happen. In these scenes in particular, Jeffries is anything but a passive voyeur, he is very much an active and embodied participant, negotiating bodily meaning with what he sees in front of him, adding his own corporeal knowledge to the images he witnesses and drawing upon the reactions they cause to understand their importance. Of course, through the processes of metafiction, the audience is going through exactly the same experience. Stam and Pearson are right then: Hitchcock indeed uses the apparatus to reflect the narrative, however, we can only understand this properly if we view cinema as a fully embodied medium, if we attribute to it something other than *visual* pleasure.

Throughout the course of the film the distant slowly becomes the near, as Thorwald gradually pollutes the safety of Jeffries' apartment with a wholly embodied presence. For the viewer, I would suggest, these scenes represent a shift in sensual perception; as Thorwald enters the apartment, vision is first partially and then completely and deliberately obscured, as the two characters (Thorwald and Jeffries) are presented to us in almost complete darkness and then, through the use of the camera flash, we are blinded, like Thorwald himself. What gives this scene its sense of menace, I would argue, is the increasing closeness of the two characters, something that obviously is based in touch, closeness and tacility rather than the removed distance of vision. It is one to thing to have realised Thorwald returns Jeffries'/our gaze in the earlier scenes, another when that gaze becomes powerless through proximity.

The image we have in these final scenes is not only one of touch but of engulfment, perhaps even what Clare Bishop, in her work on installation art calls 'mimetic darkness'. As the light of the screen dims, Thorwald, Jeffries, and the audience are plunged into the kind of darkness that, as Bishop states, very rarely occurs in the twenty-first century:

> Few of us have not lain in bed at night and felt ourselves slipping out of consciousness, our bodies enveloped in darkness as if by a soft black cloud. Yet in an age of pervasive electrical illumination we rarely experience darkness as a completely engulfing entity. Even at night, streetlamps and car headlights slip through chinks in the curtain to offer limited availability. Stepping into a pitch black installation may be one of the few times we experience total consuming darkness.[29]

We experience such moments in the cinema also, in screen blackouts and before the house lights are brought up. Darkness, on these occasions, becomes a tactile experience, not only in that we can no longer see, but in the sense that it seems to spread itself around us, to become a presence in itself. Darkness, in these moments, becomes engulfing and it is some of this sense that Hitchcock elicits in the final scenes of *Rear Window*. The language of such moments attests to the physicality of darkness and light – one is plunged, immersed, overcome and sometimes enveloped in darkness, in the same way that one is bathed, showered and struck by light.

The narrative of *Rear Window*, as Stam and Pearson suggest, is mirrored in its form and the relationship the spectator has with the screen. Each element traces the trajectory of Thorwald as he comes closer and closer to Jeffries in a journey that ends in physical engulfment. Jeffries' fear of such engulfment is attested to early on the film when Lisa is filmed looming over him. We experience a mimetic engulfment brought about by the almost total dimming of the lights in both of scenes, the darkness enfolding us and robbing us of our vision. *Rear Window* can be read as exposing the constant tension between closeness and distance; it is, as the many critics cited here state, about vision, but vision as it is related to distance and the ways in which modern man (man especially) relies on this relationship. Closeness, as Jeffries finds out, means a loss of control, a loss of self and a loss of that cool criticality that exemplifies the modern subject.

In the concluding scenes, sound is used in a haptic way to suggest the ever-increasing closeness of Thorwald. As Jeffries sits helpless in his wheelchair, he turns his head and hears the banging of his neighbour as he comes up the stairs. Again, vision has been removed here (the door to the apartment is closed), but we are still aware of what is at stake in the narrative – the engulfing presence of Thorwald. In a touch that echoes many a horror film, we hear steps outside the door getting closer and closer and Jeffries (like the audience) gets more and more agitated. We are making use of two main senses here, I would suggest, sound obviously, but also touch (the weight of the Thorwald on the stairs for instance, and the anxiety that such closeness brings). What is crucial to an understanding of embodied film theory is that sight is not relied upon; all through this scene, we can only see Jeffries' face, the rest of the apartment being blacked out through dim lightening. Far from representing a film about the importance of sight, *Rear Window* could also be seen as a film about the paucity of sight, as Hitchcock time and time again, removes it from us, asking us to fill in the blanks with our other senses.

Rear Window, then, I would assert *is* a metafictional film but in a far more complex way than had been hitherto explored. This arises perhaps not from any redefinition of the film itself but in changing notions of what cinema is. The film works as a statement on visual cinema but also as an exploration of how we receive such images when vision is denied to us, when blackness means we can no longer interact with the sight of the film, when we have to appreciate its taste, its smell but most of all its touch.

§

Like Derrida's exposition of the importance of touch in Western ontology, cinema highlights the impossibility of separating the tactile from the visual. Hitchcock manipulates his audience's understanding of space by playing with images of distance and images of proximity and with the interchange between light and darkness. We use our bodies as an index of the film's images, we feel our flesh respond when we see two bodies drawing near to each other because we know intrinsically the touch of another's skin on our own and we feel some of the wetness and heat of a face (like Jeffries') sweating in the hot morning sun because our own body has sweated. In films such as *Sabotage*, *The Birds*, or *Frenzy*, we recognise the sting of pain because our own bodies have suffered and in films such as *Notorious* or *Torn Curtain* we recognise the joy of pleasure because we too have kissed. Those of us without such experience or those of us whose experience does not equate to the levels shown on screen may not know the index of the film to its fullest extent but, through a constant process of transitivistic negotiation, we constantly offer up our own sensual memory to fill in the gaps left by the paucity of vision.

CONCLUSION

This book began as an experiment of sorts and has grown into what I see as offering a distinct perspective. Although, as has been stated many times, I do not envisage embodied film theory (or film theory of the postmodern scopic regime) as being a replacement for more traditional theories of spectatorship, such as the processes inherent within empathy, identification, screen art, and so on, I do see it as offering a valid addition to the tools we utilise to study that most complex and delicate of relationships: the screen and the viewer.

It was important that the postmodern scopic regime was examined as a far reaching and cross-discipline notion and this, inevitably, meant studying academic areas outside of the humanities such as neuroscience and biology. My intention in doing this was not to claim that film theory should be looked at with a scientific method (I leave that to theorists such as Barry Salt whose book *Film Style and Technology* utilises certain statistical analysis), but instead to suggest that there is an inherent cross-fertilisation between all disciplines when it comes to framing and conceptualising theories of vision, and that epistemic shifts affect all manner of different discourses, even those we might assume to be universal or eternal. This was at the heart of my choice to look at discourses of the self and neuroscience in the first part of this work. Had I chosen merely to look at the various aspects of embodied film theory in the first half of this work, I feel I would have been in danger of viewing postmodern vision through the lens of cinema studies and run the risk of wrongly giving the impression that it was only applicable to this rather limited area. Postmodern scopic thinking cannot be reduced to one academic discipline; instead it traverses a whole episteme.

The choice of Hitchcock to demonstrate these ideas was also a difficult one. Given the voluminous outpouring still dedicated to his work it was with some trepidation that I undertook to explore yet another angle of his films. However, in many ways, this book is no more about Hitchcock than any other director; it is about cinematic and critical tools; it is about a scopic regime; it is about how we interpret the world and perception and it is about new directions in film theory – all of which are merely exemplified through the work of one of cinematic history's most enigmatic and influential figures. I needed a central text that everyone could recognise if I was going to suggest that embodied film theory could be applied to all films and Hitch seemed the ideal choice, and his work proved a fertile ground for these theories. Time and time again I found in his work examples of sensual knowledge that were vital to the films. Often it was like finding a new layer of experience under the dusty covers of traditional thinking.

I see the ideas presented here as a first tentative step towards establishing a method of viewing spectatorship. This is already happening in certain respects: every year since this project's inception there have been more and more books and articles being publishing on the role of the senses in film and cultural theory. However, this project represents the first attempt to bring all of these somewhat disparate studies together under one conceptual term and moreover to classify and characterise the nuances between them.

One of the most important conceptual tools to arise out of this project has been the distinction between the use of the body and its sense as an index of response and as a site of reception. This simple categorisation enables us to delineate between those theories that view the process of cinema viewing as one of bodily reaction (tears, heartbeat, gut wrenching, and so on) and those theories that view it as something more akin to synaesthesia or to multi-modal spectatorship. This distinction articulates a subtle and yet important difference in many theories that might otherwise be grouped together. Of course, as we have seen, such distinctions are never simple and are rarely exclusive but I think they do add a great deal to understanding what is often a complex and unarticulated situation.

This book has also attempted to expand the remit of embodied film theory into the area of popular film and, through this perhaps, popular culture. Endemic within this mandate was the sense that embodied film theory, to be truly useful conceptually, should not only address films that are specifically about the senses they appeal to but all films. Films like *Eat Drink Man Woman* (1994) or *Like Water for Chocolate* (1992) obviously have their basis in sensual experiences beyond the purely optical; it is no surprise then that they are often cited in studies dedicated to proximal senses in cinema. However, as this work has attempted to show, these layers of spectatorial involvement are used all the time when we watch a film, we may not be aware of them, they may not be the primary response but they are there nonetheless.

Is this not the role of the critic and film writer? To uncover the layers of understanding that might ordinarily go unnoticed? Is this not what Serge Daney, Andre Bazin, Eric Rohmer, and the other critics of the cinema attempted to achieve with their various critical endeavours based on psychoanalysis and Marxism? The critic examines a text through the lens of their experience and attempts to uncover what they see as hidden meanings, covert elements and subtextual layers. The body in cinema is no different. The only way the embodied film theoretician can approach their text is through their own corporal experience and this both enriches and problematises the process.

At many points during this book I assume a universality of experience. I assume, for instance, that most readers know what taste is, that they would find certain images nauseating, that they would find certain noises painful or that they would consider certain smells diametrically opposed. This is a problem with embodied film theory but it is no different, we could suggest, from supposing everyone's experience of sexuality is similar, that claustrophobia is always a disturbing experience or that all viewers do not want to be killed in the shower by Tony Perkins (although I am sure there are some who do!).

I have been aware throughout this book of the dangers of opposing the corporal with the political. Where I do speak of embodied film theory providing an alternative to notions like ideology it is in the sense of film understanding only. I appreciate that the body should not (and perhaps even never can) be detached from the ideology that surrounds it (gender, sexuality, race, and so on). However, I also consider such considerations to be beyond the scope of the present work; at this stage of inquiry, it is enough that feelings, senses and affects be considered tools of cinematic reception. The way that they are formed is the basis for another study.

The role of the body in film maybe relatively new to critical theory but it is intimately known to anyone who has ever sat in a cinema seat or curled up in front of a DVD. The ability of a film to disgust us, to excite us, to repel us, to make us jump, sweat, laugh so our sides ache, or clutch our ears in pain provides some its most enduring memories. It is also what characterises film as medium specific – every cinema viewer knows that their body and their senses play a major role in their experience yet critical theory has only recently realised this. Eventually, I hope embodied theory of the postmodern scopic regime will be taught alongside psychoanalysis, film language and ideology, not merely because it represents a new stance but because it comes close to interrogating the real experience of many cinemagoers and movies watchers.

At its heart this book is about the construction of a new model of spectatorship. Since the 1980s a new spectator has been slowly revealed; the layers of thinking so vital to modernity have been stripped back exposing a body and its senses. This body is both universal and intensely private; it is that which separates us from out neighbour in the cinema and that which binds us inextricably together.

NOTES

Introduction

1. Henry Miller, *A Devil in Paradise* (Berkeley, 1957), p.61.
2. Gilles Deleuze, *Cinema 1: The Movement-image*, trans. Hugh Tomlinson and Barbara Habberjam (London, 2004); Gilles Deleuze, *Cinema 2: The Time-image*, trans. Hugh Tomlinson and Robert Galeta (London, 2000); Stanley Cavell, *The World Viewed* (New Jersey, 1974).
3. See Daniel Frampton, *Filmosophy* (London, 2006); Sean Cubitt, *The Cinema Effect* (Cambridge, 2003), and so on.
4. See Stephen Mulhall's discussion of film as philosophy in Stephen Mulhall, *On Film* (London, 2008), pp.129-156.
5. See David Levin, *Modernity and the Hegemony of Vision* (Berkeley, 1993); Martin Jay, *Downcast Eyes: The Denigration of Vision in Twentieth Century French Thought* (Berkeley, 1994).
6. Guy Debord, *Society of the Spectacle*, trans. Ken Kabb (London, 1992).
7. See the discussion in Chapter 4 for a more in depth examination of these reasons.
8. Ron Burnett, *Cultures of Vision: Images, Media and the Imaginary* (Bloomington, 1995), p.37; Barbara Kennedy, *Deleuze and Cinema* (Edinburgh, 2000), p.53. Anne Friedberg, *Window Shopping: Cinema and the Postmodern* (Berkeley, 1993). Vivian Sobchack, *'What My Fingers Knew', Carnal Thoughts: Embodiment and Moving Image Culture* (Berkeley, 2004), pp.53-84.
9. Jonathan Crary, *Techniques of the Observer* (Cambridge, 1992), p.31.
10. Michel Foucault, *The Order of Things* (London, 1989), p.xxii.
11. Serge Daney, 'On Salador', trans. Unknown, 1970. <available online at http://home. earthlink. net/~steevee/Daney_salador. Html>, accessed 11 August 2009.
12. Rene Descartes, 'Optics' [1637], in *Selected Philosophical Writings*, trans. John Cottingham, Robert Stoothoff and Dugland Murdoch, (Cambridge, 1992), p.63; John Locke, *An Essay Concerning Human Understanding* [1690] (London, 1972), p.147; 'I procured me a triangular glasse Prisme to

try wherewith the celebrated phenomena of colours. And in order thereto having darkened my chamber and made a small hole in my window-shuts to let in a convenient quantity of the sun's light, I placed my Prism at its entrance that it might be thereby refracted on the opposite wall.' Issac Newton, 'A Theory Concerning Light and Colours', [1704](2008) <http://www. newtonproject. ic. ac. Uk/> accessed 11 August 2009 (URL correct at the time of writing); George Berkeley, *Theory of Vision or Visual Language Vindicated and Explained* [1733] (New York, 1963), p.144.
13. See, for instance, Edward Bradford Titchner's, *A Text Book of Psychology* (London, 1910).
14. Crary, p.73.
15. Ibid, p.88.
16. Ibid, pp.90-91.
17. Ibid, p.149.
18. Gilles Deleuze, *Foucault*, trans. S. Hand (London, 2006), p. 42.
19. Michel Foucault, *The Birth of the Clinic*, trans. A. M. Sheridan, (London, 1986), p.xii.
20. Michel Foucault, *Madness and Civilisation*, trans. Richard Howard, (London, 2004).
21. Karl Marx, *Capital*, trans. Eden and Cedar Paul (London, 1933).
22. Ibid, p.151.
23. Jacqueline Rose, *Sexuality in the Field of Vision* (London, 2005), p.227.
24. Viet Erlmann, 'But What of the Ethnographic Ear?' ed. Viet Erlmann, *Hearing Cultures* (London, 2004), p.3.
25. I am indebted here to Anna Powell and her reminder that the late nineteenth century should not be seen as devoid of counter discourses to the faith in the fixed ontological subject. Symbolist poets such as Rimbaud for example strove to destroy the self with all manner of strategies from drugs to alcohol, from meditation to poetry. For them, the subject was not so fixed; in fact, it was a drunken boat floating free. However, this is a fairly marginal contemporary view as the Symbolist poets themselves might have stressed; a consideration of these liminal discourses, that skirt paradigmatic borders, is some of the complexity that is lost when one is adopting Crary's large-scale brush strokes.
26. Judith Butler, *Gender Trouble* (London, 2006); Gilles Deleuze, *The Fold*, trans. Tom Conley (London, 2006).
27. The list of these re-presentations is almost endless but we could think of David Howes anthropological anthology *Empire of the Senses* (London, 2004); Jim Drobnick's *The Smell Culture Reader* (London, 2006); the work of Claudia Benthien, *Skin: On the Cultural Border Between Self and*

the World, trans. Thomas Dunlap, (New York, 2002), Steven Connor, *The Book of Skin* (London, 2004), and so on.
28. Juhani Pallasmaa, *The Eyes of the Skin* (London, 2008).
29. Cited Pallasmaa, p.27.
30. Ibid, p.25.
31. Juhani Pallasmaa, 'Six Themes for the Next Millennium', *The Architectural Review*, Vol. 196, July 1996.
32. Jennifer Whyte, *Virtual Reality and the Built Environment* (London, 2004).
33. Marshall McLuhan, *Understanding Media* (London, 1973), p.15.
34. W. A. Ijsselsteijn; H. de Ridder; J. Freeman and S. E. Avons, 'Presence: concept, determinants and measurement', *Proceedings of the SPIE, Human Vision and Electronic Imaging V.* San Jose, California, pp.23-28, January 2000; J. Isadale, 'What is Virtual Reality?', (1998), <http://isdale.com/jerry/VR/WhatIsVR/noframes/WhatIsVR4. 1> accessed 10 August 2009.
35. Nathaniel Durlach and Anne Mavor, 'Virtual Reality: Scientific and Technological Challenges', (1995), <http://www. nap. edu/openbook. php?isbn=0309051355>, accessed 10 August 2009 (URL correct at the time of writing).
36. Ibid, p.161.
37. Jean Baudrillard, *Simulacra and Simulation*, trans. Sheila Glaser (Flint, 1990), p.34.
38. Akira Mizuta Lippit, 'Virtual Annihilation: Optics, VR and the Discourse of Subjectivity', in *Criticism*, Vol. 36, 1994.
39. 'Nintendo Hails Wii Success', (2006), <http://news.bbc.co.uk/1/hi/business/6191260.stm> accessed 23 December 2009.
40. Eugenei Shinkle, 'Video games, emotions and the six senses', *Media, Culture and Society*, Vol. 30(6), 2008.
41. Interestingly Shinkle also basis her discussion on the 'linked domains of phenomenology and cognitive neuroscience'.
42. Stephen Griffin, 'Push. Play: An Examination of the Game Play Button' delivered at the *DiGRA Conference: Changing Views – Worlds in Play*, 2005.
43. Ernest Adams, 'The Designer's Notebook: PS3 Versus Wii – The Designer's Perspective', (2009) http://www. gamasutra. com/view/feature/1753/the_designers_notebook_ps3_. Php, accessed 23 December 2009 (URL correct at the time of writing).
44. See Jeffrey Geiger, *Facing the Pacific: Polynesia and the U. S. Imperial Imagination* (Honolulu, 2007); See Yvonne Tasker, *Spectacular Bodies: Gender,*

Genre and the Action Cinema (London, 1993).

1: Film Theory and Embodiment

1. Thomas Elsaesser, '"Where were you, when…" or "I phone, therefore I am"' (2002) <http://home. hum. uva. nl/oz/elsaesser/>, accessed 24 December 2009.
2. At the time of writing works such as Barker's *The Tactile Eye; Touch and the Cinematic Experience* (Berkeley, 2009) are still being published.
3. Karin Littau, 'Eye-hunger: physical pleasure and non-narrative cinema'. *Crash Cultures: Modernity, Mediation and the Material*. Ed. Arthurs Jane and Grant, Iain. Bristol: Intellect, 2002: 35-52; Linda Williams, 'Corporealized Observers', *Fugitive Images: From Photography to Video* ed. Patrice Petro (Bloomington, 1995); Karin Littau, 'Eye-hunger: Physical Pleasure and Non-narrative Cinema' in Jane Arthurs and Iain Grant (eds) *Crash Cultures: Modernity, Mediation and the Material*, (Bristol, 2002).
4. David MacDougall, *The Corporeal Image: Film, Ethnography, and the Senses* (Princeton and Oxford, 2006), p. 25.
5. See Sobchack 'What My Fingers Knew.'
6. See Robert Lapsley and Michael Westlake, *Film Theory: An Introduction* (Manchester, 1988)
7. Andre Bazin, 'The Evolution of the Photographic Image' trans. Hugh Gray, *What is Cinema? Volume 1* (Berkeley, 1967), pp. 6-16.
8. Boorstin, p.110.
9. Linda Williams, *Hard Core* (London, 1990), p.5
10. Dziga Vertov, 'The Writings of Dziga Vertov' in Harry Geduld (ed) *Filmmakers on Filmmaking*, (London, 1962), p.92.
11. Paul Stoller, *Sensuous Scholarship*, Philadelphia: University of Pennsylvania Press, p.125.
12. Antonin Artaud, 'Cinema and Reality', trans. Helen Weaver, 'Antonin Artaud: Selected Writings', (Berkley, 1988), p.151.
13. Lee Jamison, 'The Lost Prophet of Cinema: The Film Theory of Antonin Artaud' Senses of Cinema, http://archive.sensesofcinema.com/contents/07/44/film-theory-antonin-artaud.html
14. Tom Gunning, 'An Aesthetic of Astonishment: Early Film and the (In)credulous Spectator', in Leo Braudy and Marshall Cohen (eds), *Film Theory and Criticism: Introductory Readings* (Oxford, 1999).
15. The tension and anticipation that permeated the air in the Lumiere's early shows is clearly captured by Leslie Wood 'The bill outside the hall announced: 'Wonderful Living Pictures' and the admission was one

shilling, the program lasting half an hour. The seating consisted of wooden chairs and forms…Sound effects were provided by an assistant behind the screen – the sound of the surf, the falling of the wall. As for the train entering a station, this was almost too realistic for some of the audience and they nervously started towards the exits as it steamed, head on, towards them. ' Leslie Wood, *The Miracle of the Movies* (London, 1957), p.90.
16. Many Lumiere programs were begun by the projection of a still image on the screen that would, with the flick of a switch, start into life.
17. Gunning 'An Aesthetic of Astonishment: Early Film and the (In)credulous Spectator' p.822.
18. Littau, p.46.
19. Littau, p.47.
20. Williams 'Body Genres: Corporealized Observers and the Carnal Density of Vision.'
21. Linda Williams, 'Body Genres: Gender, Genre and Excess' in *Film Quarterly* 44:4, Summer, 1991.
22. Williams' use of the term 'carnal density' highlights, I think, a common mistake amongst theorists using Crary's work. Williams, in 'Corporealized Observers' states that Crary's carnal density equates with an expansion of the remit of vision to include sensation, affect and emotion; that Crary's suggests the modern scopic regime bases vision within the 'body' of the observer. This is not strictly the case, as Anne Rutherford eloquently states in her article 'Cinema and Embodied Affect' (Anne Rutherford, 'Cinema and embodied affect'(2002) http://archive. sensesofcinema. com/ contents/03/25/embodied_affect. Html, accessed 18 August 2009) there is a marked difference between the use of physiology in optics and the use of phenomenology in optics. This difference, she says, is equitable to notions of the physiological and the lived body, between what in German, might be distinguished by the term Körper and the term Lieb. Crary suggest that, whereas the modern scopic regime stressed the physiological basis of vision (i.e. how the muscles around the eye, how blood flow to it and how changes in the brain all affected sight) it paid little attention to how sight was connected to the nerves, or the skin, to the flesh or to sensual memory that subtends cognition. In studying the importance of affect, of excitation and emotion in film, Williams' work represents more suitably the postmodern scopic regime (or the period of transition between the two) than the modern scopic ideas she aligns herself with in 'Corporealized Observers'.
23. Williams, 'Body Genres: Corporealized Observers and the Carnal Density

of Vision', p.15.
24. See Elizabeth Grosz, *Volatile Bodies: Toward a Corporeal Feminism* (Bloomington, 1994).
25. Steven Shaviro, *The Cinematic Body* (Minneapolis, 1993).
26. Gilles Deleuze and Felix Guattari, *Anti-Oedipus*, trans. Brian Massumi (London, 2004); Gilles Deleuze and Felix Guattari *A Thousand Plateaus* trans. Brian Massumi (London, 2004).
27. Shaviro, p.33.
28. Robert Stam, *Film Theory: An Introduction* (London, 2000), p.256.
29. Gregory Flaxman, 'Introduction' in *The Brain is the Screen: Deleuze and the Philosophy of Cinema* (Minneapolis, 2000), p.14.
30. Shaviro, p.51.
31. Shaviro, p.52.
32. See, for instance, the quotation that opens Chapter 3 of this book.
33. Gilles Deleuze, 'On The Time image' in *Negotiations* trans. Martin Joughin (New York, 1990).
34. Gilles Deleuze, *Francis Bacon: The Logic of Sensation* trans. Daniel Smith (London, 2004).
35. Gregg Lambert, 'Schizoanalysis and Cinema of the Brain' in Ian Buchanan and Patricia MacCormack (eds) *Deleuze and the Schizoanalysis of Cinema*, London, 2008), p.28.
36. Laura Marks, *Touch: Sensuous Theory and Multisensory Media* (Minneapolis, 2002).
37. Marks, *The Skin of the Film,* p.184.
38. Marks, *Touch,* p.50.
39. Deleuze, *Francis Bacon,* p.39.
40. Kennedy, p.90.
41. Here Deleuze borrows heavily from Bergson whose description of the evolutionary reason for this is highly illuminating: 'if we follow, step by step, the progress of external perception from the monera to the higher vertebrates, we find that living matter, even as a simple mass of protoplasm, is already irritable and contractile, that is open to the influence of external stimulation, and answers to it by mechanical, physical and chemical reactions. As we rise in the organic series, we find a division of physiological labour' (Henri Bergson, *Matter and Memory* trans. Nancy Margaret Paul and W. Scott Palmer (London, 2004), p.17.
42. Ronald Bogue, *Deleuze on Music, Painting and the Arts* (London, 2003), p.150.
43. Kennedy, p.51.
44. Sobchack, 'What My Fingers Knew', p.57.

45. Sobchack, 'What My Fingers Knew', p.61.
46. Sobchack, 'What My Fingers Knew', p.60.
47. Sobchack, 'What My Fingers Knew', p.63.

2: Critical Theory and Embodiment

1. Maurice Merleau-Ponty, *The Phenomenology of Perception* trans. Colin Smith (London, 2005), p.214.
2. Maurice Merleau-Ponty, *The Visible and the Invisible* trans. Alphonso Lingis (Illinois, 1968); Luce Irigaray, 'The Invisible of the Flesh', in *An Ethics of Sexual Difference* trans. Carolyn Burke and Gillian Gill (London, 1993).
3. Didier Anzieu, *The Skin Ego* trans. C. Turner (New York, 1990).
4. Genevieve Lloyd, *The Man of Reason* (London, 1984).
5. See Mary Douglas, *Purity and Danger* (London, 2002).
6. Sigmund Freud, *Beyond the Pleasure Principle* trans. James Strachey in *The Essentials of Psychoanalysis* [1920] (London, 1991).
7. Ibid, p.233.
8. Ibid, p.234.
9. Ibid, p.236.
10. Anzieu, p.96.
11. See, for instance, S. F. Mason, *Main Currents of Scientific Thought*, (London, 1953)p.344. 'In this work Haeckel revived and amplified the biogenetic principle of Meckel, namely, the view that the individual organism during the course of its embryological development passed through the main stages in the evolution of its species'.
12. Freud, *Beyond the Pleasure Principle,* p.236.
13. Ibid, p.238.
14. 'As nature has uncovered from under (the) hard shell the seed for which she most tenderly cares – the propensity and vocation to free thinking – this gradually works back upon the character of the people' Immanuel Kant, *What is Enlightenment?* [1784] in Isaac Kramnick (ed) *The Portable Enlightenment Reader* (London, 1995), p.7.
15. Anzieu, p.9. *My italics.*
16. Ernest Jones, *The Life and Work of Sigmund Freud* (London, 1953), p.88.
17. Nicholas Abraham and Maria Torok. *The Shell and the Kernel: Renewals in Psychoanalysis*, trans. Nicholas Reid (Chicago, 1994), p.91.
18. Sigmund Freud, 'Instincts and their vicissitudes' [1915], trans. James Strachey, in *The Essentials of Psychoanalysis*, (London, 1991); Sigmund Freud, 'Three essays on sexuality' [1905] trans. James Strachey in *The Essentials of Psychoanalysis* (London, 1991).

19. Anzieu, p.17.
20. Anzieu, p.63.
21. Robert Brain, *The Decorated Body* (Hutchinson, 1979).
22. Ibid, p.73.
23. Anzieu, p.157.
24. Deleuze and Guattari, *A Thousand Plateaus* p.342.
25. John Macquarrie, *Existentialism* (London, 1973), p.68.
26. Jean Paul Sartre, *Being and Nothingness* trans. Hazel Barnes (London, 2005), pp.327-328
27. Sartre, *Being and Nothingness,* p.280.
28. Jacques Lacan, *The Four Fundamental Concepts of Psychoanalysis* trans. Alan Sheridan, (London, 1986), p.84-84.
29. Jean Paul Sartre, *Nausea* trans. Robert Baldick (London, 1980), p.22.
30. Grosz, p.86.
31. Monika Langer, *Merleau-Ponty's Phenomenology of Perception* (London, 1989)
32. Langer, pp.104-105.
33. As Hayim Gordon and Shlomit Tamari, assert, Merleau-Ponty's conceptions of the body differ also from a great many other Western thinkers: 'In his discussions of the human body, Merleau-Ponty frequently goes further than the thoughts presented by other thinkers who learned from Husserl's phenomenology. He also differs from most major Western philosophers, such as Augustine, Descartes, Spinoza, and Hegel, who rarely dedicated their thinking to the human body, and did not view the human body as a phenomenological source. In contrast to these great thinkers, Merleau-Ponty studied the human body as central to perception, and hence as central to our existence and our engagements in the world. In these detailed studies, he endeavored to obtain a phenomenological understanding of the human body. Haim Gordon and Schlomit Tamari, *Maurice Merleau-Ponty's Phenomenology of Perception: A Basis for Sharing the Earth* (London, 2004), p.63.
34. Gordon and Tamari, p.72
35. Merleau-Ponty, p.240
36. Langer, p.105
37. Irigaray, *This Sex Which is Not One*, pp.151-152.
38. Merleau-Ponty, *Phenomenology of Perception,* p.154.
39. See, for instance, Magda Arnold, *Memory and the Brain* (London, 1984)
40. As Moniker Langer points out the original French term *Le Sentir* could

also be translated as 'Sensing', a word that, perhaps better describes its place within Merleau-Ponty's oeuvre.
41. Heinz Werner, *Untersuchungen uber Empfindung und Empfinden*, published in Ztschr f. Psychologie, 1930; V. Goldstein and O. Rosenthanl, *Zum Problem der Wirkung der Farben auf den Organismus*, published in *Archiv fur Neurologie and Psychiatie*, 1930.
42. Merleau-Ponty, *Phenomenology of Perception*, p.243.
43. Merleau-Ponty, *Phenomenology of Perception*, p.243.
44. Merleau-Ponty, *Phenomenology of Perception*, pp.244-245.
45. Merleau-Ponty, *Phenomenology of Perception*, p.268.
46. Merleau-Ponty, *The Visible and the Invisible*, p.142.
47. Merleau-Ponty, *The Visible and the Invisible*, p.143.
48. S. Brent Plate, 'Religious Cinematics: The Immediate Body in the Media of Film', in *Postscript*, 1. 2/1. 3, 2005, p.261.
49. Brent Plate, pp.259-275.
50. Merleau-Ponty, *Phenomenology of Perception*, p.258.
51. Plato, *Symposium* [385 B.C], trans. Benjamin Jowett (London, 1972).
52. William Harvey, *An Anatomical Disquisition on the Motion of the Heart and Blood in Animals* [1628] (London, 1972), p.273.
53. Simone de Beauvoir, *The Second Sex*, trans. H.M Parshley, (London, 1997), pp.63-64.
54. Irigary, *This Sex which is Not One*, p.24.
55. Luce Irigaray, *Speculum of the Other Woman* (New York, 1995), p.7.
56. Laura Mulvey, 'Visual Pleasure and Narrative Cinema', in Leo Braudy and Marshell Cohen (eds), *Film and Criticism: Introductory Readings* (Oxford, 1999).
57. See the discussion of Beharry's film *Seeing is Believing* in Marks, *The Skin of the Film*.
58. Julia Kristeva, 'New Maladies of the Soul' in *The Portable Kristeva* (New York, 1997), p.374.
59. Marks, *Touch,* p.18.
60. Hélène Cixous, *The Laugh of the Medusa* in Elaine Marks and Isabelle de Courtivron (eds) *New French Feminisms* (London, 1980), p.252.
61. Douglas, p.47.
62. Julia Kristeva, 'The Powers of Horror', *The Portable Kristeva*, ed. Kelly Oliver (New York, 1997)
63. Luce Irigaray, 'The Mechanics of Fluids', trans. Catherine Porter, *This Sex Which is Not One* (New York, 1985).
64. Cixous, p.254.

3: Neuroscience and Embodiment

1. Francisco Varela, 'The Re-enchantment of the Concrete', Jonathan Crary and Sanford Kwinter, eds. , *Incorporations v. 6*, (New York, 1992), p.340.
2. Gilles Deleuze, 'The Brain is the Screen: An Interview with Gilles Deleuze', trans. Marie Therese Guirgis, ed. Gregory Flaxman, *The Brain is the Screen: Deleuze and the Philosophy of Cinema* (Minneapolis, 2000), p.366.
3. Eleanor Turk, *The History of Germany* (London, 1999), p.105.
4. Stephen Rose, *The Conscious Brain* (London, 1976).
5. Kuhn, p.111.
6. I use here the term 'epistemic shifts' specifically in order to distance this notion from the Kuhnian 'paradigm shift'. As Kuhn himself states in the preface to the 1970 edition of *The Structure of Scientific Revolutions*, natural science is characterised by paradigm shifts that is, large scale shifts of thinking linked to certain accepted theories and formulations that enable almost universal consensus between practitioners. This does not apply to the social sciences and other disciplines that retain the heterogeneity of conflicting discourses. The terms episteme and regime, as used by Crary via Foucault, suggest a far looser conception, one that is based more on a sense of generalised thinking that carries across disciplinary borders.
7. Crary, p.150.
8. Purkyne's major work, for instance, was *Beitrage zur Kenntniss des Sehens in subjectiver Hinsicht* (*Contributions to the Understanding of Vision in its Subjective Aspect*), cited in Nicholas J. Wade, *A Natural History of Vision* (Cambridge, 1998), p.158.
9. Henry Gray, *Gray's Anatomy*, available online at http://www.bartleby.com/107/1.html, (1918) accessed 30 December 2009 (URL correct at the time of writing).
10. See Rudolph Arnheim, *Art and Visual Perception* (Berkeley, 2004).
11. Alhazen, quoted in David Lindberg, *Theories of Vision from al-Kindi to Kepler*, Chicago, 1981), p.69.
12. Antonio Damasio, *Descartes' Error* (London: Papermac, 1994); Andrew Ellis and Andrew Young, *Human Cognitive Neuropsychology* (London: Psychology Press, 1996).
13. Richard Cytowic, *Synesthesia: A Union of the Senses* (Cambridge, 2002), p.10.
14. It must also be said here, however, that the limbic system thesis, arising mainly in the work of Richard Cytowic has been challenged by various writers (Frith and Paulescu, 1997), for instance, C. D. Frith and E. Paulescue, 'The Physiological Basis of Synaesthesia', in Simon Baron Cohen

and John Harrison (eds), *Synaesthesia: Classic and Contemporary Readings*, London, 1997). and should not be considered as broadly accepted.
15. Arthur Rimbaud, *Vowels*, trans. Paul Schmidt, in *The Complete Works* (London, 1988), p.123.
16. Robert Robertson, 'Eisenstein, Synaesthesia, Symbolism and the Occult Traditions', http://www. offscreen. com/biblio/phile/essays/eisenstein_synaesthesia/ (2006), accessed 30 December 2009 (URL correct at the time of writing).
17. Noam Sagiv, 'Synesthesia in perspective', in L. C Robertson and Noam Sagiv (eds) *Synesthesia: Perspectives from Cognitive Neuroscience* (New York, 2005).
18. Richard Cytowic, *The Man Who Tasted Shapes* (London, 1993).
19. Cytowic *The Man Who Tasted Shapes* p.153.
20. Ibid, p.147.
21. Ibid, p.147.
22. Susan Greenfield, *The Human Brain* (London, 2001), p.15.
23. Michael O'Shea, *The Brain: A Very Short Introduction* (Oxford, 2005), p.56.
24. A. R. Luria, *The Mind of a Mnemonist*, trans. Lynn Solotaroff (Cambridge, 1987).
25. Ibid, p.25.
26. Cytowic (2002), Daphne Maurer, 'Neonatal synaesthesia: implications for the processing of speech and faces', in Simon Baron-Cohen, John Harrison (eds.) *Synaesthesia: Classic and Contemporary Readings*; (Oxford: Blackwell, 1997); Simon Baron Cohen, 'Is There a Normal Phase of Synaesthesia in Development?', in *Psyche*, 2(27), June 1996.
27. Cytowic (1993); Sean Day, 'Synaesthesia and synaesthetic metaphors', 1996. <http://psyche. cs. monash. edu. au/v2/psyche-2-32-day. html> accessed 10 August 2009.
28. V. S. Ramachandran, 'Mirror Neurons and Imitation Learning as the Driving Force Behind the Great Leap Forward in Human Evolution'. 2000. < http://edge. org/3rd_culture/ramachandran/ramachandran_p1. html> accessed 11 August 2009.
29. G. Rizzolatti and L. Craighero, 'The Mirror Neuron System', in *Annual Review of Neuroscience*, 27, 2004.
30. Ibid, p.171.
31. G. Rizzolatti, L. Fadiga, V. Gallese and L. Fogasi, 'Premotor Cortex and the Recognition of Motor Actions', in *Cognitive Brain Research*, 3, 1996.
32. Bryan Kolb and Ian Whishaw, *Fundamentals of Human Neuropsychology*, (London:, 2003), 212.

33. L. Fogassi; P. Francesco Ferrari,; B. Gesierich; S. Rozzi; F. Chersi; G. Rizzolatti, 'Parietal Lobe: From Action Organization to Intention Understanding' in *Science* 308: 662-667, 2005.
34. Rizzolatti and Craighero (2004).
35. Vittorio Gallese, 'Intentional Attunement: The Mirror Neuron System and its Role in Interpersonal Relations'. 2005. <http://www.interdisciplines.org/mirror/papers/1> accessed 10 August 2009 (URL correct at the time of writing).
36. Gallese, p.1.
37. Cytowic, *Synesthesia: A Union of the Senses,* p.72.
38. J. E. Steiner, 'The Gustofacial Response: Observation on Normal and Anencephalic New Born Infants', in J. F. Bosman (ed), *Fourth Symposium on Oral Sensation and Perception* (U. S Department of Health, Education and Welfare, Bethesda, MD, 1973).
39. Ibid, p.320.
40. Ibid, p.329.
41. Robert Jutte, *A History of the Senses* (London, 2005), p.239.
42. David Howes, 'Introduction', Davod Howes (ed) *Empire of the Senses* (London, 2005), p.5.
43. Ibid, p.4.
44. Carl Plantinga and Greg Smith, *Passionate Views: Film, Cognition and Emotion* (Washington, 1999).

4: On Hitchcock

1. *Hands of Mr Ottermole, The. Hitchcock Presents, Season 2. Dir. Robert Stevens. Shamley Productions , 5 May 1957.*
2. Frampton, p.32.
3. Eric Rohmer and Claude Chabrol, *Hitchcock: The First Forty Four Films*, trans. Stanley Hochman (1957; New York, 1979).
4. Jack Sullivan, *Hitchcock's Music* (New Haven, 2007); Jean Pierre Dufreigne, *Hitchcock's Style* (New York, 2004); Mark Wolff and Tony Nourmand, *Hitchcock Poster Art* (London, 1999); Pat Hitchcock O'Connell and Laurent Bouzereau, *Alma Hitchcock: The Woman Behind the Man* (New York, 2003).
5. Robert Kapsis, *Hitchcock: The Making of a Reputation* (Chicago, 1992); Tania Modelski, *The Women Who Knew Too Much* (London, 1989); David Bordwell and Kristin Thompson, *Film Art: An Introduction* (New York, 2006); Patricia Pisters, *The Matrix of Visual Culture,* (Stanford, 2003).
6. Spoto states 'The contrast between manner and mockery so evident in the

common vaudeville entertainment is in fact a perfect reflection of the struggle that existed in Hitchcock's society and in his personal world. As a clever, lonely boy, pampered by a doting mother, he was caught between the Victorian world of class and privilege and the Cockney's inbred resentment of the World.' Donald Spoto, *The Dark Side of Genius*, (London, 1994), p.22
7. Deleuze, *Cinema 1: The Movement-image*, p.204.
8. Raymond Durgnat, *The Strange Case of Alfred Hitchcock* (London, 1974).
9. This point is exemplified with Durgnat's description of the 1944 films *Bon Voyage* (1944) and *Aventure Malgache* (1944); Durgnat admits having to reply on rather sketchy memories of a partial screening he observed seventeen years prior to the writing of his book. Both of these films have now been released by Image Entertainment and Milestone Film and Video and have been available since 1994.
10. Films such as Tom Tyker's 2006 *Perfume*, those works from the 1980s and 90s discussed by Laura Marks (2000) or even a film such as *The Piano* (1993) that forms the basis of Sobchack's compelling essay 'What My Fingers Knew'.
11. Ian Cameron and V. F. Perkins, *Movie*, No. 6, pp. 4-6, 1963.
12. Claude Chabrol, *Cahiers du Cinéma* , 39-44, 1954.
13. Janet Masin, Alfred Hitchcock, *Boston After Dark*, 3, no,24, 1972. My italics.
14. Jean Douchet, 'Hitch and his Public', *A Hitchcock Reader*, eds. Marshall Deutelbaum and Leland Poague (London, 1960), p. 8.
15. G. K. Chesterton, 'A Defence of Penny Dreadfuls', in *The Defendant* (Calfary, 2000), p.84.
16. Quoted in Spoto, *The Dark Side of Genius*, p.406.
17. Douchet, p.9.
18. George Toles, '"If thine eye offend..." Psycho and the Art of Infection', *Alfred Hitchcock's Psycho: A Casebook*, ed. Robert Phillip Tolker (Oxford, 2004); Slavoj, 'In My Bold Gaze My Ruin is Writ Large', Slavoj Žižek (ed), *Žižek Everything You Always Wanted to Know About Hitchcock but Were Afraid to Ask Lacan*, (London, 2002).

5: On Taste and Digestion

1. Jean Brillat Savarin, *The Philosopher in the Kitchen* (London, 1981).
2. James Lyons, 'What About the Popcorn? Food and the Film Watching Experience', *Reel Food*, ed. Anne Bower (London, 2004).
3. Alexander Lucas, *Demystifying Anorexia Nervosa* (Oxford, 2004).

4. Laurent Bouzereau, *The Alfred Hitchcock Quote Book* (London, 1993), p.128; Michael Walker, *Hitchcock's Motifs* (Amsterdam, 2005), p.187.
5. Ibid, p.187.
6. As Jeffrey Geiger and R.L. Rutsky state this is an integral methodological aspect of film theory, film theory, 'To read a film is to look beyond its obvious meaning – what it says or what happens in its narrative – in order to find the unnoticed meanings, assumptions and beliefs around which it is organised.' Jeffrey Geiger and R. L. Rutsky, 'Introduction', in *Film Analysis: A Norton Reader*, eds. Jeffrey Geiger and R. L. Rutsky (London, 2005). 19. Film theory of the postmodern scopic regime merely attempts to add an extra layer to these sometimes unnoticed experiences.
7. Hitchcock made this link between food and sex explicit in an off the record conversation with Samuel Raphaelson, 'As they get on, after five or six years in most married couples 'that old feeling' begins to dissipate. Food oftentimes takes the place of sex in a relationship. ' (quoted, Spoto pp.519-520).
8. Dick Stromgen, 'Now to the banquet we press: Hitchcock's gourmet and gourmand offerings', published in Paul Loukides and Linda Fuller (eds), *Beyond the Stars III: The Material World of American Popular Film* (Bowling Green OH, 1993), p.39.
9. Donald Spoto, *The Art of Alfred Hitchcock* (London, 1992), p.251.
10. Ibid, p.257.
11. Ibid, p.251.
12. 'Eventually he [Robie] returns, happily enough, to resume his contended solitude in the villa. She [Francine] must pursue him and declare her love, frankly albeit she is allowed to do so by requesting him to declare his love for her...She translates that old music hall lament. And her mother came too into a suaver form of bourgeois appropriation...Marriage is the biggest theft of all' (Durgnat p.247).
13. J. G Frazer, *The Golden Bough* (London, 1993), p.480; Ibid p.488; Claude Levi Strauss, *The Raw and the Cooked*, trans. John and Doreen Weightman (London, 1964).
14. It is interesting to compare this scene also with the dining scene in the 1956 version of *The Man Who Knew Too Much* (1956). Here we again see eating with fingers but this time it is within the context of an awkward cultural exchange as Ben and Jo McKenna learn to eat in the Arabic style in a restaurant. Notice how, in each scene, embodied knowledge is used to underpin the larger mandates of the film: the most noticeable aspect of Ben McKenna's character in this scene is his physical discomfort, a discomfort that (through embodied knowledge and mirror neurons)

the audience also feels. This discomfort arises out of his place as an alien abroad, a psychological state that is underpinned and suggested through physical correlative.
15. An ideal example of this can be seen in the famous scene from the 1963 film *Tom Jones* (1963), where Tony Richardson draws on a whole gamut of sensual and erotically charged haptic experiences to convey the sense of a lust fuelled meal between Tom and Mrs Waters.
16. Merleau-Ponty, *Phenomenology of Perception,* p.154.
17. Victoria Gilman, 'Food Coloring', in *Science and Technology*, Volume 81, Number 34, 2003. There is, however, a story about a dinner party thrown by Hitchcock at which all of the food was dyed blue.
18. FDA/IFIC, *Food Color Facts*, International Food Information Council: Washington, 1993.
19. E. T. Rolls; M. J. Burton and F. Mora, 'Hypothalamic neuronal responses associated with the sight of food', in *Brain Res*, Jul 23;111(1):53–66, 1976;T. Ono; R. , Tamura; H. , Nishijo; K. , Nakamura and E. Tabuchi , 'Contribution of amygdalar and lateral hypothalamic neurons to visual information processing of food and nonfood in monkey', *Physiol Behav* 45: 411–421, 1989.
20. Edmund T. Rolls, 'Neural Processing Related to Feeding in Primates', Legg, C and Booth, D (eds), *Appetite: Neural and Behavioural Bases*, eds. C. Legg and D. Booth (Oxford, 1994), p.13.
21. Diane Phillips, 'How Does it Make Me Feel? A Consumer's Satisfaction Response to Food Products', in *Journal of Food Products Marketing*, Volume 6, Issue 2, 2000, p. 15.
22. Compare for the instance the wedding scene in Arau's *Like Water for Chocolate* (1992) with the similar scene in Pasolini's *Salo* (1975).
23. Levi Strauss, p.135.
24. John Ratey, *A User's Guide to the Brain* (London: Little, 2001), p.75
25. Published in Deutelbaum and Poague (1989) as 'Male Desire, Male Anxiety', p.219-230
26. Modleski, p.106.
27. Ibid, p.107.
28. Ibid, p.109.
29. Leslie Brill, *The Hitchcock Romance* (New Jersey, 1988), p.140.
30. This technique of adopting the gaze of an inanimate object is, of course, typical of Hitchcock, see the same type of shot in *Psycho* when Marion Crane not so much stares at the stolen money as is stared at by it,
31. Karl Abraham, *Oral Eroticism and Character* (London, 1979), p.403.
32. William Pechter, 'The Hitchcock Problem', Commentary, V. 54, quoted

Jeanne Thomas Allen, 'The Representation of Violence to Women: Hitchcock's Frenzy', *Film Quarterly*, Vo. 38, Spring, 1985.
33. Wood, 'The Fear of Spying', p.221.
34. Not counting the initial dead body floating in the Thames.
35. Raymond Bellour, *The Analysis of Film* (Bloomington, 2001).
36. Brillat Savarin, p.45.
37. Brill, p.139.
38. Spoto, *The Art of Alfred Hitchcock,* p.441.
39. Interestingly in Arthur Le Bern's original novel this body is that of Miss Barling, Brenda Blaney's secretary; in Hitchcock's film this rather spinsterish woman has been replaced by a young blond.
40. Adam Lowenstein, 'The Master, the Maniac, and Frenzy', *Hitchcock: Past and Future*, eds. Richard Allen and Sam Ishi Gonzales (London, 2004), p.182.

6: On Smell

1. Hellen Keller, 'Sense and Sensibility'. *The Smell Culture Reader*. Ed. Jim Drobnick (London, 2006), p. 181
2. Constance Classen, David Howes and Anthony Synnot, *Aroma: The Cultural History of Smell*, (London, 1994).
3. Luca Turin, *The Secret of Scent* (London, 2008).
4. Compare this Benjaminian vision of the twentieth century metropolis with descriptions of seventeenth century Paris contained in Alain Corbin, *The Foul and the Fragrant*, trans. M. Kochan (London, 1986).
5. Gale Largey and Rod Watson, 'The Sociology of Odors' *The Smell Culture Reader*. Ed. Jim Drobnick (London, 2006); See, for instance, the entry in Otto Lowenstein's 1966 book *The Senses* where he states 'Continental Europeans derive more enjoyment from scents than the inhabitants of the British Isles, where a 'perfumed person' is regarded with a certain amount of suspicion. One sometimes wonders whether the climate may have something to do with this. ' (Otto Lowenstein, *The Senses* (London, 1966), p. 173).David Stoddart, *The Scented Ape* (Cambridge, 1990).
6. Georg Hegel, *Introductory Lectures on Aesthetics*, trans. Bernard Bosanquet (London, 1975), p.622.
7. Laura Marks, *Touch*, p.115.
8. Sigmund Freud, 'Civilization and its Discontents' [1930], trans. James Strachey, *Civilization, Society and Religion*, ed. Albert Dickinson (London, 1991), p.288.
9. The poverty turns out to be a trick her father plays upon her.

10. Diane Ackerman, *A Natural History of the Senses* (London, 1990).
11. Marco Iacoboni; Istvan Molnar-Szakacs; Vittorio Gallese; Giovanni Buccino; John C. Mazziotta and Giacomo Rizzolatti, 'Grasping the Intentions of Others With One's Own Mirror Neuron System' in *PloS Biology*, Volume 3, Issue 3, 2005.
12. Maurice Merleau-Ponty, 'The Film and the New Psychology', *Sense and Non Sense*, trans. Hubert L. Dreyfus and Patricia Dreyfus (Chicago, 1964), p.50.
13. Marks, *Touch,* p.118.
14. Slavoj Žižek, *Looking Awry* (Cambridge: Massachusetts, 1992), p. 93.
15. Ibid, p.93.
16. Marks, *The Skin of the Film,* p.196.
17. Helen Gilbert, 'Dance, Movement and Resistance Politics', *The Post-Colonial Studies Reader*, eds. Bill Ashcroft, Gareth Griffiths and Helen Tiffin (London, 1999).
18. Ibid, p.341.
19. Marks, *The Skin of the Film,* p.209.
20. Paul Gauguin, *Paul Gauguin's Intimate Journals* (London, 1986), p.96.
21. Marcel Proust, 'Another Memory'. *The Smell Culture Reader*. Ed. Jim Drobnick (London, 2006).
22. Alan Hirsch, 'Nostalgia, The Odors of Childhood and Society.' *The Smell Culture Reader*. Ed. Jim Drobnick (London, 2006).
23. Devon Hinton, Vuth Pich, Dara Chhean and Mark Pollack, 'Olfactory Triggered Panic Attacks Among Khmer Refugees.' *The Smell Culture Reader*. Ed. Jim Drobnick (London. Berg, 2006).
24. S. Van Toller, S. Hotson and M. Kendal-Reed, 'The Brain and the Sense of Smell: Can We Begin to Make Sense of Cortical Information After an Odour Has Been Received', in S. Van Toller, and G. H. Dodd, (eds), *Fragrance: the Psychology and Biology of Perfume* (London, 1992).
25. David Martin-Jones, *Deleuze, Cinema and National Identity* (Edinburgh, 2006), p.72.
26. Eleanor Margolis, 'Vagueness gridlocked: A map of the smells of New York'. *The Smell Culture Reader*. Ed. Jim Drobnick (London, 2006); Martin Manalansan, 'Immigrant lives and the politics of olfaction in the global city' in Drobnick (2006).
27. J. Douglas Porteous, 'Smellscape'. *The Smell Culture Reader*. Ed. Jim Drobnick (London, 2006),
28. Wood, *Hitchcock's Films: Revisited,* pp. 288-302.
29. William Rothman, *The Murderous Gaze* (Cambridge, 2002); Durgnat (1974) and so on.

30. Spoto, *The Art of Alfred Hitchcock,* p.263.
31. Notice how Charles Tobin (Otto Kruger) in *Saboteur* is pictured as being all the more evil because of his position as head of a young family.
32. Wood, *Hitchcock's Films Revisited,* p.297.
33. Ibid, p.298.
34. This is especially noticeable when Uncle Charlie returns home and greets his sister, both are framed by the boughs of the trees, as the camera pans along the street, we are presented with images of white and (supposedly) fragrant blossom.
35. Marks, *The Skin of the Film,* p.163.

7: On Hearing

1. Michel Chion, *Audio-Vision,* trans. Claudia Gorbman (New York, 1994), p.34.
2. David Sonnenshein, *Sound Design* (California, 2001); Kaja Silverman, *The Acoustic Mirror* (Bloomington, 1988).
3. Silverman, p.42.
4. Cavell, p.150.
5. Murray Schaffer, 'Open Ears', in Michael Bull and Les Back (eds), *The Auditory Culture Reader* (London, 2005).
6. Mary Ann Doane, 'The Voice in Cinema: The Articulation of Body and Space', eds. *Film Theory: Introductory Readings, Leo Braudy and Marshall Cohen* (Oxford, 1999).
7. V. I. Pudovkin, 'Asynchronism as a Principle of Film Sound' [1929], *Film Sound: Theory and Practice,* eds. Elizabeth Weis and John Belton (New York, 1985).
8. Pudovkin, p.86.
9. Sonnenshein, p.xxii.
10. Ibid, p.71.
11. J. Blitz, *Elements of Acoustics* (Washington, 1964).
12. Sonnenshein, p.70.
13. Anna Powell, *Deleuze and Horror Film* (Edinburgh, 2006), p.206.
14. Pascal Wyse. 2003. <http://arts.guardian.co.uk/print/0,,4669399-110760,00.html> accessed 10 August 2009.
15. Sarah Anglis, Ciaran O'Keefe, Richard Lord and Richard Wiseman, 'Infrasonic – The Experiment'. 2003.<http://www. spacedog. biz/Infrasonic/results. htm> 10 August 2009 (URL correct at the time of writing).
16. Melanie Ferguson, Adrian Davis and Elizabeth Lovell, 'Cinemas – do they

pose a risk to hearing', in *Noise and Health*, Vol. 2: 8, 2000.
17. Kate van Orden, 'Descartes on Musical Training and the Body', *Music, Sensation and Sensuality*, eds. Linda Phyllis Austern (London, 2002); Daniel Schneck and Dorita Berger, *The Music Effect* (London, 2006).
18. van Orden, p.26.
19. Adam Mars Jones, 'Quiet Please', published in *Granta*, 86, 2006.
20. Interestingly Sullivan (2006) uses the embodied description 'chilling' to describe this scene.
21. Sullivan, p.304.
22. Deleuze, *Cinema 2: The Time-image,* p.12.
23. Durgnat, *The Strange Case of Alfred Hitchcock,* p.105.
24. Michel Chion makes the parallel between this use of sound and the visual close-up.
25. Phillip J. Skerry, *Psycho in the Shower: The History of Cinema's Most Famous Scene* (New York, 2009); Rothman etc.
26. Sullivan; Roy Prendergast, *Film Music: A Neglected Art* (London, 1992) and so on.
27. Close analysis of the soundtrack reveals that there are, in fact, two clearly discernibly different screams in the scene: one that is recognisably that of Janet Leigh, the other a more distant, higher, younger sounding voice that serves to add texture to the closely miked screams of the star.
28. Louis Giannetti, *Understanding Movies* (London, Longman, 1972) p.112.
29. Prendergast, p.144
30. Sergi Eisenstein,'Synchronization of the Senses', in *The Film Sense*, trans. Jay Leyda (London, 1980), p.67.
31. Ibid, p.63.
32. Craig Sinclair, 'Audition: making sense of cinema', *The Velvet Light Trap*, March 22, 2003, p.8.
33. Ibid, p.6.
34. For a discussion of music and sound as it relates to sensuality see Linda Phyllis Austen (ed), *Music, Sensation and Sensuality* (London, 2002).
35. As Hugo Munsterberg notes in *The Photoplay*, the notion of flatness is always a difficult one when dealing with moving pictures, they are on the one hand physically flat but they are also, on the other, psychologically imbued with depth so that, leading Munsterberg to conclude that: 'We have no right whatsoever to say that the scenes which we see on the screen appear to us as flat pictures' (1918: 18). Hugo Munsterberg, *The Photoplay* (New York, 1918).
36. Hitchcock however does provide numerous examples of the feminine voice taking precedence over the male gaze, most notably of course in the

remake of *The Man Who Knew Too Much* (1956), where it is the musical female voice of Jo that guides the eye (camera) up the stairs and into the room where her son is being held captive. Hitchcock himself, in the script notes to the film stressed the importance of having the voice in this scene lead the camera, he states 'When Doris starts to sing we must make sure that she is deliberately projecting her voice and this is most essential when we come to voice loud over the exit door of the ballroom. And when we come into the hallway for out first pan we should still feel conscious she is singing loud deliberately' (Hitchcock, cited, Sullivan, 2006: 203). It of course also Jo's voice that proves the key narrative element in the Albert hall sequence also.

37. Leon Alberti, *On Painting*, trans. John Spencer (New Haven, 1977), p.51.
38. Elizabeth Weis, 'The Evolution of Hitchcock's Aural Style and Sound in The Birds', in Weis and Belton (1985); Angelo Restivo, 'The Silence of The Birds', *Hitchcock Past and Future*, eds. Richard Allen and S. Ishi Gonzales (London, 2004).
39. Sullivan, p.259.
40. 'The murderous birds have their own music, they don't need anyone else's, not even Bernard Herrmann's' ((Ibid).
41. Elizabeth Weis, *The Silent Scream* (New Jersey, 1982), p.138.
42. Ibid, p.138.
43. Penelope Houston, 'The figure on the carpet', in *Sight and Sound*, Autumn, 1963.
44. Wood, *Hitchcock's Films Revisited*, p.154.
45. Durgnat, *The Strange Case of Alfred Hitchcock,* p.354.
46. Weis, *The Silent Scream,* p.141.
47. Ibid, p.188.
48. Gianluca Sergi, 'The sonic playground: Hollywood cinema and its listeners', *Hollywood Spectatorship*, eds. Melvyn Stokes and Richard Maltby (London, 2001) , p.125.
49. Chion, p.10.
50. Francois Truffaut, *Truffaut/Hitchcock* (London, 1983), p.296.
51. Truffaut, p.297.

Chapter 8: On Touching

1. Derrida, p. 53.
2. Ashley Montague, *Touching: The Human Significance of Skin* (New York: Harper Perennial, 1986).
3. As Jacques Derrida shows touch has often provided a counterpoint to the

hegemony of the visual in Western culture; Kant's hierarchy of the senses, for instance, places touch at the forefront of the senses, again because it is common to all living creatures and is key to the recognition of form (see Derrida, 2004 p.42)
4. Montague, p.3.
5. Murray Pomerance, *An Eye for Hitchcock* (New Jersey, 2004), p.63.
6. Wood, *Hitchcock's Films: Revisited,* p.202.
7. Walter Benjamin, 'The Work of Art: Second Version', trans. Edmund Jephcott and Harry Zohn, *The Work of Art in the Age of its Technological Reproducibility and Other Writings on Media* , eds. Michael Jennings, Brigid Doherty and Thomas Levin (Cambridge, 2008), p.23.
8. Margaret Iverson, *Alois Riegl* (Cambridge, 1993), pp.15-16.
9. Alfred Hitchcock, *Alfred Hitchcock Interviews* (Jackson, 2003), p.100.
10. Bernard Berenson, *Aesthetics and History* (London, 1950); Bernard Berenson, *The Florentine Painters of the Renaissance* (London, 2005).
11. Berenson, *The Florentine Painters of the Renaissance,* pp.4-5.
12. Berenson, *Aesthetics and History,* p.60.
13. Deleuze, *Cinema 1: The Movement-image,* p.203.
14. Marks, *Touch,* p.18.
15. Marks, *Touch,* p.10.
16. Sobchack, 'What My Fingers Knew', p.83.
17. Cited in Tom Ryall, *Alfred Hitchcock and the British Cinema* (London, 1996), p.110.
18. Merleau-Ponty, *Phenomenology of Perception,* p.267.
19. Laine, p.96.
20. Sobchack, *What My Fingers Knew,* p.84.
21 Montague, p.292.
22. Stefan Sharff, *The Art of Looking in Hitchcock's Rear Window* (New York: Limelight Editions, 1997). See also the entry in Rohmer and Chabrol (1988): 'To begin in the most modest and objective way possible, let us merely say that the theme concerns the very essence of cinema, which is seeing, spectacle. ', p.124.
23. Ibid, p.3.
24. See Durgant, Mulvey, and so on.
25. Durgnat, p. 240.
26. Robert Stam and Roberta Pearson, 'Hitchcock's Rear Window: Reflexivity and the Critique of Voyeurism', Deutlebaum and Poague (1986).
27. Ibid, p.201.
28. Ibid, p.205.
29. Clare Bishop, *Installation Art* (London, 2005).

Conclusion

1. Barry Salt, *Film Style and Technology: History and Analysis* (New York, 1993).

WORKS CITED

Abraham, Karl. *Oral Eroticism and Character*. London: Karnac, 1979.

Abraham, Nicholas and Maria Torok. *The Shell and the Kernel: Renewals in Psychoanalysis*, trans. Nicholas Reid. Chicago: University of Chicago Press, 1987/1994.

Ackerman, Diane. *A Natural History of the Senses*. London: Vintage, 1990.

Alberti, Leon. *On Painting*, trans. John Spencer. New Haven: Yale University Press, 1977.

Allen, Jeanne Thomas. 'The Representation of Violence to Women: Hitchcock's Frenzy'. *Film Quarterly*. 38. Spring. 1985: 30-38.

Anglis, Sarah; Ciaran O'Keefe; Richard Lord and Richard Wiseman. 'Infrasonic – The Experiment'. 2003. <www. spacedog. biz/Infrasonic/results. Htm> 15 August 2009 (URL correct at the time of writing).

Anzieu, Didier. *The Skin Ego*, trans. C. Turner. New Haven: Yale University Press, 1990.

Arnheim, Rudolph. *Art and Visual Perception*. Berkeley: University of California Press, 2004.

Arnold, Magda. *Memory and the Brain*. London: Lawrence Erlbaum Associates, 1984.

Artaud, Antonin. 'Cinema and Reality', trans. Helen Weaver, *Selected Writings*. Berkley: University of California Press, pp.150-155.

Austen, Linda Phyllis. Ed. *Music, Sensation and Sensuality*. London: Routledge, 2002.

Barker, Jennifer. *The Tactile Eye; Touch and the Cinematic Experience*. Berkeley: University of California Press, 2009.

Baron Cohen, S. 'Is There a Normal Phase of Synaesthesia in Development?' *Psyche*. 2(27). June 1996.

Baudrillard, Jean. *Simulacra and Simulation*, trans. Sheila Glaser. Flint: University of Michigan Press, 1990.

Baudrillard, Jean. *The System of Objects*, trans. James Benedict. London: Verso, 2005.

Bazin, Andre. *What is Cinema, Vol. 1*, trans. H Gray. Berkeley: University of California Press, 1992.

Bellour, Raymond. *The Analysis of Film*. Bloomington: University of Indiana Press, 2001.
Benjamin, Walter. 'The Work of Art: Second Version', in *The Work of Art in the Age of its Technological Reproducibility and Other Writings on Media*. Cambridge: Harvard, 2008, pp. 19-56.
Benthien, Claudia. *Skin: On the Cultural Border Between Self and the World*, trans. Thomas Dunlap. New York: Columbia University Press, 2002.
Berenson, Bernard. *The Florentine Painters of the Renaissance*. London: Indypublish, 2005.
Berenson, Bernard. *Aesthetics and History*. London: Constable, 1950.
Bergson, Henri, *Matter and Memory*, trans. Nancy Margaret Paul and W. Scott Palmer. London: Dover, 2004.
Berkeley, George. *Theory of Vision or Visual Language Vindicated and Explained*. New York: Library of the Liberal Art, 1733/1963.
Bishop, Clare. *Installation Art*. Tate Publishing, 2005.
Blitz, J. *Elements of Acoustics*. Washington: Butterworths, 1964.
Bogue, Ronald. *Deleuze on Music, Painting and the Arts*. London: Routledge, 2003.
Boorstin, Jon. *Making Movies Work: Thinking Like a Filmmaker*. Los Angeles: Silman James Press, 1995.
Bordwell, David and Kristin Thompson. *Film History: An Introduction*. New York: McGraw Hill, 1994.
Bordwell, David and Kristin Thompson. *Film Art: An Introduction*. New York: McGraw Hill, 2006.
Bouzereau, Laurent. *The Alfred Hitchcock Quote Book*. London: Citadel Press, 1993.
Bradford Titchner, Edward. *A Text Book of Psychology*. London: Macmillan, 1910.
Brain, Robert. *The Decorated Body*. Hutchinson: London, 1979.
Brent Plate, S. 'Religious Cinematics: The Immediate Body in the Media of Film'. *Postscript*. 1. 2/1. 3, 2005: 257-273.
Brill, Leslie. *The Hitchcock Romance*. New Jersey: Princeton University Press, 1988.
Brillat Savarin, Jean. *The Philosopher in the Kitchen*, trans. Anne Drayton. London: Penguin, 1825/1981.
Burnett, Ron. *Cultures of Vision: Images, Media and the Imaginary*. Bloomington: University of Indiana Press, 1995.
Butler, Judith. *Gender Trouble*. London: Routledge, 2006.
Cameron, Ian and V. F. Perkins, in *Movie*. No. 6. 1963: 4-6.

Cavell, Stanley. *The World Viewed*. Cambridge: Harvard University Press, 1979.

Chabrol, Claude, *Cahiers du Cinéma* , 1954

Chesterton, G. K. 'A defence of penny dreadfuls', in *On Lying in Bed and Other Essays*. Calgary: Bayeux Arts, 2000. 76-81.

Chion, Michel. *Audio-Vision*, trans. Claudia Gorbman. New York: Columbia University Press, 1994.

Cixous, Helene. 'The Laugh of the Medusa', trans. Keith Cohen and Paula Coehn. Elaine Marks and Isabelle de Courtivron. Ed. *New French Feminisms*. London: Harvester, 1980: 245-264.

Classen, Constance, David Howes and Anthony Synnot. *Aroma: The Cultural History of Smell*. London: Routledge, 1994.

Connor, Steven. *The Book of Skin*. London: Reaktion Books, 2004.

Corbin, Alain. *The Foul and the Fragrant*, trans. M. Kochan. London: Berg, 1986.

Crary, Jonathan. *Techniques of the Observer: On Vision and Modernity on the Nineteenth Century*. Cambridge: MIT Press, 1992.

Cubitt, Sean. *The Cinema Effect*. Cambridge: MIT Press, 2003.

Cytowic, Richard. *Synesthesia: A Union of the Senses*. Cambridge: MIT Press, 2002.

Cytowic, Richard. *The Man Who Tasted Shapes*. London: Abacus, 1993.

Damasio, Antonio. *Descartes' Error*. London: Papermac, 1994.

Daney, Serge. 'On Salador', trans. Unknown. 2009. http://home.earthlink.net/-steevee/Daney_salador, 15 August 2009.

Day, Sean. 'Synaesthesia and synaesthetic metaphors'. 1996. http://psyche.cs.monash.edu.au/v2/psyche-2-32-day.html, 15 August 2009.

de Beauvoir, Simone. *The Second Sex*, trans. H. M. Parshely. London: Vintage, 1997.

Debord, Guy. *Society of the Spectacle*. trans. Ken Kabb, London: Rebel Press, 1992.

Deleuze, Gilles and Felix Guattari. *A Thousand Plateaus*, trans. Brian Massumi. London: Continuum, 2004a.

Deleuze, Gilles and Felix Guattari. *Anti-Oedipus*, trans. Brian Massumi. London: Continuum, 2004c.

Deleuze, Gilles. 'On The Time image', trans. Martin Joughin. *Negotiations*. New York: Columbia University Press, 1990: 57-61.

Deleuze, Gilles. 'The brain is the screen: An interview with Gilles Deleuze', trans. Marie Therese Guirgis. Ed. Gregory Flaxman. *The Brain is the Screen: Deleuze and the Philosophy of Cinema*. Minneapolis: University of Minnesota Press, 2000: 365-374.

Deleuze, Gilles. *Cinema 1: The Movement-image*, trans Hugh Tomlinson and Barbara Habberjam. London: Continuum, 2004.
Deleuze, Gilles. *Cinema 2: The Time-image*, trans. Hugh Tomlinson and Robert Galeta. London: Continuum, 2000.
Deleuze, Gilles. *Francis Bacon: The Logic of Sensation*, trans. Daniel Smith. London: Continuum, 2004b.
Deleuze, Gilles. *Foucault*, trans. S. Hand. London: Continuum, 2006a.
Deleuze, Gilles. *The Fold*, trans. Tom Conley. London: Continuum, 2006.
Derrida, Jacques. *On Touching: Jean Luc Nancy*, trans. Christine Irizarry. Palo Alto: Stanford University Press, 2005.
Descartes, Rene. 'Optics', trans. John Cottingham, Robert Stoothoff and Murdoch Dugland. *Selected Philosophical Writings*. Cambridge: Cambridge University Press, 1637/1992: 57-72.
Doane, Mary Ann. 'The voice in cinema: The articulation of body and space'. *Film Theory and Criticism*. Ed. Leo Braudy and Marshall Cohen. 1999: 363-375.
Donald Spoto. *The Art of Alfred Hitchcock*. London: Anchor, 1992.
Douchet, Jean. 'Hitch and his Public', trans. Verena Conley. *A Hitchcock Reader*. Ed. Marshall Deutelbaum and Leland Poague. London: Blackwell, 1960/1986: 7-15.
Douglas Porteous, J. 'Smellscape'. *The Smell Culture Reader*. Ed. Jim Drobnick. London: Berg, 2006: 89-106.
Douglas, Mary. *Purity and Danger*. London: Routledge, 2002.
Dufreigne, Jean Pierre. *Hitchcock's Style*. New York: Assouline, 2004.
Durgnat, Raymond. *The Strange Case of Alfred Hitchcock*. London: Faber and Faber, 1974.
Durlach, Nathaniel and Anne Mavor. Eds. 'Virtual reality: Scientific and technological challenges'. 1995. http://www.nap.edu/openbook. php?isbn=0309051355, 15 August 2009.
Eisenstein,Sergi. 'Synchronization of the senses', trans. Jay Leyda. *The Film Sense*. Ed. Jay Leyda. London: Faber and Faber, 1980: 60-91.
Ellis, Andrew and Andrew Young. *Human Cognitive Neuropsychology*. London: Psychology Press, 1996.
Elsaesser, Thomas, '"Where were you, when…" or "I phone, therefore I am"'. 2002. <http://home. hum. uva. nl/oz/elsaesser/> 15 August 2009;.
Erlmann, Viet. 'But what of the ethnographic ear?' *Hearing* Cultures. Ed. Viet Erlmann, . London: Berg, 2004: 1-20.
FDA/IFIC, *Food Color Facts*, International Food Information Council: Washington, 1993.

Ferguson, Melanie, Adrian Davis and Elizabeth Lovell. 'Cinemas – do they pose a risk to hearing', in *Noise and Health*, Vol. 2: 8, 2000: 55-58.
Flaxman, Gregory. 'Introduction'. *The Brain is the Screen: Deleuze and the Philosophy of Cinema*. Ed. Gregory Flaxman. Minneapolis: University of Minnesota Press, 2000: 1-57.
Fogassi, L., P. Francesco Ferrari, B. Gesierich ; S. Rozzi, F. Chersi and G. Rizzolatti, 'Parietal lobe: from action organization to intention understanding'. *Science*. 308. 2005: 662-667.
Foucault, Michel. *Madness and Civilisation*, trans. Richard Howard. London: Routledge, 2004.
Foucault, Michel. *The Archaeology of Knowledge*, trans. A. M Sheridan Smith. London: Routledge, 2002.
Foucault, Michel. *The Birth of the Clinic*, trans. A. M. Sheridan. London: Routledge, 1986.
Foucault, Michel. *The Order of Things*. London: Routledge, 1989.
Frampton, Daniel. *Filmosophy*. London: Wallflower Press, 2006.
Frazer, J. G. *The Golden Bough*. London: Wordsworth, 1993.
Freud, Sigmund. 'Civilization and its Discontents', trans. James Strachey. *Civilization, Society and Religion*. Ed. Albert Dickson. London: Penguin, 1930/1991: 243-340.
Freud, Sigmund. 'Instincts and Their Vicissitudes', trans. James Strachey. *The Essentials of Psychoanalysis*. Ed. Anna Freud. London, Penguin, 1915/1991: 197-217.
Freud, Sigmund. 'Three Essays on Sexuality', trans. James Strachey. *The Essentials of Psychoanalysis*. Ed. Anna Freud. London, Penguin, 1905/1991: 277-375.
Freud, Sigmund. 'Beyond the Pleasure Principle', trans. James Strachey. *The Essentials of Psychoanalysis*. Ed. Anna Freud. London, Penguin, 1920/1991: 218-268.
Friedberg, Anne. *Window Shopping: Cinema and the Postmodern*. Berkeley: University of California Press, 1993.
Frith, C. D. and E. Paulescue. 'The Physiological Basis of Synaesthesia'. Simon Baron Cohen and John Harrison. Eds. *Synaesthesia: Classic and Contemporary Readings*. London: Wiley Blackwell, 1997: 123-147.
Gallese, Vittorio. 'Intentional Attunement: The Mirror Neuron System and its Role in Interpersonal Relations'. 2005. http://www.interdisciplines.org/mirror/papers/1, 15 August 2009 (URL correct at the time of writing).
Gauguin, Paul. *Paul Gauguin's Intimate Journals*, trans. Van Wyck Brooks. London: Liverlight, 1949.

Geiger, Jeffrey and R. L. Rutsky. 'Introduction'. *Film Analysis: A Norton Reader*. Ed. Jeffrey Geiger and R.L. Rutsky. London: Norton, 2005: 17-41.

Geiger, Jeffrey. *Facing the Pacific: Polynesia and the U. S. Imperial Imagination*. Honolulu: University of Hawaii Press, 2007.

Giannetti, Louis. *Understanding Movies*. London; Longman, 1972.

Gilbert, Helen. 'Dance, Movement and Resistance Politics'. *The Post-Colonial Studies Reader*. Ed. Bill Ashcroft, Gareth Griffiths and Helen Tiffin. London: Routledge, 1999: 341-345.

Gilman, Victoria. 'Food Coloring', in *Science and Technology*, Volume 81, Number 34, 2003: 34.

Goldstein, V. and Rosenthanl, O. *Zum Problem der Wirkung der Farben auf den Organismus*, published in *Archiv fur Neurologie and Psychiatie*, 1930.

Gombrich, E. H. *The Story of Art*. London: Phaidon, 1972.

Gordon, Haim and Schlomit Tamari. *Maurice Merleau-Ponty's Phenomenology of Perception: A Basis for Sharing the Earth*. London: Praeger, 2004.

Gray, Henry. *Gray's Anatomy*. 1918. <http://www.bartleby.com/107/1.html> 15 August 2009 (URL correct at the time of writing).

Greenfield, Susan. *The Human Brain*. London: Ted Smart, 2001.

Griffin, Stephen. 'Push. Play: An Examination of the Game Play Button', delivered at the *DiGRA Conference: Changing Views – Worlds in Play*, 2005.

Grosz, Elizabeth. *Volatile Bodies: Toward a Corporeal Feminism*. Bloomington: Indiana University Press, 1994.

Gunning, Tom. 'An Aesthetic of Astonishment: Early Film and the (In)credulous Spectator'. *Film Theory and Criticism*. Ed. Leo Braudy and Marshall Cohen. Oxford: Oxford University Press, 1999: 818-832.

Gunning, Tom. 'Tracing the Individual Body: Photography, Detectives and Early Cinema'. *Cinema and the Invention of Modern Life*. Ed. Leo Charney and Vanessa Schwartz. Berkeley: University of California Press, 1995: 13-45.

Harvey, William. *An Anatomical Disquisition on the Motion of the Heart and Blood in Animals*. London: William Benton, 1972.

Hegel, Georg. *Introductory Lectures on Aesthetics*, trans. Bernard Bosanquet. London: Penguin, 1975.

Hinton, Devon, Vuth Pich, Dara Chhean and Mark Pollack, 'Olfactory Triggered Panic Attacks Among Khmer Refugees'. *The Smell Culture Reader*. Ed. Jim Drobnick. London: Berg, 2006: 68-84.

Hirsch, Alan. 'Nostalgia, the Odors of Childhood and Society'. *The Smell Culture Reader*. Ed. Jim Drobnick. London: Berg, 2006: 187-189.

Hitchcock O'Connell, Pat and Laurent Bouzereau. *Alma Hitchcock: The Woman Behind the Man*. New York: Berkley Publishing Group, 2003.

Hitchcock, Alfred. *Alfred Hitchcock Interviews*. Jackson: University Press of Mississippi, 2003.

Houston, Penelope. 'The Figure in the Carpet', in *Sight and Sound*, Autumn, 1963: 487-501.

Howes, David. 'Introduction'. *Empire of the Senses*. Ed. David Howeds. Oxford: Berg, 2005: 1-20.

Iacoboni, Marco, Istvan Molnar-Szakacs, Vittorio Gallese, Giovanni Buccino, John C. Mazziotta and Giacomo Rizzolatti, 'Grasping the Intentions of Others With One's Own Mirror Neuron System'. *PloS Biology*. Volume 3, Issue 3. 2005: e79.

Ijsselsteijn, W. A., H. de Ridder, J. Freeman and S. E. Avons. 'Presence: concept, determinants and measurement', *Proceedings of the SPIE, Human Vision and Electronic Imaging V*. San Jose, California, 23-28, January 2000.

Irigaray, Luce. 'The Invisible of the Flesh', trans. Carolyn Burke and Gillian Gill. *An Ethics of Sexual Difference*. London: Athlone Press, 1993: 151-184.

Irigaray, Luce. 'The Mechanics of Fluids', trans. Catherine Porter. *This Sex Which is Not One*. New York: Cornell University Press, 1985: 106-119.

Irigaray, Luce. *Speculum of the Other Woman*, trans. Gillian C. Gill. New York: Cornell, 1995a.

Irigaray, Luce. *This Sex Which is Not One*, trans. Catherine Porter. Ithaca: Cornell University Press, 1993.

Isadale, J. 'What is virtual reality?'. 1998. <http://isdale. com/jerry/VR/WhatIsVR/noframes/WhatIsVR4.> 15 August 2009.

Iverson, Margaret. *Alois Riegl*. Cambridge: MIT Press, 1993.

Jay, Martin. 'Scopic Regimes of Modernity'. *Vision and Visuality*. Ed. Hal Foster. London: New Press, 1988: 3-28.

Jay, Martin. *Downcast Eyes: The Denigration of Vision in Twentieth Century French Thought*. Berkeley: University of California Press, 1994.

Jones. Ernest. *The Life and Work of Sigmund Freud*. London: Pelican, 1953.

Jutte, Robert. *A History of the Senses*. London: Polity, 2005.

Kant, Immanuel. *What is Enlightenment?*, published in Isaac Kramnick. Ed. *The Portable Enlightenment Reader*. London; Penguin, 1784/1995: 1-6.

Kapsis, Robert. *Hitchcock: The Making of a Reputation*. Chicago: University of Chicago Press, 1992.

Keller, Hellen. 'Sense and Sensibility'. *The Smell Culture Reader*. Ed. Jim Drobnick. London: Berg. 2006: 181-183.

Kennedy, Barbara. *Deleuze and Cinema*. Edinburgh: Edinburgh University Press, 2000.
Kolb, Bryan and Ian Whishaw. *Fundamentals of Human Neuropsychology*. London: W. H. Freeman, 2003.
Kristeva, Julia. 'The Powers of Horror'. *The Portable Kristeva*. Ed. Kelly Oliver. New York: Columbia University Press, 1997a: 229-264.
Kristeva, Julia. 'New Maladies of the Soul'. *The Portable Kristeva*. ED. Kelly Oliver. New York: Columbia University Press, 1997: 203-208.
Kuhn, Thomas. *The Structure of the Scientific Revolutions*. Chicago: University of Chicago Press, 1970.
Lacan, Jacques. *The Four Fundamental Concepts of Psychoanalysis*, trans. Alan Sheridan. London: Penguin, 1986.
Lambert, Gregg. 'Schizoanalysis and Cinema of the Brain'. *Deleuze and the Schizoanalysis of Cinema*. Ed. Ian Buchanan and Patricia MacCormack. London: Continuum, 2008: 27-38.
Lane, Tarja. 'Cinema as second skin: Under the membrane of horror film', in *New Review of Film and Television Studies*. 4:2, 2006: 93-106.
Langer, Monika. *Merleau-Ponty's Phenomenology of Perception*. London: Palgrave, 1989.
Largey, Gale and Rod Watson. 'The Sociology of Odors'. *The Smell Culture Reader*. Ed. Jim Drobnick. London: Berg, 2006: 29-40.
Levi Strauss, Claude. *The Raw and the Cooked*, trans. John and Doreen Weightman. London: Jonathan Cape, 1964.
Levin, David. *Modernity and the Hegemony of Vision*. Berkeley: University of California Press, 1993.
Lindberg, David. *Theories of Vision from Al-Kindi to Kepler*. Chicago: University of Chicago Press, 1981.
Lippit, Akira Mizuta. 'Virtual Annihilation: Optics, VR and the Discourse of Subjectivity', in *Criticism*. Vol. 36, 1994: 595-610.
Littau, Karin. 'Eye-hunger: physical pleasure and non-narrative cinema'. *Crash Cultures: Modernity, Mediation and the Material*. Ed. Arthurs Jane and Grant, Iain. Bristol: Intellect, 2002: 35-52.
Lloyd, Genevieve. *The Man of Reason*. London: Methuen, 1984.
Locke, John. *An Essay Concerning Human Understanding*. London: William Benton, 1690/1972.
Lowenstein, Adam. 'The Master, the Maniac, and Frenzy'. *Hitchcock: Past and Future*. Ed. Richard Allen and Sam Ishi Gonzales. London: Routledge, 2004: 179-192.
Lowenstein, Otto. *The Senses*. London: Pelican, 1966.

Lucas, Alexander. *Demystifying Anorexia Nervosa*. Oxford: Oxford University Press, 2004.

Luria, A. R. *The Mind of a Mnemonist*, trans. Lynn Solotaroff. Cambridge: Harvard University Press, 1987.

Lyons, James. 'What about the popcorn? Food and the film watching experience'. *Reel Food*. Ed. Anne Bower. London: Routledge, 2004: 311-334.

MacDougall, David. *The Corporeal Image: Film, Ethnography and the Senses*. Princeton and Oxford: Princeton University Press.

Macquarrie, John. *Existentialism*. London: Pelican, 1973.

Margolis, Eleanor. 'Vagueness Gridlocked: A Map of the Smells of New York'. *The Smell Culture Reader*. Ed. Jim Drobnick. London: Berg, 2006: 107-117.

Marks, Laura. *The Skin of the Film*. Durham and London: Duke University Press, 2000.

Marks, Laura. *Touch: Sensuous Theory and Multisensory Media*. Minneapolis: University of Minnesota Press, 2002.

Mars Jones, Adam. 'Quiet Please', published in *Granta*, 86, 2006: 249.

Martin Manalansan. 'Immigrant Lives and the Politics of Olfaction in the Global City'. *The Smell Culture Reader*. Ed. Jim Drobnick. London: Berg, 2006: 41-53.

Martin-Jones, David. *Deleuze, Cinema and National Identity*. Edinburgh, University of Edinburgh Press, 2006.

Marx, Karl. *Capital*, trans. Eden and Cedar Paul. London: Dent and Sons, 1933.

Masin, Janet. *Alfred Hitchcock*, in *Boston After Dark*. 3, no,24. 1972: 1-23.

Mason, S. F. *Main Currents of Scientific Thought*. London: Routledge, 1953.

Maurer, Daphne. 'Neonatal Synaesthesia: Implications for the Processing of Speech and Faces'. *Synaesthesia: Classic and Contemporary Readings*. Ed. Simon Baron-Cohen, John Harrison. Oxford: Blackwell, 1997: 224-243.

McGilligan, Patrick. *Alfred Hitchcock: A Life in Darkness in Light*. London: Harper Collins, 2003.

McLuhan, Marshall. *Understanding Media*. London: Abacus, 1973.

Merleau-Ponty, Maurice. 'The Film and the New Psychology', in *Sense and Non Sense*, trans. Hubert L. Dreyfus and Patricia Dreyfus. Chicago: Northwestern University Press, 1964: 48-62.

Merleau-Ponty, Maurice. *The Phenomenology of Perception*, trans. Colin Smith. London: Routledge, 2005.

Merleau-Ponty, Maurice. *The Visible and the Invisible*, trans. Alphonso Lingis. Illinois: Northwestern University Press, 1968.
Metz, Christian. *The Imaginary Signifier*, trans. Celia Britton, Annwyl Williams, Ben Brewster and Alfred Guzzetti. Bloomington: University of Indiana Press, 1977.
Miller, Henry. *A Devil in Paradise*. Berkeley: University of California Press, 1957.
Miller, James *The Passion of Michel Foucault*. London: Harper Collins, 1993.
Mitry, Jean. *The Aesthetics and Psychology of Cinema*, trans. Christopher King. London: Athalone, 2000.
Modelski, Tania. *The Women Who Knew Too Much*. London: Routledge, 1989.
Montague, Ashley. *Touching: The Human Significance of Skin*. New York: Harper Perennial, 1986.
Mulhall, Stephen. *On Film*. London: Routledge, 2008.
Mulvey, Laura. 'Visual Pleasure and Narrative Cinema'. *Film and Criticism*. Ed. Leo Braudy and Marshall Cohen. Oxford; Oxford University Press, 1999: 833-844.
Munsterberg, Hugo. *The Photoplay*. New York: D Appleton and Company, 1918.
Newton, Issac. *A Theory Concerning Light and Colours*. 1671. <http://www.newtonproject. ic. ac. uk> 15 August 2009 (URL correct at the time of writing).
O'Shea, Michael. *The Brain: A Very Short Introduction*. Oxford: Oxford University Press, 2005.
Olkowski, Dorothea. *Gilles Deleuze and the Ruin of Representation*. Berkeley: University of California Press, 1999.
Ono, T., R. Tamura, H. Nishijo, K. Nakamura and E. Tabuchi. 'Contribution of Amygdalar and Lateral Hypothalamic Neurons to Visual Information Processing of Food and Nonfood in Monkey'. *Physiol Behav*. 45. 1989:411–421.
Pallasmaa, Juhani. 'Six themes for the next millennium'. *The Architectural Review*. Vol. 196, July 1996.
Pallasmaa, Juhani. *The Eyes of the Skin*. London: John Wiley and Sons, 2008.
Phillips, Diane. 'How Does it Make Me Feel? A Consumer's Satisfaction Response to Food Products'. *Journal of Food Products Marketing*. Volume 6, Issue 2. 2000: 15-33.
Pisters, Patricia, *The Matrix of Visual Culture*. Stanford: Stanford University Press, 2003.

Plantinga, Carl and Greg Smith. *Passionate Views: Film, Cognition and Emotion*. Washington: Johns Hopkins University Press, 1999.

Plato, *Symposium*, trans. Benjamin Jowett. London: William Benton, 385 B.149-174.C/1972:

Pomerance, Murray. *An Eye for Hitchcock*. New Jersey: Rutgers University Press, 2004.

Powell, Anna. *Deleuze and Horror Film*. Edinburgh: University of Edinburgh Press, 2006.

Prendergast, Roy. *Film Music: A Neglected Art*. London: Norton, 1992.

Proust, Marcel. 'Another memory', trans. Joachim Neugroschel. *The Smell Culture Reader*. Ed. Jim Drobnick. London: Berg, 2006: 210-211.

Pudovkin, V. I. 'Asynchronism as a Principle of Film Sound'. *Film Sound: Theory and Practice*. Ed. Elizabeth Weis and John Belton. New York: Columbia University Press, 1929/1985: 86-91.

Fabbri, Paolo. 'Free/indirect/discourse'. *Pier Paolo Pasolini: Contemporary Perspectives*. Ed. Patrick Allen Rumble and Bart Testa. Toronto: University of Toronto Press: 78-87.

Ramachandran, V. S. 'Mirror Neurons and Imitation Learning as the Driving Force Behind the Great Leap Forward in Human Evolution'. 2000. <http://edge. org/3rd_culture/ramachandran/ramachandran_p1.html> 15th August 2009.

Ratey, John. *A User's Guide to the Brain*. London: Little, Brown and Company, 2001.

Restivo, Angelo. 'The Silence of *The Birds*'. *Hitchcock Past and Future*. Ed. Richard Allen and S. Ishi Gonzales. London: Routledge, 2004: 164-178.

Rimbaud, Arthur. *Vowels*, trans. Paul Schmidt, in *The Complete Works*. London: Picador, 1988.

Rizzolatti, G. and L. Craighero. 'The Mirror Neuron System', in *Annual Review of Neuroscience*. 27. 2004: 169-192.

Rizzolatti, G., L. Fadiga, V. Gallese and L. Fogasi. 'Premotor Cortex and the Recognition of Motor Actions', in *Cognitive Brain Research*. 3. 1996: 593-609.

Robert Robertson, 'Eisenstein, Synaesthesia, Symbolism and the Occult Traditions'. 2006. <http://www. offscreen. com/biblio/phile/essays/eisenstein_synaesthesia> 15th August 2009 (URL correct at the time of writing).

Rohmer, Eric and Claude Chabrol. *Hitchcock: The First Forty Four Films*, trans. Stanley Hochman. New York: Continuum, 1957/1979.

Rolls, E. T., M.J. Burton and F. Mora, 'Hypothalamic Neuronal Responses Associated with the Sight of Food', in *Brain Res*, Jul 23;111(1). 1976: 53–66.

Rolls, Edmund T. 'Neural Processing Related to Feeding in Primates', in C. Legg and D. Booth. Eds. *Appetite: Neural and Behavioural Bases*. Oxford: Oxford University Press, 1994.

Rose, Jacqueline. *Sexuality in the Field of Vision*. London: Vintage, 2005.

Rose, Stephen. *The Conscious Brain*. London: Pelican, 1976.

Rothman, William. *The Murderous Gaze*. Cambridge: Harvard University Press, 2002.

Rutherford, Anne. 'Cinema and embodied affect'. 2002. <http://archive.sensesofcinema.com/contents/03/25/embodied_affect.html> 15 August 2009.

Ryall, Tom. *Alfred Hitchcock and the British Cinema*. London: Continuum, 1996.

Sagiv, Noam. 'Synesthesia in Perspective'. *Synesthesia: Perspectives from Cognitive Neuroscience*. Ed. L. C Robertson and Noam Sagiv. New York: Oxford University Press, 2005: 3-10.

Salt, Barry, *Film Style and Technology: History and Analysis*. New York, Starword, 1993.

Sartre, Jean Paul. *Being and Nothingness*, trans. Hazel Barnes. London: Routledge, 2005.

Sartre, Jean Paul. *Nausea*, trans. Robert Baldick. London: Penguin, 1980.

Schaffer, Murray. 'Open Ears'. *The Auditory Culture Reader*. Ed. Michael Bull and Les Back. London: Berg, 2005: 25-40.

Schneck, Daniel and Dorita Berger. *The Music Effect*. London: Jessica Kingsley Publishers, 2006.

Sergi, Gianluca. 'The Sonic Playground: Hollywood Cinema and its Listeners'. *Hollywood Spectatorship*. Ed. Melvyn Stokes and Richard Maltby. London: BFI, 2001: 121-131.

Sharff, Stefan. *The Art of Looking in Hitchcock's Rear Window*. New York: Limelight Editions, 1997.

Shaviro, Steven. *The Cinematic Body*. Minneapolis: University of Minnesota Press, 1993.

Shinkle, Eugenie. 'Video games, emotions and the six senses', in *Media, Culture and Society*. 30(6). 2008: 907-915.

Silverman, Kaja. *The Acoustic Mirror*. Bloomington: Indiana University Press, 1988.

Sinclair, Craig. 'Audition: making sense of cinema'. *The Velvet Light Trap*, March 22, 2003.

Skerry, Phillip J. *Psycho in the Shower: The History of Cinema's Most Famous Scene*. New York: Continuum, 2009.

Sobchack, Vivian. 'What My Fingers Knew'. *Carnal Thoughts: Embodiment and Moving Image Culture*. Berkeley: University of California Press, 2004: 53-84.

Sonnenshein, David. *Sound Design*. California: MWP, 2001.

Spoto, Donald. *The Art Of Alfred Hitchcock*. London: Hopkins and Blake, 1992.

Spoto, Donald. *The Dark Side of Genius: The Life of Alfred Hitchcock*. London: Plexus, 1994.

Stam, Robert and Roberta Pearson. 'Hitchcock's Rear Window: Reflexivity and the Critique of Voyeurism'. *A Hitchcock Reader*. Ed. Marshall Deutlebaum and Leland Poague. 1986: 193-206.

Stam, Robert. *Film Theory: An Introduction*. London: Blackwell, 2000.

Steiner, J. E. 'The Gustofacial response: Observation on normal and anencephalic new born infants'. *Fourth Symposium on Oral Sensation and Perception*. Ed. J. F. Bosman. U. S Department of Health, Education and Welfare, Bethesda, MD, 1973.

Stoller, Paul. *Sensuous Scholarship*. Philadelphia: University of Pennsylvania Press.

Stoddart, David. *The Scented Ape*. Cambridge: Cambridge University Press, 1990.

Stromgen, Dick. 'Now to the Banquet We Press: Hitchcock's Gourmet and Gourmand Offerings'. *Beyond the Stars III: The Material World of American Popular* Film. Ed. Paul Loukides and Linda Fuller. Bowling Green OH: Popular Press, 1993: 38-50.

Sullivan, Jack. *Hitchcock's Music*. New Haven: Yale University Press, 2007.

Tasker, Yvonne. *Spectacular Bodies: Gender, Genre and the Action Cinema*. London: Routledge, 1993.

Taylor, John Russell. *Hitch: The Life and Work of Alfred Hitchcock*. London: Sphere, 1981.

Toles, George. '"If thine eye offend…" Psycho and the Art of Infection'. *Alfred Hitchcock's Psycho: A Casebook*. Ed. Robert Phillip Tolker. Oxford: Oxford University Press, 2004: 120-146.

Truffaut, Francois. *Truffaut/Hitchcock*. London: Simon and Schuster, 1983.

Turin, Luca. *The Secret of Scent*. London: Faber and Faber, 2008.

Turn, Eleanor. *The History of Germany*. London: Greenwood Press, 1999.

van Orden, Kate. 'Descartes on Musical Training and the Body'. *Music, Sensation and Sensuality*. Ed. Linda Phyllis Austern. London; Routledge, 2002: 17-38.

Van Toller, S., S. Hotson and M. Kendal-Reed. 'The Brain and the Sense of Smell: Can We Begin to Make Sense of Cortical Information After an Odour has been Received'. *Fragrance: the Psychology and Biology of Perfume.* Ed. S. Van Toller, and G. H. Dodd. Elsevier Applied Science, London, 1992: 195-220.

Varela, Francisco. 'The Re-enchantment of the Concrete'. *Incorporations v. 6.* . Ed. Jonathan Crary and Sanford Kwinter. New York: Zone Books, 1992: 320-338.

Vertov, Dziga. 'The Writings of Dziga Vertov'. *Filmmakers on Filmmaking.* Ed. Harry Geduld. London: Pelican, 1962: 92-95.

Wade, Nicholas J. *A Natural History of Vision.* Cambridge: MIT Press, 1998.

Walker, Michael. *Hitchcock's Motifs*, Amsterdam; University of Amsterdam Press, 2005.

Weis, Elizabeth. 'The Evolution of Hitchcock's Aural Style and Sound in *The Birds*'. Film Sound: Theory and Practice. Ed. Elizabeth Weis and John. Belton, 1985: 298:311.

Weis, Elizabeth. *The Silent Scream.* New Jersey: Fairleigh Dickinson University Press. 1982.

Werner, Heinz. *Untersuchungen uber Empfindung und Empfinden*, published in Ztschr f. Psychologie, 1930.

Whyte, Jennifer. *Virtual Reality and the Built Environment.* London: Architectural Press, 2004.

Williams, Linda. 'Body Genres', in *Film Quarterly.* 44: 4, Summer, 1991.

Williams, Linda. 'Corporealized Observers'. *Fugitive Images: From Photography to Video.* Ed. Patrice Petro. Bloomington, Indiana: Indiana University Press, 1995: 3-41.

Williams, Linda. *Hard Core.* London: Pandora, 1990.

Wolff, Mark and Tony Nourmand . *Hitchcock Poster Art.* London: Aurum Press, 1999.

Wood, Leslie. *The Miracle of the Movies.* London: Burke Publishing, 1957.

Wood, Robin. 'The Fear of Spying', in Deutlebaum and Poague, 1986.

Žižek, Slavoj. Ed. *Everything You Always Wanted to Know About Lacan but Were Afraid to Ask Hitchcock.* London: Verso, 2002.

Žižek, Slavoj. *Looking Awry.* Cambridge: Massachusetts, 1992.

FILMOGRAPHY

Aventure Malgache. Dir. Alfred Hitchcock. Ministry of Information, 1944.
Birds, The. Dir. Alfred Hitchcock. Universal Pictures, 1963.
Bitter Tears of Petra Von Kant, The. Dir. Ranier Maria Fassbinder. Filmverlag der Autorun, 1972.
Blackmail. Dir. Alfred Hitchcock. BIP, 1929.
Blow Up. Dir. Michelangelo Antonioni. Bridge Films, 1966.
Blue Velvet. Dir. David Lynch. DEG, 1986.
Blue. Dir Derek Jarman. Basilisk Communications, 1993.
Bon Voyage. Dir. Alfred Hitchcock. Ministry of Information, 1944.
Champagne. Dir. Alfred Hitchcock. BIP, 1928.
Dial M for Murder. Dir. Alfred Hitchcock. Warner Brothers, 1954.
Downhill. Dir. Alfred Hitchcock. Gainsborough Pictures, 1927.
Easy Virtue. Dir. Alfred Hitchcock. Gainsborough Pictures, 1927.
Eat Drink Man Woman. Dir. Ang Lee. Central Motion Pictures Corporation, 1994.
Exorcist, The. Dir. William Friedkin. Hoya Productions, 1973.
Frenzy. Dir. Alfred Hitchcock. Universal Pictures, 1972.
Hands of Mr Ottermole, The. *Hitchcock Presents, Season 2*. Dir. Robert Stevens. Shamley Productions , 5 May 1957.
Jamaica Inn. Dir. Alfred Hitchcock. Mayflower Pictures, 1939.
Juno and the Paycock. Dir. Alfred Hitchcock. BIP, 1930.
Lady Vanishes, The. Dir. Alfred Hitchcock. Gainsborough Pictures, 1938.
Lamb to the Slaughter. *Hitchcock Presents, Season 3*, Dir. Alfred Hitchcock. Shamley Productions, 13 April 1958.
Lawrence of Arabia. Dir. David Lean. Horizon Pictures, 1962.
Let Him Have it. Dir. Peter Medak. British Screen productions, 1991.
Lifeboat. Dir. Alfred Hitchcock. Twentieth Century Fox, 1944.
Like Water for Chocolate. Dir. Alfonso Arau. Arau Films International, 1992.
Lodger, The. Dir. Alfred Hitchcock. Carlyle Blackwell Productions, 1932.
Man Who Knew Too Much, The. Dir. Alfred Hitchcock. Filwite Productions, 1956.

Man Who Knew Too Much, The. Dir. Alfred Hitchcock. Gaumont British Pictures, 1934.
Manxman, The. Dir. Alfred Hitchcock. BIP, 1928.
March of the Penguins. Dir. Luc Jacquet. Bonne Pioche, 2005.
Marnie. Dir. Alfred Hitchcock. Universal Pictures, 1964.
Modern Times. Dir. Charlie Chaplin. Charles Chaplin Productions, 1936.
Mountain Eagle, The. Dir. Alfred Hitchcock. Gainsborough Pictures, 1926.
Mr and Mrs Smith. Dir. Alfred Hitchcock. RKO Radio Pictures, 1941.
Murder! Dir. Alfred Hitchcock. BIP, 1930.
Mysteries of July. Dir. Reece Auguiste. NBPC, 1990.
North by Northwest. Dir. Alfred Hitchcock. MGM, 1959.
Notorious. Dir. Alfred Hitchcock. Vanguard Films, 1946.
Number 17. Dir. Alfred Hitchcock. BIP, 1932.
Perfume. Dir. Tom Twyker. Constantin Film Produktion, 2006.
Piano, The. Dir. Jane Campion. Australian Film Commission, 1993.
Pleasure Garden, The. Dir. Alfred Hitchcock. Gainsborough Pictures, 1925.
Polyester. Dir. John Waters. New Line Cinema, 1981.
Psycho. Dir. Alfred Hitchcock. Shamley Productions, 1960.
Rear Window. Dir. Alfred Hitchcock. Paramount Pictures, 1954.
Rebecca. Dir. Alfred Hitchcock. Selznick International Pictures, 1940.
Rich and Strange. Dir. Alfred Hitchcock. BIP, 1931.
Ring, The. Dir. Alfred Hitchcock. BIP, 1927.
Rope. Dir. Alfred Hitchcock. Transatlantic Pictures, 1948.
Sabotage. Dir. Alfred Hitchcock. Gaumont British Pictures, 1936.
Saboteur. Dir. Alfred Hitchcock. Frank Lloyd Productions, 1942.
Salo. Dir. Pier Paolo Passolini. PEA, 1975.
Scent of Mystery, The. Dir. Jack Cardiff. Michael Todd Jr., 1960.
Secret Agent. Dir. Alfred Hitchcock. Gaumont British Pictures, 1936.
Shadow of a Doubt. Dir. Alfred Hitchcock. Skirball Productions, 1943.
Supersize Me. Dir. Morgan Spurlock. Bathbur Pictures, 2004.
Suspicion. Dir. Alfred Hitchcock. RKO, 1941.
To Catch a Thief. Dir. Alfred Hitchcock. Paramount Pictures, 1955.
Tom Jones. Dir. Tony Richardson. Woodfall Film Productions, 1963.
Topaz. Dir. Alfred Hitchcock. Universal Pictures, 1969.
Torn Curtain. Dir. Alfred Hitchcock. Universal Pictures, 1966.
Train Arriving at the Station, The. Dir. The Lumiere Brothers, 1895.
Trouble with Harry, The. Dir. Alfred Hitchcock. Alfred Hitchcock Productions, 1955.
Under Capricorn. Dir. Alfred Hitchcock. Transatlantic Pictures, 1949.
Vertigo. Dir. Alfred Hitchcock. Alfred Hitchcock Productions, 1958.

INDEX

Abraham, Karl
  Oral Eroticism and Character 115
Ackerman, Diane 127
Adams, Ernest 18
advertising 11
aesthetics 1, 20, 27, 39, 41, 79-80, 125, 131
Alhazen 78
Al Kindi 77
anthropology 3
Antonioni, Michelangelo
  Blow Up (1966) 144
Anzieu, Didier 3, 14, 46
  Skin Ego, The 52–54
architecture 3, 8, 10, 14-15
Aristotle 77–78
Artaud, Antonin 28
Aryton, John 11
auteur theory 5

Bacon, Francis
  Logic of Sensation, The 39
Baudelaire, Charles 79
Baudrillard, Jean 16
  System of Objects, The 10
Bazin, Andre 184
  'The Evolution of the Photographic Image' 26
de Beauvoir, Simone
  The Second Sex 66
Beharry, Shauna 67

Benjamin, Walter
  'The Work of Art in the Age of Mechanical Reproduction' 167
Bentham, Jeremy 10
Benthien, Claudia
  Skin: On the Cultural Border Between Self and the World 164
Berenson, Bernard 36, 167
  Aesthetics and History and The Florentine Painters of the Renaissance 168-170
Berkeley, George 7–8, 62
biology 8, 35, 50-52, 55, 58, 63, 65, 73, 75-76, 78, 81, 84, 116, 183
body, the
  as an acoustic site 145–147
  as an index of audition 147–150
  as a site of reception 24–25, 32–34
  as index of response 2, 24, 25–32
Bogue, Ronald 40
Boorstin, Jon 26-27
  Making Movies Work 26
Brain, Robert
  Decorated Body, The 53
Brewster, Sir David 11
Bruno, Giordano 80
Bruynel, Ton 147

camera obscura 6–9, 17-18
Campion, Jane
  Piano, The (1993) 42-43, 164, 172-173
Cardiff, Jack
  Scent of Mystery (1960) 142
Cartesianism 6, 33, 39, 55–57, 62, 70, 81, 86, 168, 172
Cahiers du Cinéma 95, 97-98
Cavell, Stanley 1, 143
Chabrol, Claude 5, 97
Chaplin, Charlie
  Modern Times (1936) 143
Charcot, Jean Martin 10
Chesterton, G. K.
  Defence of Penny Dreadfuls, A 98
cinema spectatorship 5
  multi-modal experience of 5
cinesthesia 172–174
Connor, Steven
  Book of Skin, The 164
corporeality
  importance of 5
Crary, Jonathan 6-9, 13, 31, 46, 64, 76-77
  Techniques of the Observer: On Vision and Modernity in the Nineteenth Century 6, 8, 76
Cronenberg, David 33
Cytowic, Richard 78, 80-86, 172
  Man Who Tasted Shapes, The 81–84

Daguerrotype 11
Damasio, Antonio 78, 172
  Descartes' Error 78
Daney, Serge 7, 184
Debord, Guy 2
Deleuze, Gilles 1, 10, 14, 20, 27, 33-41, 54, 87, 95, 116-117, 126, 134, 149-150, 169-170, 174-175
  and film theory 35–36
  death of 33
Deleuzian philosophy 13, 20
Derrida, Jacques
  On Touching - Jean Luc Nancy 164
Descarteś, Rene 7-8, 75, 77, 148
  (See Cartesianism)
  Optics 7
Doane, Mary Ann 144
Douchet, Jean 5, 99, 100
  Hitch and His Public 176
Douglas, Mary 113
  Purity and Danger 69
Durgnat, Raymond 96, 106, 132, 150, 173, 177
  Strange Case of Alfred Hitchcock, The 96

Edison, Thomas
  kinetoscope 11
  The Edison company 28
  Irwin-Rice Kiss, The (1896) 174
Eisenstein, Sergei 25, 80, 82, 152
Elsaesser, Thomas 23, 26
epistemic shifts 183
Erlmann, Viet 12
Fassbinder, Rainer Werner (Dir.)
  Bitter Tears of Petra Von Kant, The (1972) 171
feminism 3-4, 13, 20, 41, 54, 63–69, 94, 113
  second wave 13, 41
Foucault, Michel 9-10
  Madness and Civilization 10
Frampton, Daniel
  Filmosophy 93-94

Index

Freud, Sigmund 11-12, 47–52, 126
  Beyond the Pleasure Principle 47, 50
  Civilisation and Its Discontents 126
  and psychoanalysis 11–12
Friedberg, Anne 6

Galen 75- 78
gender politics 46
gender studies 3
Giannetti, Louis
  Understanding Movies 151
Goethe, Johann Wolfgang von 8
Goldstein and Rosenthal
  Zum Problem der Wirkung der Farben auf den Organismus 59
Griffin, Stephen 18
Gropius, Walter 14
Grosz, Elizabeth 46-47, 52, 55-56
  Volatile Bodies 47
Guattari, Felix 27, 33-36, 39, 54, 116, 170
Gunning, Tom 28–29
  'An Aesthetic of Astonishment: Early Film and the (In)credulous Spectator' 28
Haeckel, Ernst 49-50
haptic vision 24, 39, 118, 168, 170-172
Harvey, William 64, 75
  Anatomical Disquisition on the Motion of the Heart and Blood in Animals, An 64
Hegel, Georg Wilhem Friedrich
  Lectures on Aesthetics 125
Heidegger, Martin 15
Hitchcock, Alfred
  and embodiment 96–99
  and two important kinds of murder 165–168
  as historical paradigm 94–96
  Alfred Hitchcock Presents, Lamb to the Slaughter (1958) 111
  Birds, The (1963) 114, 118, 129, 154-162, 181
  Blackmail (1929) 112, 150, 169
  Champagne (1928) 127, 171
  Easy Virtue (1927) 96
  Frenzy (1972) 95, 103-104, 112–118, 181, 121, 125-126, 149-150, 156, 166, 181
  and taste and digestion 103–122
  Hands of Mr Ottermole, The 101
  Jamaica Inn (1939) 173
  Lady Vanishes, The (1938) 165
  Lifeboat (1944) 131, 156
  Man Who Knew Too Much, The (1934) 130, 165
  Man Who Knew Too Much, The (1956) 96
  Murder! (1930) 130
  Manxman, The (1928) 96
  Marnie (1964) 100, 114, 125
  Mountain Eagle, The (1926) 96
  Mr and Mrs Smith (1941) 104
  North by Northwest (1959) 155
  Notorious (1946) 114, 174-175, 181
  Number 17 (1932) 171
  Pleasure Garden, The (1925) 95, 131-132, 138, 171
  Psycho (1960) 98, 100, 104, 116, 151, 155-156, 169, 170
  Rear Window (1954) 96, 98, 100, 104, 114, 132, 163, 166, 176–180

Rich and Strange (1932) 103, 111
Ring, The (1927) 130, 164
Rope (1948) 96, 104, 121, 166
Sabotage (1936) 125, 165-166, 181
Secret Agent (1936) 165-166
*Shadow of a Doub*t (1943) 123, 135-137, 139-152, 156
To Catch a Thief (1954) 103, 106, 109, 170
Topaz (1969) 166
Torn Curtain (1966) 98, 166, 181
Trouble With Harry, The (1955) 96, 169-170
Under Capricorn (1949) 170
Vertigo (1957) 16, 96, 100, 134, 155
Hollywood 4
  golden age of 2
Hopital de la Salpetriere 10
Horner, George
  zoetrope 11
Howes, David 88, 123
Huitzilopochti
  in Aztec culture 107
IMAX 20, 96
Impressionists 8
iPod 88
Irigaray, Luce 3, 41, 46, 58, 61, 65-69, 153
  Speculum of the Other Woman 67
Jamison, Lee 28
Jarman. Derek
  Blue (1993) 19
Jay, Martin
  Downcast Eyes: The Denigration of Vision in Twentieth Century French Thought 12

Jutte, Robert 87-88
  A History of the Senses 87

Kahn, Fritz 74-75
  Der Mensch als Industriepalast ('Man as an Industrial Palace') 74
kaleidoscope 11
Kant, Immanuel 50
  thought of (Kantian) 5
Kapsis, Robert 94
Kennedy, Barbara 6, 32, 39-42, 45
  and sensation 39–41
  Deleuze and Cinema 39
Kristeva, Julia 68-69, 113
Kuhn, Thomas 75-76
  The Structure of Scientific Revolutions 75

Lacanian psychoanalysis 94, 100
Lambert, Greg 36
Lane, Tarja
  'Cinema as Second Skin' 164
Lawrence of Arabia (1962) 40
Le Corbusier (Charles-Edouard Jeanneret) 14
Lee, Ang
  Eat Drink Man Woman, aka *Yin shi nan nu* (1994) 184
Lehman, Ernest 99
Levi-Strauss, Claude 36, 107, 110, 113
Levin, David
  Modernity and the Hegemony of Vision 12
Lewis, Jerry 33
Leytonstone 95
Like Water for Chocolate (1992) 184

Lippit, Akira Mizuta
  'Virtual Annihilation: Optics, VR and the Discourse of Subjectivity' 16
Littau, Karin 24, 29-30, 40
  'Eye Hunger: Physical Pleasure and Non-narrative Cinema' 29
Locke, John 7
Lumiere Brothers 11
  Arrival of a Train at the Station? (1895) 28
Lyons, James
  'What About the Popcorn? Food and the Film Watching Experience' 103
Lyotard, Jean-François 13

MacDougall, David
  The Corporeal Image 25
March of the Penguins (2005) 40
Marks, Laura 17, 20, 32, 36-39, 42, 68, 125-126, 128-131, 134, 138, 141, 159, 164, 168, 170-171
  and embodied film theory 36–39
  and haptic vision 170
  and smell 125–126
  The Skin of the Film 36, 141, 164
  Touch: Sensuous Theory and Multisensory Media 170
  use of Deleuze 37–38
Marxism 25-26, 70, 185
Marx, Karl 10
McLuhan, Marshall 15
Merleau-Ponty, Maurice 3, 14, 46-47, 54, 56-62, 65, 68, 87, 108-109, 128, 173
  Phenomenology of Perception 46, 54, 56, 58, 62

Visible and the Invisible, The 46, 54–60
Millbank prison 10
Modernists 8
Modleski, Tania 103, 112-114, 121, 177
  Women Who Knew Too Much, The 103, 112
Monet, Claude
  paintings 9
Montague, Ashley 163-164, 175
  Touching: The Human Significance of Skin 163
Muller, Johannes
  Handbuch des Physiologie des Menschen 8
Mulvey, Laura 67, 100, 153
  'Visual Pleasure and Narrative Cinema' 67, 100
Munsterberg, Hugo 25
Mysteries of July (1990) 130-132, 134, 138

National Research Council of America 16
neuroscience 3-4, 13, 34-36, 58, 71, 73-89, 93, 172, 183
Newton, Isaac 7
  Optics 7
nineteenth-century science and the body 77
Nintendo Wii 17-20, 25

Oedipus complex 51
Pallasmaa, Juhani 14-15, 19
  'Six Themes for the Next Millennium' 15
  Eyes of the Skin: Architecture and the Senses, The 14
Panoptical prison 10

Pascal, Blaise 78
Pechter, William 117
Perkins, Anthony 100, 185
phenomenology 3, 54–59
Phillips, Diane 109
philosophy 15, 20, 30, 46, 54, 66, 77-78, 94, 153
physiology 8
Plateu, Joseph
  Phenakistoscope 11
Plato 64, 77-78
political ideology 4
Pomerance, Murray 166
Ponti, Carlo
  Megalethoscope 11
pornography 26, 31
post-colonialism 20
psychoanalysis 3-4, 11-12, 17, 25, 33, 35, 40, 46–48, 51, 54-56, 65, 73, 85, 94, 100, 104, 113, 184
Pudovkin, V. I. 25, 145

Ramachandran, Vilayanur 84
Ratey, John 111
Rimbaud, Arthur 79
Ring, The (1998) 130, 164
Robertson, Robert 80
Rohmer, Eric 5, 94, 96, 184
Rose, Jacqueline 11
  'Sexuality in the Field of Vision' 11
Rose, Stephen 78
  Conscious Brain, The 75
Royal Society 11
Russell, William 151

Salt, Barry
  Film Style and Technology 183
  statistical analysis 183

Sartre, Jean-Paul
  Being and Nothingness 54–57, 69
Schaulust, or eye hunger 29
Schopenhauer, Arthur 8
screen kiss 174–175
Semiotics 12, 25, 26, 144
sensual revolution 88
Shaviro, Steven
  The Cinematic Body 33-34
Shinkle, Eugenie 17-18
Silence of the Lambs (1991) 164
Silverman, Kaja
  The Acoustic Mirror 143
Skinner, B. F.
  and behaviorism 79
Sobchack, Vivian 6, 32, 41–43, 45, 67, 128, 164, 168, 172-175
  cinesthesia and phenomenology 41–43
  Address of the Eye, The 41-42, 128
  'What My Fingers Knew' 6, 41, 164, 172
Sonnenschein, David 145-148, 151, 161
  Sound Design 145
Sony Eye Toy 18
spectatorship
  theories of 183
Spoto, Donald 95, 105-106, 115, 119, 136,
stereoscope 7, 8
Stewart, James 100, 176

Stroller, Paul 27-28
  Sensuous Scholarship 28
Stromgem, Dick 105
Sullivan, Jack 149, 154

Super Size Me (2004) 110
synaesthesia 3, 4, 24, 79–81, 128

Taylor, John Russell 95
 Exorcist (1973), *The* 110
thaumatrope 11
theosophy 79, 80
Turk, Eleanor 75
Turner, Joseph Mallord William
 paintings 9
 Morning After the Deluge, The 9
Twyker, Tom
 Perfume (2006) 142

van Orden, Kate
 'Descartes on Musical Training and the Body' 148
Varela, Franciso J. 86-87
 'The Re-enchantment of the Concrete' 86
Vertov, Dziga 27
virtual reality 15, 16, 17, 20
de Vlieger, Simon 9
Volkman, A. W.
 Tachitoscope 11
von Stampfer, Simon
 stroboscope 11

Wade, Nicholas J.
 Natural History of Vision, A 77
Walker, Michael 104
Waters, John
 Polyester (1981) 125, 142
Watson, Walden O. 124, 151
Weis, Elisabeth 155-158
 'The Evolution of Hitchcock's Aural Style and Sound in The Birds' 155
 Silent Scream, The 155
Werner, Heinz
 Untersuchungen uber Empfindung und Empfinden 59
Wheatstone and Brewster 7
Wheatstone, Charles
 first stereoscope demonstration 11
Williams, Linda 24, 26, 30, 31-33, 42, 98
 'Body Genres: Corporealized Observers and the Carnal Density of Vision' 31
 'Body Genres: Gender, Genre and Excess' 31
 Hard Core 26
Window on the World (WoW) 15
Wittgenstein, Ludwig 166
Wood, Robin 5, 106, 113, 117, 135-138, 142, 156, 166-167
 Hitchcock's Films 106
 on Hitchcock's *Shadow of a Doubt* 136–139
 'The Fear of Spying: Can Hitchcock Be Saved for Feminism?' 113
Wright, Lloyd 14

Young, Iris 65-66, 69, 78

Žižek, Slavoj 94, 100, 129, 159
 'In My Bold Gaze My Ruin is Writ Large' 100